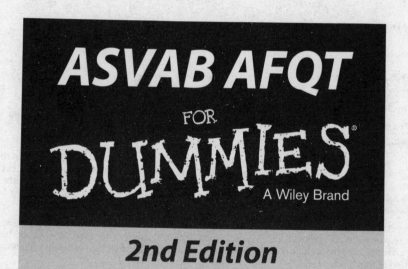

ASVAB AFQT

FOR DUMMIES®

A Wiley Brand

2nd Edition

by Rod Powers

FOR DUMMIES®

A Wiley Brand

ASVAB AFQT **For Dummies®, 2nd Edition**

Published by:
John Wiley & Sons, Inc.
111 River Street
Hoboken, NJ 07030-5774
www.wiley.com

For general information on our other products and services, please contact our Customer Care Department within the U.S. at 877-762-2974, outside the U.S. at 317-572-3993, or fax 317-572-4002. For technical support, please visit www.wiley.com/techsupport.

Wiley publishes in a variety of print and electronic formats and by print-on-demand. Some material included with standard print versions of this book may not be included in e-books or in print-on-demand. If this book refers to media such as a CD or DVD that is not included in the version you purchased, you may download this material at http://booksupport.wiley.com. For more information about Wiley products, visit www.wiley.com.

Library of Congress Control Number: 2014931919

ISBN 978-1-118-81778-0 (pbk); ISBN 978-1-118-83076-5 (ebk); ISBN 978-1-118-83077-2 (ebk)

Manufactured in the United States of America

10 9 8 7 6 5 4 3 2 1

Contents at a Glance

Table of Contents

Introduction

Because you're reading this book, there's a very good chance that you're interested in joining the U.S. military. I say that because the military recruiting commands are the only people in the entire world who care about the Armed Forces Qualification Test (AFQT) score. The AFQT score is derived from four of the nine Armed Services Vocational Aptitude Battery (ASVAB) subtests. It's used to determine your overall qualification to join the military branch of your choice.

Perhaps you've read my best-selling *ASVAB For Dummies* (Wiley), or some other ASVAB prep book, and you want more practice so you can achieve the highest possible AFQT score. Maybe you've already taken the ASVAB, you want to retest for a higher AFQT score, and you're looking for an advantage. In any case, you've chosen the right book!

Ever since *ASVAB For Dummies* hit the bookshelves, I've received hundreds of e-mails from readers, asking for ways to score higher on the AFQT portion of the ASVAB. That's why I decided to write this book. Although the entire ASVAB is an important qualification for the military job you want, the four subtests that make up the AFQT score are ultra-important because the AFQT score determines whether you can even get into the military.

Long gone are the days when someone could just walk into a recruiter's office and get into the military as long as he had a pulse. Today's all-volunteer military members are the cream of the crop. For example, did you know that under current regulations, you need a minimum of a high school education to join, and that no more than 10 percent of all recruits can have a GED?

Something else you may not know: The military services can't just grow to whatever size they want. Like any other government agency, they have a budget, and they have to operate within that budget. Every year, when Congress passes the annual Defense Authorization Act, it tells each military branch how many members it's allowed to have at any given time. By law, the services can't go over the size mandated by congressional leaders (who hold the military purse strings).

Did you also know that of every ten people who walk into a military recruiter's office, only three ultimately are allowed to enlist? Sure, some are disqualified because of medical history or criminal history, but many are turned away because their AFQT scores are too low or because other qualified applicants have higher AFQT scores.

Today's military is high-tech. Even the "common" infantry soldier has to learn how to use and maintain complicated electronic gadgets to survive on today's battlefield. The services use the AFQT to determine whether someone is "trainable" in the high-tech military.

About This Book

Full-disclosure doctrine requires me to inform you that much of the information in this book can be found in *ASVAB For Dummies*. The AFQT is, after all, part of the ASVAB, and I wouldn't cheat you by putting part of the information in one book and part of the information in another.

So why should you spend some of your hard-earned money on this book, particularly if you've already bought *ASVAB For Dummies?* Because here you find expanded, more-detailed information about the AFQT and the four subtests that make up the AFQT score. If you're worried about your AFQT score, I guarantee this book will help you get the highest score possible.

Even if you're not worried about your AFQT score, this book contains four — count 'em, four! — additional practice tests for the four most important subtests of the ASVAB. Extra practice is never a bad thing, as my high-school football coach was fond of saying.

As you read through this book, you'll see a couple of special conventions:

✔ Whenever I use a new term, I italicize the term and define it nearby, often in parentheses.

✔ I put web addresses and e-mail addresses in monofont so you can easily distinguish them from the surrounding text.

When this book was printed, some web addresses may have needed to break across two lines of text. If that happened, rest assured that I haven't put in any extra characters (such as hyphens) to indicate the break. So when using one of these web addresses, just type in exactly what you see in this book, pretending as though the line break doesn't exist (or simply click the link if you're reading an e-book).

This book has a few sidebars (shaded boxes) sprinkled throughout. They're full of interesting information about topics described in those chapters, but you don't have to read them if you don't want to; they don't contain anything you must know about the AFQT, so if you're in a hurry, you can skip them. You can also skip anything marked with a Technical Stuff icon. These tidbits are nonessential, too.

Foolish Assumptions

While writing this book, I made a few assumptions about you — namely, who you are and why you picked up this book. I assume the following:

✔ You aren't a dummy. You just want information to help you get the highest AFQT score possible.

✔ You're a high-school graduate or have a GED or at least 15 college credits. You just want to brush up on your high-school math and/or English skills as they apply to the AFQT. (If you aren't a high-school graduate, or you don't have a GED or at least 15 college credits, you need to get back to school because you're not eligible to enlist in the military.)

✔ You want to join the U.S. military and want to take advantage of all the enlistment goodies, such as enlistment bonuses or additional education benefits, that are available. Depending on current recruiting needs, the services often tie enlistment incentives to high AFQT scores.

Icons Used in This Book

Throughout this book you find icons — little pictures in the margins — that help you use the material in this book to your best advantage. Here's a rundown of what they mean:

The Tip icon alerts you to helpful hints regarding the subject at hand. Tips can help you save time and score higher on the AFQT.

The Remember icon highlights important information you should read carefully.

The Warning icon flags information that may prove hazardous to your plans of acing the AFQT. Often, this icon accompanies common mistakes people make when taking the test or qualifying for enlistment. Pay special attention to the Warning icon so you don't fall into one of these pitfalls.

The Example icon points out sample questions that appear in the review chapters.

The Technical Stuff icon points out information that's interesting, enlightening, or in depth but that isn't necessary for you to read. You don't need this information to maximize your AFQT score, but knowing it may make you a better informed test taker — or at least help you impress your friends!

Beyond the Book

ASVAB AFQT For Dummies, 2nd Edition has eight full practice exams located online at `learn.dummies.com`. All you have to do to access them is register by following these simple steps:

1. **Find your PIN code.**

   • **Print-book users:** If you purchased a hard copy of this book, turn to the front of this book to find your PIN.

   • **E-book users:** If you purchased this book as an e-book, you can get your PIN by registering your e-book at `www.dummies.com/go/getaccess`. Simply select your book from the drop-down menu, fill in your personal information, and then answer the security question to verify your purchase. You'll then receive an e-mail with your PIN.

2. **Go to** `http://learn.dummies.com`.

3. **Enter your PIN.**

4. **Follow the instructions to create an account and establish your own login information.**

Now you're ready to go! You can come back to the online program as often as you want — simply log on with the username and password you created during your initial login. No need to enter the PIN a second time.

If you have trouble with your PIN or can't find it, contact Wiley Product Technical Support at 877-762-2974 or go to `http://support.wiley.com`.

You can use the online exams to determine exactly what areas you need to review. As you take the practice tests, the software will keep track of the areas in which you score well and the areas in which your scores aren't so hot. From there, you can focus your study time on the topics that trip you up so you can improve your performance in those areas when you take the ASVAB.

But wait — that's not all! In addition to the online tests, this product also comes with some other goodies you can find on the web. Stressed out about the math subtests you'll face? Find some helpful tips and handy formulas to know on the free Cheat Sheet at `www.dummies.com/cheatsheet/asvabafqt`. I also give you a rundown of the minimum AFQT score standards for each branch of the military.

You can also access bonus articles on double-checking your algebra answers, improving your vocabulary, and ways parents can help their kids prep for the AFQT. Head to www.dummies.com/extras/asvabafqt for these goodies.

Where to Go from Here

You don't have to read this book from cover to cover in order to maximize your AFQT score. If you decide to skip around, look over the table of contents and choose which topics you're interested in.

You may want to brush up on word problems but already know that you'll ace the Paragraph Comprehension subtest. If so, head to Chapters 10 and 11, but skip Chapters 6 and 7.

You may want to jump straight to Chapter 12 and take the first AFQT practice exam — that way, you can get an idea of what subjects you need to study more. Early on in your reading of the book, check out Chapter 2, which provides invaluable information regarding how the AFQT score is computed and how the score applies to military enlistment.

No matter where you start, I wish you all the best in your future military endeavors. I enjoyed every single second of my 23-year military career, and I'm confident you'll enjoy your time in the military as well.

Part I
Getting Started with ASVAB AFQT

getting started with

ASVAB AFQT

In this part . . .

- ✔ Get an overview of the ASVAB AFQT, how it's scored, and how to prepare for it.

- ✔ Check out the differences between the paper and computerized test, find out what your score means, and get details on the possibility of retaking the test.

- ✔ Figure out what study strategy works best for you, take advantage of study tips, and prepare yourself for test day.

Chapter 1

Examining the AFQT

If you're thinking about joining the U.S. military, your AFQT score may well be the most important score you achieve on any military test. Sure, other tests determine which military jobs you may get or whether you get promoted, but what good are those if you can't get into the military in the first place? You need a qualifying score on the AFQT, or your plans for enlistment may be compromised. You could be a young Rambo in the making, in perfect health, able to run three miles in three minutes, and it wouldn't matter if you didn't have a qualifying AFQT score.

The services have years and years of research to back up their policy of using the AFQT score as qualifications for enlistment. Study after study has shown that an individual's AFQT score is the single most significant factor in determining whether a recruit will make it through basic training and the first enlistment period. It costs the military more than $50,000 to process a new recruit for enlistment and send that person through basic training (and that's not even including the cost of additional specialized schooling after you've graduated), so you can see why the services want to maximize their chances of getting their money's worth.

Thankfully, with a little review, there's absolutely no reason that you shouldn't be able to score well on the AFQT. The score is, after all, composed of four areas that you studied intensely during your high-school years: basic math, math word problems, vocabulary, and reading. That's where *ASVAB AFQT For Dummies*, 2nd Edition, comes in. Other test-prep books, such as my *ASVAB For Dummies* (Wiley), try to prepare you for the entire Armed Services Vocational Aptitude Battery (ASVAB) and may be a great addition to your review, but this book is specifically designed to help you boost the most important ASVAB score of all: the AFQT score.

Getting a Close-Up View of the AFQT

The AFQT isn't a stand-alone test. You can't just walk into a recruiter's office and say you want to take the AFQT. You have to take the entire ASVAB, which consists of nine separate subtests. Four of those subtests make up the score that's known as the *AFQT score*. The AFQT score determines whether you're qualified to join the service of your choice. (Turn to Chapter 2 for the minimum qualifying scores for each service.)

In the beginning, there was no AFQT

When you start basic training, you learn about military history. Why not start a little sooner and find out where this whole testing thing came from?

The Army began general testing of draftees during World War I. In order to provide a method for classifying these soldiers, the Army developed the Army Alpha Test, which consisted of 212 multiple-choice and true/false questions, including common-sense questions and vocabulary and arithmetic problems. But many of the draftees couldn't read or write, so the Army developed the Army Beta Test, which required little word knowledge and relied on pictures and diagrams. Nearly 2 million soldiers took one of these tests during World War I.

During World War II, the Army General Classification Test (AGCT) replaced the Alpha and Beta tests. The new test had 150 questions — mostly vocabulary and arithmetic. The AGCT was used by the Army and Marine Corps to assign recruits to military jobs. Of the 9 million soldiers and marines who took this test during World War II, just over 60 percent could read and write above a third-grade level. During this time, a completely separate aptitude test was given to Navy recruits; it was called the Navy General Classification Test (NGCT). (The Air Force didn't have a test because the United States technically didn't have an Air Force as you know it today; the Air Force was part of the Army back then.)

In 1948, Congress required the Department of Defense to develop a uniform screening test to be used by all the services. In 1950, the Department of Defense came up with the Armed Forces Qualification Test (AFQT). This test consisted of 100 multiple-choice questions in areas such as math, vocabulary, spatial relations, and mechanical ability. The military used this test until the mid-1970s. In addition to the AFQT, service-specific tests classified prospective recruits into jobs. The Army Classification Battery, the Navy Basic Test Battery, and the Airman Qualification Examination (to name a few) were used for classification purposes from the late 1950s to the mid-1970s.

In the 1960s, as military jobs began getting more diverse and technical, the Department of Defense decided to develop a standardized military selection and classification test and administer it in high schools. That's where the ASVAB enters the picture. The first ASVAB test was given in 1968, but the military didn't use it for recruiting purposes for several years. In 1973, the draft ended and the nation entered the contemporary period in which all military recruits are volunteers. That year, the Air Force began using the ASVAB; the Marine Corps followed in 1974. From 1973 to 1975, the Navy and Army used their own test batteries for selection and classification. In 1976, the ASVAB became the official military job classification test used by all services, and the AFQT score became the official entry standard.

Here are the four subtests that make up your AFQT score:

- **Arithmetic Reasoning:** The Arithmetic Reasoning subtest consists of 30 math word problems. The subtest is multiple-choice. On the paper version, you get 36 minutes to correctly solve as many of the 30 problems as you can; on the computerized-adaptive test (the *CAT version* or *CAT-ASVAB*), it's 16 questions in 39 minutes. Chapter 10 leads you step-by-step through solving math word problems. Take a look at Chapter 11 for some tips on doing well on this subtest.

- **Word Knowledge:** The Word Knowledge subtest is a vocabulary test, plain and simple. You have to find words that are "closest in meaning" to underlined words in the question stem. You have 35 words to define in 11 minutes on the paper version, or 16 questions in 8 minutes on the CAT version. You can boost your vocabulary knowledge by following the advice in Chapter 4 and get an idea of what the subtest is all about in Chapter 5.

- **Paragraph Comprehension:** The Paragraph Comprehension subtest requires you to read a paragraph and then answer one to four questions about information contained in that paragraph. The paper version has 15 questions in all, and you're expected to complete the subtest in 13 minutes; the CAT version has 11 questions in 22 minutes. Chapter 6 can help you improve your reading comprehension skills, and you can get a little practice with the Paragraph Comprehension subtest in Chapter 7. (*Note:* Many other standardized tests refer to this type of question as "reading comprehension." The military likes to do things its own way, so it refers to them as "paragraph comprehension" questions. Different name, same thing.)

✔ **Mathematics Knowledge:** This subtest measures your ability to solve high-school level math problems. You have to solve 25 basic math problems in 24 minutes on the paper version or 16 questions in 20 minutes on the CAT version. Like the other subtests of the AFQT, all the questions are multiple-choice. To make sure your math skills measure up, see Chapter 8. Chapter 9 gives you an idea about the test format, as well as a little added math practice.

The AFQT isn't the only qualifying standard the military uses. You have to meet all the set standards in order to qualify for enlistment, including age, weight, number of dependents, medical history, education level, and criminal history.

Reaping the Benefits of Getting the Highest Possible Score

Chapter 2 gives you the minimum AFQT qualifying scores for each service. But you don't want to be satisfied with making just the minimum. You want to score as high as possible.

The services put great stock in your AFQT score. Not only does a high AFQT score give you a greater chance of enlistment, but it also means you may have access to special treats, such as the following:

✔ **Enlistment incentives:** Depending on current recruiting needs, individual services often tie the AFQT score to enlistment incentives, such as monetary bonuses or education benefits. For example, the Army often requires a minimum AFQT score of 50 to qualify for a bonus or to qualify for the Student Loan Repayment Program and other programs and benefits.

✔ **Enlistment programs:** Most military jobs are tied to individual line scores derived from the entire ASVAB, but certain enlistment programs sometimes require a minimum AFQT score that is significantly higher than the minimum score needed for a regular enlistment. For example, some Navy jobs (such as those in the nuclear field) require a higher AFQT score.

✔ **Education level:** You have to have a high-school diploma in order to join any of the services. The services can, however, take a limited number of GED applicants each year. To qualify with a GED, you must score higher on the AFQT than a qualified high-school diploma holder.

✔ **Quotas:** During times when the services are doing well meeting their recruiting goals, they often get more people who want to join than they have room for. At these times, the services get to pick and choose whom they let join and whom they don't. Branches commonly raise their AFQT minimum scores temporarily to separate the best-qualified applicants from the rest. Sometimes enlistment gets so competitive that the services may require a minimum score of 50 just to be considered. As of this writing, minimum scores for the services tend to rest in the 30s.

✔ **Waivers:** One past study indicated that only four out of ten people who walked into a recruiter's office were qualified for enlistment. Certain factors — such as criminal history, age, education level, number of dependents, or medical history — made them ineligible. Some of these eligibility criteria can be waived (sometimes with difficulty and processing delays). However, when the military grants a waiver, it's taking a chance on an otherwise ineligible recruit. For example, if you have too many criminal misdeeds in your past and require a waiver to enlist, a service is much more likely to grant the waiver if you score 85 on the AFQT than it is if you score 45.

Enlistment standards, programs, quotas, and incentives change — sometimes on a week-by-week basis, depending on the service's current recruiting needs. For the latest information, check with a military recruiter or visit `http://usmilitary.about.com`.

The AFQT is scored as a percentile. That means, for example, that if you score 70, you've scored higher than 70 percent of the thousands of people who've taken the test before you. The highest possible score on the AFQT is 99.

The AFQT isn't a one-shot deal. If you don't achieve a qualifying score, you can retest. After your first test, you have to wait at least 30 days to take a second test. After the second test, in most cases, you have to wait six months before you can test again. Keep in mind the age requirements and needs of the service. Although you can retest, getting a qualifying score upfront is the best way to keep your recruiter happy and your training and placement on schedule.

Establishing a Study Program

If you're not planning to make a study plan, you should plan again. A study plan is essential if you want to score well on the AFQT.

I can't give you one best way to prepare a study plan. Each person has different ways of studying and learning that work the best for him. Still, people generally fall into one of three categories:

- **Auditory learners:** These people learn best by hearing something. They do really well in lecture classes, and they love listening to audiobooks.

- **Visual learners:** These folks prefer to learn by seeing something. They would rather read a book or look at a diagram.

- **Tactile learners:** These people get the best results by doing something. Instead of listening to an explanation or reading an instruction manual, they need to do it in order to learn it.

Try to figure out what type of learner you are before developing a plan of study. Chapter 2 can help with this process and give you some tips about what to include in your study plan based on your own individual learning style.

Most people don't look forward to sitting down for a study session. Because of that, they try to make study more enjoyable by spending time on the subjects they're already good at. After all, studying familiar information is much easier than learning something new. Try not to fall into this trap! If you're already an avid reader, you probably don't need to spend much of your time improving your reading comprehension skills. You're already going to ace that portion of the AFQT, right? Instead, spend most of your time boning up on the areas where you need improvement, such as math and math word problems.

Try to dedicate one to two hours per day to your AFQT studies. Pick a time and place where you won't be interrupted. Having your dad yell at you to cut the grass probably won't be beneficial to your study session. Also, turn off your cellphone. Is that call as important as your future military career? You won't be allowed to use your cellphone in basic training anyway, so this is a good time to get into the practice of not texting your BFF that OMG, J4I, UBD is making me AAK.

Having raised twin daughters, I happen to be an expert on this texting stuff. Your BFF is your "best friend forever." And "OMG, J4I, UBD is making me AAK" translates to "Oh my God, just for info, user brain damage is making me asleep at the keyboard."

Guessing Smart

All the questions on the ASVAB/AFQT are multiple-choice with four possible answers. That means if you answer eeny-meeny-miny-mo, by the law of averages, you'd get one-fourth of the questions right.

Of course, you can increase these odds immensely by studying. But the chances are good that no matter how much time you put into advanced study, you'll come across at least one question on the test that leaves you scratching your head.

When this happens, you can improve your odds of guessing correctly by guessing smart. Chapter 3 includes tips and techniques about smart guessing in general. Flip to Chapter 5 for tips on intelligent guessing for the Word Knowledge subtest, Chapter 7 for techniques you can use on the Paragraph Comprehension subtest, Chapter 9 for Mathematics Knowledge subtest guessing plans, and Chapter 11 to discover how to make intelligent guesses on the Arithmetic Knowledge subtest.

Using the Practice Exams to Your Advantage

This book includes four full-length AFQT practice exams, with questions that are very similar to the ones you see on the ASVAB subtests that comprise the AFQT score. The practice exams included in this book can help increase your confidence and ensure that you're ready to take the actual ASVAB, but you have to use them correctly.

When I wrote my first book, *ASVAB For Dummies,* many readers contacted me. Some were disappointed that the practice tests included in the book weren't the exact same as the questions they found on the actual ASVAB. I'll let you in on a little not-so-secret secret: No ASVAB or AFQT preparation book includes the exact same questions as what you find on the actual test. Not only would that be unethical, but it would probably also result in several federal law-enforcement agents knocking on the author's door — not my idea of a good time. Actual ASVAB test questions are controlled items; that means that the military keeps them to itself. If you see any questions on the actual ASVAB or AFQT that are the exact same as the ones you find in this book (or any other preparation guide), it's pure coincidence.

However, just because the practice exams don't include the exact same questions that you see on the AFQT doesn't mean that the practice exams aren't valuable — just use them the way they were designed to be used:

- ✔ **Practice Exam 1:** The first practice test is intended as an initial assessment tool. Take this test before you set up your study plan. You can use the results of Practice Exam 1 to determine which areas of the AFQT you need to spend the most time on.

- ✔ **Practice Exam 2:** Use this test as a progress check after a week or two of study. Adjust your study plan accordingly.

- ✔ **Practice Exam 3:** Take this practice exam about a week before you're scheduled to take the actual ASVAB. Use the results to determine which AFQT subjects need a little extra attention.

- ✔ **Practice Exam 4:** Take the final practice exam a day or two before the ASVAB to make sure you're ready and to boost your confidence. If you don't score well, you may want to consider asking your recruiter to reschedule your ASVAB test for a later date to give you more time to study.

You may find your recruiter trying to rush you to take the ASVAB and medical exam so he can get you signed up quickly. Recruiters live and die off their recruiting goals. Make sure you don't let the recruiter schedule your exam until you're sure you're ready to take the test.

The mini-AFQT computerized test (see Chapter 2) that recruiters have in their offices is a pretty good indicator of whether you're ready for the real test. Usually, people's AFQT scores are within five or six points of what the mini-AFQT predicts.

Although you can't equate scores on the practice exam with actual AFQT scores (because of the method of scoring the AFQT; see Chapter 2), shoot for a minimum of 80 percent on each subtest, keeping in mind whether your practice test mimics the paper version, the computerized version, or a random number of questions replicating the question type:

- **Arithmetic Reasoning:** For the paper version, this subtest has 30 questions. If you miss more than 6 on a practice exam, you should dedicate more study time to solving math problems. For the CAT-ASVAB, you have 16 questions. If you miss more than 3, you should concentrate on improving this score.

- **Word Knowledge:** The Word Knowledge subtest has 35 questions on the paper version. You need to focus more attention on this area if you miss more than 7 questions. You must complete 16 questions on the computer version, so you should study more if you miss more than 3 questions.

- **Paragraph Comprehension:** If you miss more than 3 of the 15 Paragraph Comprehension questions on the paper version or 2 out of 11 on the CAT version, dedicate more study time to your reading skills.

- **Mathematics Knowledge:** Missing more than 5 questions on this 25-question subtest indicates you need further study. Concentrate on your math skills if you miss more than 3 on a CAT-ASVAB practice test.

Chapter 2

Facing the AFQT Head-on

In This Chapter

▶ Considering computer versus paper tests

▶ Understanding how the AFQT is scored

▶ Knowing what score you need to get in

▶ Taking the test again to get a better score

*E*veryone looking to enlist in the U.S. military has to take the Armed Services Vocational Aptitude Battery (ASVAB). The ASVAB consists of nine separately timed subtests, which the military primarily uses to determine your aptitude to learn various military jobs.

Four of the ASVAB subtests are used to compute the Armed Forces Qualification Test (AFQT) score. This score determines whether you're qualified to join the military service of your choice. Each branch of military service has its own minimum AFQT score standards. Your AFQT score tells the military what your chances are of making it successfully through your enlistment period. The services have conducted countless studies over the years, and the results are very clear: The higher your AFQT score, the greater the chances that you'll successfully complete your enlistment contract.

As you can imagine, the AFQT score is very important to the military recruiting commands. If you have a high AFQT score, you can expect your recruiter to be wining and dining you, offering you all kinds of enlistment incentives, and telling all his coworkers that you're his very best friend. On the other hand, if your AFQT score is below the minimum standards set by that service, you can expect your recruiter to say, "Don't call us; we'll call you." If you have a qualifying AFQT score that's mediocre, you can probably still enlist, but you'll most likely miss out on many enlistment goodies, such as enlistment bonuses. (Maybe you'll get a free T-shirt.)

In this chapter, I explain which of the four ASVAB subtests are used to compute your AFQT score and how the military calculates the score. I also tell you the minimum qualifying AFQT scores for each service branch, and explain how you can request a retest if your score is too low.

Looking at the Big ASVAB Picture

Depending on where and for what purpose you take the test, you may encounter several versions of the ASVAB. However, for the purposes of this discussion, I can separate them into just two: the computerized version and the pencil-and-paper version.

The computerized version of the ASVAB (CAT-ASVAB) contains nine separately timed subtests. On the CAT-ASVAB, Auto Information and Shop Information are separated into two different tests, whereas they're combined on the paper version. In Table 2-1, I outline the nine ASVAB subtests in the order that you take them; the bolded subtests are used to calculate the AFQT score.

Table 2-1	Details about the ASVAB Subtests		
Subtest	**Questions/Time (Paper Version)**	**Questions/Time (CAT-ASVAB)**	**Content**
General Science	25 questions, 11 minutes	16 questions, 8 minutes	General principles of biological and physical sciences
Arithmetic Reasoning	**30 questions, 36 minutes**	**16 questions, 39 minutes**	**Math word problems**
Word Knowledge	**35 questions, 11 minutes**	**16 questions, 8 minutes**	**Correct meaning of a word and best synonym or antonym for a given word**
Paragraph Comprehension	**15 questions, 13 minutes**	**11 questions, 22 minutes**	**Questions based on paragraphs (usually a few hundred words) that you read**
Mathematics Knowledge	**25 questions, 24 minutes**	**16 questions, 20 minutes**	**High-school math**
Electronics Information	20 questions, 9 minutes	16 questions, 8 minutes	Electricity and electronic principles and terminology
Mechanical Comprehension	25 questions, 19 minutes	16 questions, 20 minutes	Basic mechanical and physical principles
Auto and Shop Information	25 questions, 11 minutes	11 Auto Information questions, 7 minutes; 11 Shop Information questions, 6 minutes	Knowledge of automobiles, shop terminology, and tool use
Assembling Objects	16 questions, 15 minutes	16 questions, 15 minutes	Spatial orientation

You can't take just the four AFQT subtests of the ASVAB. You have to take all nine subtests in order to get a qualifying AFQT score. The military isn't set up to give *partial* ASVAB tests. For example, if you take the ASVAB and get line scores that qualify you for the military job(s) you want, but your AFQT score is too low to join, you have to retake the entire ASVAB — not just the four subtests that make up the AFQT — to get a higher AFQT score.

During the initial enlistment process, your service branch determines your military job or enlistment program based on minimum *line scores* it has established. Line scores are computed from the various subtests of the ASVAB. If you get an appropriate score in the appropriate areas, you can get the job you want — as long as that job is available and you meet other established qualification factors.

The computerized ASVAB (CAT-ASVAB)

Nobody really cares about the AFQT score except the military — and it cares *a lot!* So, because you're reading this book, I'm willing to bet that you're interested in joining the military. And if you're interested in joining the military, you're most likely to take the computerized version of the ASVAB. That's because most of those taking the ASVAB for the purpose of joining the military take it at a Military Entrance Processing Station (MEPS), and all these places use the computerized test.

The computerized version of the ASVAB — called the *CAT-ASVAB* (CAT stands for Computerized Adaptive Testing) — has the same questions as the paper version. The CAT-ASVAB adapts the questions it offers you based on your level of proficiency. (That's why it's called *adaptive*.) The first test item is of average difficulty. If you answer this question correctly, the next question is more difficult. If you answer the first question incorrectly, the computer gives you an easier question. (By contrast, on the pencil-and-paper ASVAB, hard and easy questions are presented randomly.) On the ASVAB, harder questions are worth more points than easier questions, so you want to get to them sooner to maximize your score.

Pros of taking the CAT-ASVAB

Maybe it's because young people today are more comfortable in front of a computer than they are with paper and pencil, but military recruiters have noted that among applicants who've taken both the paper-based version and the computerized version of the ASVAB, recruits tend to score slightly higher on the computerized version of the test.

When you take the CAT-ASVAB, the computer automatically calculates and prints your standard scores for each subtest and your line scores for each service branch. (If you're interested in line scores, which are used for military job-classification purposes, you may want to pick up a copy of *ASVAB For Dummies* [Wiley].) This machine is a pretty smart cookie; it also calculates your AFQT score on the spot. With the computerized version, you usually know whether you qualify for military enlistment on the same day you take the test and, if so, which jobs you qualify for.

Cons of taking the CAT-ASVAB

Unlike the pencil-and-paper version, you can't skip questions or change your answers after you enter them on the CAT-ASVAB. This restriction can make taking the test harder for some people. Instead of being able to go through and immediately answer all the questions you're sure of and then come back to the questions that require you to do some head scratching, you have to answer each question as it comes. Also, judging how much time to spend on a difficult question before guessing and moving on can be tough. Finally, if you have a few minutes at the end of the test, you can't go back and check to make sure you marked the correct answer to each question.

The pencil-and-paper test

Most people take the pencil-and-paper version of the ASVAB under the *Career Exploration Program,* a cooperative program between the Department of Education and the Department of Defense at high schools all across the United States. Although the results of this version can be used for military enlistment purposes (if taken within two years of enlistment), its primary purpose is to serve as a tool for high-school guidance counselors to use when recommending possible careers to high-school students.

You can also take the pencil-and-paper version for purposes of enlistment through a recruiter, but that's not done very often these days. In unusual circumstances, when it's impractical for an applicant to travel to a MEPS location, arrangements can be made to administer the pencil-and-paper version locally.

A final pencil-and-paper version of the ASVAB is the Armed Forces Classification Test (AFCT). This version of the ASVAB is used by folks already in the military who want to improve their ASVAB scores for the purposes of retraining into a different military job. Except for the name of the exam, the AFCT is exactly the same as the other versions of the ASVAB.

The mini-AFQT

You may take a sort of "mini-AFQT" in the recruiter's office. This test is called the Computer Adaptive Screening Test (CAST). Another version in use is called the Enlistment Screening Test (EST).

The CAST and EST aren't qualification tests; they're strictly recruiting tools that recruiters may use at their discretion. The CAST and EST contain questions similar (but not identical) to questions appearing on the ASVAB. They help estimate an applicant's probability of obtaining a qualifying AFQT score. If you take one of these mini-tests and score low, you probably don't want to take the actual ASVAB until you've put in some extensive study time. In fact, many recruiters won't even schedule you for the ASVAB unless you score well on the CAST or EST.

Pros of taking the paper-and-pencil test

The paper-based test allows you to skip questions that you don't know the answer to and come back to them later. You can't do so on the CAT-ASVAB. This option can be a real help when you're racing against the clock and want to get as many answers right as possible. You can change an answer on the subtest you're currently working on, but you can't change an answer on a subtest after the time for that subtest has expired.

You can mark up the exam booklet as much as you want. If you skip a question, you can circle the number of the question in your booklet to remind yourself to go back to it. If you don't know the answer to a question, you can cross off the answers that seem unlikely or wrong to you and then guess based on the remaining answers.

Cons of taking the paper-and-pencil test

On the pencil-and-paper version, harder questions are randomly intermingled with easier questions, so you may find yourself spending too much time trying to figure out the answer to a question that's too hard for you, and you may miss answering some easier questions at the end of the subtest because you ran out of time. The result: Your overall score will be lower.

The paper answer sheets are scored by an optical scanning machine. The machine has a conniption when it comes across an incompletely filled-in answer circle or stray pencil marks and will often stubbornly refuse to give you credit for these questions, even if you answered correctly.

Scoring the AFQT

If the military would simply score the subtests of the ASVAB as "number correct," or even "percent correct," a recruiter's life would be much easier. But, the military being the military, it does it the hard way.

The AFQT is often mistakenly called the "overall ASVAB score." You commonly hear someone say, "I got a 67 on the ASVAB," or "My ASVAB score was 92." That's not correct; it implies that the AFQT is derived from all nine subtests of the ASVAB, and it's not. The AFQT score is computed from just four of the ASVAB subtests — the four subtests of the ASVAB that measure your math and communicative ability (see "Looking at the Big ASVAB Picture" earlier in this chapter).

In this section, I explain how the AFQT is scored.

Understanding raw scores

The military scores each subtest of the ASVAB by using a raw score. A *raw score* is the total number of points you receive on each subtest of the ASVAB. You don't see your raw scores on the printout you receive from your recruiter after completing the test. The recruiter walks you back to the waiting area and retrieves two or three copies of your scores on a printout that includes all your line scores for each branch, your AFQT, and some other information.

You can't use the practice tests in this book (or any other ASVAB or AFQT study guide) to calculate your probable ASVAB scores. ASVAB scores are calculated using raw scores, and raw scores aren't determined simply from the number of right or wrong answers. On the actual ASVAB, harder questions are worth more points than easier questions.

Computing the verbal expression score

The military uses the verbal expression (VE) score to measure your communicative ability. The score goes toward computing the AFQT score as well as many of the military's line scores. The military brass (or at least their computers) determine your VE score by first adding the value of your Word Knowledge (WK) raw score to your Paragraph Comprehension (PC) raw score. The result is then converted to a scaled score ranging from 20 to 62.

Getting the AFQT score formula

To get your *AFQT raw score,* the computer doubles your VE score and then adds your Arithmetic Reasoning (AR) score and your Mathematics Knowledge (MK) score to it. Here's the formula:

AFQT raw score = 2VE + AR + MK

You don't get to see what your AFQT raw score is on your ASVAB score sheet. The computer converts the score into a percentile score.

Normalizing the percentile score

Your AFQT raw score is converted to an AFQT *percentile score,* ranging from 1 to 99. How does that work? In 1997, the Department of Defense conducted a "Profile of American Youth" study, which examined the AFQT raw scores of a national probability sample of 18- to 23-year-olds who took the ASVAB during that year.

Your AFQT percentile score is derived by comparing your AFQT raw score to those of the approximately 14,000 young people who took part in the study. For example, an AFQT percentile score of 50 means that you scored better than 50 percent of the individuals included in the 1997 study.

Making Sense of Minimum Qualifying Scores

The primary purpose of the AFQT percentile score is to determine whether you qualify for the military service of your choice. Each of the branches has its own priorities, so they all have different minimum qualifying scores.

Considering the AFQT tier categories

AFQT scores are grouped into five categories based on the percentile score ranges shown in Table 2-2. People who score in Categories I and II tend to be above average in trainability; those in Category III, average; those in Category IV, below average; and those in Category V, markedly below average.

Table 2-2	AFQT Tiers
Category	*Percentile Score*
I	93–99
II	65–92
III A	50–64
III B	31–49
IV A	21–30
IV B	16–20
IV C	10–15
V	0–9

If your AFQT percentile score falls into Category I, all the military services want you — very badly. They also want you if your score falls into Category II or Category IIIA.

If your score falls into Category IIIB, you may or may not be able to enlist, depending in large part on how the branch is currently doing on making its recruiting goals.

Congress has directed that the military can't accept Category V recruits or more than 4 percent of recruits from Category IV. If you're in Category IV, you must have a high-school diploma to be eligible for enlistment; you can't do it with a GED. Even so, if your score falls into Category IV, your chances of enlistment are very small.

Making the military cut

Each of the services has established minimum AFQT qualification scores within its respective recruiting regulations. Keep in mind that minimum scores change instantly depending on the needs of the services at that given time, so getting a high score is your best bet in order to remain competitive:

- **Army (including Army National Guard and Army Reserves):** The Army requires a minimum AFQT score of 31 for those with a high-school diploma and 50 for those with a GED. At times when the Army is experiencing high recruiting and reenlistment rates, it has been known to temporarily increase its qualifying AFQT score minimum to as high as 50.

- **Air Force (including Air National Guard and Air Force Reserves):** Air Force recruits must score at least 36 points on the AFQT to qualify for enlistment. In actuality, the vast majority (over 70 percent) of those accepted for an Air Force enlistment score 50 or above. For those who have a GED rather than a high-school diploma, the minimum is 65.

You're more likely to be struck by lightning than to enlist in the Air Force without a high-school diploma. Only about 0.5 percent of all Air Force enlistments each year are GED holders.

✔ **Navy:** Navy recruits must score at least 35 on the AFQT to qualify for enlistment. For GED holders, the minimum score is 50.

✔ **Navy Reserves:** The Navy is the only branch for which the requirements for the Reserves are different from the requirements for the branch itself. The Navy Reserves requires a minimum score of 31 on the AFQT for those with a high-school diploma and 50 for those with a GED.

✔ **Marine Corps (including Marine Corps Reserves):** Marine Corps recruits must score at least 32. Very few exceptions are made (about 1 percent) for some otherwise exceptionally qualified recruits with scores as low as 25. Candidates with a GED must score a minimum of 50 on the AFQT to be considered. The Marine Corps limits GED enlistments to no more than 5 percent per year.

✔ **Coast Guard (including Coast Guard Reserves):** The Coast Guard requires a minimum of 40 points on the AFQT. A waiver is possible for applicants with prior service if their ASVAB line scores (which are computed from the various ASVAB subtests) qualify them for a specific job and they're willing to enlist in that job. For the very few people (less than 5 percent) who are allowed to enlist with a GED, the minimum AFQT score is 50.

Just because you've met the minimum qualifying score for the service of your choice, that's no guarantee of enlistment. During good recruiting times, a branch commonly gets more qualified applicants than it has slots for. During these times, the military has to pick and choose which applicants to accept and which ones to turn away. Quite often, it does so based on AFQT scores.

Also, enlistment incentives such as enlistment bonuses and college funds (educational assistance) are often tied to minimum AFQT scores. As with quotas, this situation is subject to change at any time based on the service's current recruiting needs.

Retaking the Test

You can't actually "fail" the AFQT, but you can fail to achieve a high enough score to enlist in the service you want. If your AFQT score is too low, you need to work on one (or more) of four areas: math knowledge, arithmetic reasoning, reading comprehension, and word knowledge. These are the four subtests that are used to calculate your AFQT score. Parts II and III of this book are specifically designed to help you improve your scores on these four subtests. When you're sure you're ready, you can apply (through your recruiter) for a retest.

ASVAB tests are valid for two years as long as you aren't in the military. In most cases, after you join the military, your ASVAB scores remain valid as long as you're in. In other words, except in a few cases, you can use your enlistment ASVAB scores to qualify for retraining years later.

After you take an initial ASVAB test (taking the ASVAB in high school doesn't count as an initial test), you can retake the test after 30 days. After the retest, you must wait at least six months before taking the ASVAB again. There's no lifetime limit on how many times you can retest as long as you still meet the other requirements and a recruiter is still willing to work with you.

When you retake the ASVAB, the score on your *most recent* test is what counts. If you score lower on the retest, that's the score that's used for your military enlistment.

The bad news is that you can't retake the ASVAB on a whim or whenever you feel like it. Each of the services has its own rules.

Army

The Army allows a retest only if

- Your previous ASVAB test has expired. *Remember:* Test scores are valid for two years.

- You failed to achieve an AFQT score high enough to qualify for enlistment.

- Unusual circumstances occur. For example, if you're called away from the test because of an emergency, you can retake the test.

Army recruiters aren't allowed to schedule a retest for the sole purpose of increasing scores so you can qualify for enlistment incentives, job qualifications, or other special enlistment programs.

Air Force

The Air Force doesn't allow you to retest after you've enlisted in the Delayed Entry Program (DEP). Current policy allows retesting of applicants who aren't in the DEP, but already have a qualifying AFQT score. Retesting is authorized when the applicant's current line scores limit the ability to match an Air Force skill with his qualifications.

These days, you can't just take the ASVAB and a medical examination and head straight out to basic training. You have to wait your turn. The military has only so many basic training slots each month, and it has to reserve a slot for you (often several months in the future). To ensure your commitment, the services enlist you in the DEP. Under this program, you're enlisted in the inactive reserves while waiting for your basic training date to arrive.

Navy

The Navy allows you to retake the test if your previous ASVAB test has expired or you've failed to achieve a qualifying AFQT score for enlistment in the Navy.

In most cases, individuals in the DEP can't retest. One notable exception is the Navy's DEP Enrichment Program. This program provides for the provisional DEP enlistment of high-school diploma graduates with AFQT scores between 28 and 30. Individuals enlisted under the program are enrolled in academic enhancement training, retested with the ASVAB, and accessed onto active duty as long as they score 31 or higher on the subsequent ASVAB retest.

Marine Corps

The Marine Corps will authorize a retest if your previous test is expired. Otherwise, recruiters can request a retest as long as the initial scores don't appear to reflect your true capability (considering your education, training, and experience).

Additionally, the retest can't be requested *solely* because your initial test scores didn't meet the standards prescribed for specific military job qualification.

Coast Guard

For Coast Guard enlistments, six months must elapse since your last test before you may retest for the sole purpose of raising scores to qualify for a particular enlistment option. The Coast Guard Recruiting Center may authorize retesting after 30 days have passed from an initial ASVAB test if substantial reason exists to believe that your initial AFQT score or subtest scores don't reflect your education, training, or experience.

Chapter 3

Mastering the Art of Studying and Test Taking

• •

In This Chapter

▶ Reading the right way

▶ Discovering your learning style

▶ Making time to study

▶ Sitting down to the test

• •

A military career is all about taking tests. You take tests to enter the military, you take tests in basic training, you take tests when learning your new military job, you take tests to re-certify in your military job every few years, and you even take tests to earn promotions!

As a first sergeant, if I had a dime for every time I heard someone say, "I just can't take tests," well, I'd have a lot of dimes. I said it then to the troops, and I'll say it to you now: There's no such thing. If you couldn't take tests, you never would've made it through high school or gotten a GED, and one of the two is required in order to join the military. The truth of the matter is that when people get out of a school environment, they quickly lose the motivation and skills to study properly. Lack of success in test taking has more to do with ineffective study skills and techniques than intellectual ability.

Effective studying doesn't happen overnight. Studying requires time and patience. Getting the highest possible AFQT score is very much an individual affair; no one path will always produce the best results for everyone. Studying is a process that you learn through trial and error. You have to discover a strategy that works for you.

By incorporating the reading rules, study strategies, and test-taking techniques covered in this chapter, you should increase your chances of achieving the study and test-taking goals you set for yourself.

Reading for Study

I know what you're thinking: "Wait a minute. You talk about reading comprehension in Chapter 6. Why am I reading about reading here?" Reading for the purposes of study is a different kind of reading. *Reading comprehension* just requires you to place information into short-term memory long enough to answer a question about it a few seconds later. To read for the purposes of study, you need to commit important information to your long-term memory — at least long enough to take the ASVAB.

Checking out the survey, question, read, recall, and review method

This method is affectionately known as the SQR[3] method by those who make a living teaching students how to study. It helps you separate the important information from the chaff.

- ✔ **Survey:** The first step is to survey the material to get the big picture. This quick preview allows you to focus your attention on the main ideas and to identify the sections you want to read in detail. The purpose is to determine which portions of the text are most applicable to your task. Read the table of contents, introduction, section headings, subheadings, summaries, and the bibliography. Skim the text in between. Be sure to look at any figures, diagrams, charts, and highlighted areas.

- ✔ **Question:** After you've gained a feel for the substance of the material, compose questions about the subject you want answered. First, ask yourself what you already know about the topic and then generate your questions.

- ✔ **Read:** Now go back and read those sections you identified during your survey and search for answers to your questions. Look for the ideas behind words.

- ✔ **Recall:** To help retain the material, make a point to summarize the information you've read at appropriate intervals, such as the end of paragraphs, sections, and chapters. Your goal isn't to remember *everything* you've read — just the important points. Recite these points silently or aloud. Reciting the points helps you improve your concentration. You can also jot down any important or useful points. Finally, determine what information you still need to obtain.

- ✔ **Review:** This last step involves reviewing the information you've read. Skim a section or chapter immediately after you finish reading it. You can do so by skimming back over the material and by looking at any notes you made. Go back over all the questions you posed and see if you can answer them.

Taking notes

Reading something once isn't enough to really learn it. That's why note taking is so important. Clearly written, accurate notes help to capture information for later study and review. Taking notes also helps you to focus and learn during your study time.

Here are some note-taking and note-studying tips:

- ✔ **Organize the information.** Arrange data or ideas into small groups that make sense to you. The smaller groups make remembering the information easier.

- ✔ **Make the information relevant.** Connect the new information with the information you already know. Recalling the information you already know about a subject helps you recall the new stuff more easily.

- ✔ **Learn actively.** Use all your senses. Don't just speak aloud when reviewing your notes; get your entire body into the act. Get up and move around as if you're practicing for a speech.

- ✔ **Use your long-term memory.** To commit information to your long-term memory, review the material several times. Take advantage of your ability to remember best what you read last by changing the order of the information you recite during your review.

Putting Study Strategies to Work for You

Knowing how to study is like knowing how to fish: It's a set of learning skills that lasts a lifetime and brings many rewards. Just as there are many ways to fish, there are many ways to study. The key is finding the techniques that work best for you.

Working with your own learning style

Individuals learn best in individual ways. Some people may learn more quickly by hearing something. For others, seeing something may be the way. Still others may learn best by doing something. No one style of learning is better than another. However, by identifying your dominant learning style, you can adjust your study techniques to your individual learning abilities.

Auditory learners

Auditory learners use hearing to process information. When given a choice, strong auditory learners sit where they can easily hear the speaker and where outside sounds won't interfere. Some auditory learners sit to one side (on the side of their strongest ear). Many times, auditory learners have an easier time understanding the words from songs on the radio and announcements on public address systems than other people do.

Here are some characteristics of auditory learners:

- They prefer to hear information.
- They have difficulty following written directions.
- They have difficulty with reading and writing.
- They may not look the speaker in the eye; instead, they may turn their eyes away so they can focus more on listening.

If you're an auditory learner, keep in mind the following study suggestions:

- Listen to readings and lectures on CDs or online recordings (when available).
- Participate in discussions, ask questions, and repeat given information.
- Summarize or paraphrase written material and record the information.
- Discuss the material with someone else.

Visual learners

Visual learners need to see the big picture. They may choose a seat where they can see the whole stage or screen. They may like the back seat so everything is out in front and they can see it all. Visual learners survey the scene, like to sightsee, and see the forest despite the trees.

Visual learners share the following characteristics:

- They need to see it to learn it; they must have a mental picture.
- They have artistic ability.
- They have difficulty with spoken directions.
- They find sounds distracting.
- They have trouble following lectures.
- They may misinterpret words.

If you're a visual learner, follow these suggestions:

- Use visuals (graphics, films, slides, illustrations, doodles, charts, notes, and flashcards) to reinforce learning.
- Use multicolored highlighters to organize your notes.
- Write down directions.
- Visualize words, phrases, and sentences to be memorized.
- Write everything down; review often.

Tactile learners

Tactile learners have the need to touch and feel things. They want to feel or experience the lesson themselves. Given a choice, strong tactile learners are right in the middle of the action. They tear things apart to see how they work and put them back together without the directions. Tactile learners immediately adjust the seat, mirror, radio, and temperature when they get in the car.

Here are some characteristics of tactile learners:

- They prefer hands-on learning or training.
- They can often put objects together without the directions.
- They have difficulty sitting still.
- They learn better when they can get involved.
- They may be coordinated and have athletic ability.

If you're a tactile learner, try the following strategies:

- Make a model, do lab work, role-play, "be the ball."
- Take frequent breaks.
- Copy letters and words to learn how to spell and remember facts.
- Use a computer to study as much as possible.
- Write facts and figures over and over.
- Read and walk, talk and walk, repeat and walk.

Getting the most out of your study time

Whether you're studying for the ASVAB, the AFQT, military promotion tests, or a college course, proper study techniques can help you attain your goals.

Staying motivated

Studying and learning can take you far in life, yet getting down to those tasks can be so hard. Whether you're studying for college or to advance your career, studying can be one of the most important things you should be doing. Modern life — whether commercials, the Internet, friends, or TV — continually demands your attention, and all these things can feel easier to attend to than study. So what can you do to help stay motivated?

✔ **Give your study the attention it deserves.** If you were totally isolated, say on a desert island, you'd study every last morsel of your subject until you were completely versed in it because nothing else would be there to distract you. Imagine being in a cell with no TV and nothing except *ASVAB AFQT For Dummies.* You'd certainly read it cover to cover — and maybe many times! You'd know this book inside out because it's all you'd have to do. Having too much choice over what you pay attention to means that you need to exert willpower now more than ever to stay motivated.

✔ **Think about your goals.** Consider why you're studying and what you're studying for, because presumably it connects to what you want your life to be. All kinds of things may distract you when you're not studying. But ask yourself whether you want your life to be about drinking coffee, playing computer games, watching TV, and chatting with friends. Or do you have bigger fish to fry? Your life is about what you do with it, day in and day out.

✔ **Feed and develop your mind.** In today's culture of entertainment, everything is supposed to be fun and exciting. If you buy into this idea too much, then you stop benefiting from the more subtle stimuli because they don't immediately excite you. Your mind needs the rigor of study as well as the relaxation of entertainment. When you study well, you find it has its own subtle pleasures and satisfactions above and beyond the good results it can bring into your life. Imagine what feeling compelled to study hard and well would be like.

Managing your time

You may have all the time in the world, but if you don't use it wisely, it won't help you meet your goals. Procrastination is a problem for many people studying for the ASVAB or AFQT. The following tips can help you deal with this issue:

✔ **Clear your schedule.** Recognize that your obligations and the resulting stress are as important as other people's needs. Set limits around being interrupted or rescheduling your work time to accommodate others. Omit or reschedule some of your other obligations. You want to give full concentration to your studies without feeling guilty about what you're *not* doing.

✔ **Create a work area that's free from distractions and commit to staying there for at least one to two hours.** If you get side-tracked, remind yourself how this activity will help you to meet your goals.

✔ **Prioritize.** What has to be done first? What's worth more in terms of your AFQT score? (Chapter 2 can help you with this decision.) What's worth more in terms of your personal, educational, or career goals?

✔ **Use a daily to-do list.** This list helps you reach your goals and prioritize your daily tasks. As soon as you've completed a task, check it off your list. If you like keeping things on your computer, check out Remember The Milk (www.rememberthemilk. com), a free online to-do list.

✔ **Break down your study into chunks.** Estimate how much time you need to complete the task. Don't try to do it all at once. Break it down so it's doable and not so overwhelming. Stay up to date on assignments to help avoid overload.

✔ **Recognize that you don't have to be perfect.** Some people are so afraid that they won't perform perfectly that they don't do anything at all. Make sure you understand your goals. Then evaluate how important your study is and what level of performance is acceptable to you. Then just do it!

If you score better than the 50th percentile on the AFQT, you become a very attractive candidate to the military. You don't need a perfect score to get recruiters to chase you all over town.

✔ **Make study enjoyable.** Work on this task first, while you have more energy. Reward yourself when you check tasks off your daily to-do list.

You're only human, so you probably gravitate toward studying the subject areas that you have an interest in or that you're good at. If you're an avid reader, don't spend too much of your time studying reading comprehension. (You're already likely to sail through that part of the test.) On the other hand, if you had a hard time in math in high school, you'll want to spend extra time brushing up on your arithmetic skills.

Finding the right place to study

After you've found the time to study, commit to a time and place that meets your needs. Ask yourself whether the environment in which you're studying matches your learning style. If you don't know your dominant learning styles, refer to the "Working with your own learning style" section earlier in this chapter. Here are some aspects of the study environment you may need to consider:

- ✔ **Time of day:** Whenever possible, schedule your most challenging courses and most intense study sessions during the time of day when you're most alert. Some people are at their best in the morning; others don't get rolling until late afternoon. You know how you work, so plan to study when you can give your best to it.

- ✔ **Posture and mobility:** Recognizing your posture and mobility needs helps you plan where and when you should study. Some people prefer to sit at a table or desk (in a formal posture) in order to concentrate and study effectively. Others are able to learn more easily while sitting comfortably on a sofa or lying on the floor (in an informal posture). Still others need to move about in order to learn; reading while walking on a treadmill may be appropriate for them. Some people can sit and study for long periods of time (they have high persistence), while others need to take frequent breaks (they have low persistence).

- ✔ **Sound:** Contrary to popular belief, not everyone needs to study in a perfectly quiet environment. If you do choose to study to music, choose baroque classical music, such as Johann Sebastian Bach and Antonio Vivaldi. The tempo and instrumentation of this music seems to be most compatible with study and learning.

  Several studies have shown that baroque music, with a 60-beats-per-minute beat pattern, activates the left and right brain. The simultaneous left- and right-brain action maximizes learning and retention of information, according to one study conducted by the Center for New Discoveries in Learning.

- ✔ **Lighting:** Light does make a difference, so study in the environment that best matches your learning preferences. Studies have shown that some people become depressed because of light deprivation during the winter months. If you're one of those people, try to study and spend as much time as possible in highly lit places.

  Other studies have shown reading ability can be affected by the light contrast between print and paper color. Black letters printed on white paper create a high contrast. Some people find have a better time reading black print on blue or gray paper, which has less contrast and is easier on their eyes. (You can't always choose the paper your study material is printed on, but you can choose it for note-taking and reviewing purposes.)

- ✔ **Temperature:** You can't always control the temperature of a room, but you should be aware of your preference for either a cool or warm environment. Dress in layers so you can adjust to differences in room temperatures. Study in the environments in which you feel most comfortable.

Setting goals

Setting goals is a good way to accomplish a particularly difficult task. Developing study skills is one such task that takes time and effort to master. By setting S.M.A.R.T. goals related to an area of your study skills that needs improvement, you'll be studying like a pro in no time!

S.M.A.R.T. goals are

- ✔ **Specific:** After you decide what you want to work on, narrow it down to one thing. Be as specific as possible. Working out one problem at a time makes reaching your goal without spreading yourself too thin much easier. "I want to be a better reader" is too broad. Be more specific; for example, you may say, "I want to improve my reading speed." Write down this specific goal.

- ✔ **Measurable:** Goals are only achievable if you can measure them in some way. For example, rather than "I want to improve my reading speed," a measurable goal would be "I want to improve my reading speed by ten words per minute."

- ✔ **Action:** This step is where you decide how you're going to achieve your goal. Write this part as an "I will" statement. Following the example I give in the preceding bullet, your goal would now look something like, "I want to improve my reading speed by ten words a minute. I will do this by skimming over words like *the* and *an.*"

- ✔ **Realistic:** Make sure your goals are within reach. "I will improve my reading speed by memorizing every word in the dictionary" isn't reasonable for most people. Everyone has limits due to time, resources, or ability. Don't ignore these restraints, or you'll be setting yourself up to fail.

- ✔ **Timeline:** Set a date to accomplish the goal. Make sure this date is both specific and realistic for you. "I will meet this goal sometime over the summer" is vague. Try something more like, "I will meet this goal by the first day of school next fall." This wording gives you a definite time to shoot for and helps keep you working toward the goal. Goals can take only a few days to achieve; they may take months or years. Just be sure to make it a realistic timeline for you and your lifestyle.

Taking the Test: Putting Your Best Foot Forward

Sooner or later, the time for you to actually sit down and take the ASVAB will arrive. It may get here before you think you're ready. Or you may think that test day can't get here fast enough. Regardless of which group you fall into, you can improve your test-taking ability by understanding test-taking techniques, keeping a positive attitude, and overcoming your fears.

Approach the big test as you'd approach a giant jigsaw puzzle. It may be tough, but you can do it! A positive attitude goes a long way toward success. Use the practice tests in Part IV to familiarize yourself with the test structure and to build your confidence in the subject matter. Although the questions aren't the exact questions you'll see on the ASVAB, they're very, very similar. If you score well on the practice tests, you'll likely score well on the AFQT.

Some of the tricky problems can knock you off balance. However, if you prepare a plan of attack for what to do if you get stuck, you won't get worried or frustrated. In each of the chapters where I describe the individual tests (Chapters 5, 7, 9, and 11), I give you tips about what to do when all looks bleak. Go over these individual techniques before the test and make sure you have them down pat.

The day before

On the afternoon or evening before the test, get some exercise. Exercise can help you remain mentally sharp.

Cramming doesn't work. If you've followed a study plan, the night before the test you should do a quick review and get to bed early. **Remember:** Your brain and body need sleep to function well, so don't stay up late! The night before the test isn't the best time to go out for a few beers with your friends. Headaches and the ASVAB don't work well together.

Test day

The military has a saying: "If you're on time, you're late." You hear this tenet more than once in basic training. If you're taking the ASVAB for the purposes of joining the military (and chances of that are pretty good, if you're reading this book), then you're likely taking the test at a Military Entrance Processing Station (MEPS) and your recruiter has probably arranged your transportation.

At some stations, they conduct the ASVAB test in the afternoon and then set you up with a hotel room (depending on your travel site) to continue processing (medical examination, job selection, security clearance interview, and so on) early the next morning.

Arrive prepared

Your recruiter should brief you about what to expect and, in some cases, may even drive you to the MEPS herself. In other cases, depending on how far you live from the closest MEPS, you may be provided with public transportation. In any case, you want to make sure you're on time and ready:

- ✔ **Eat a light meal before the test (breakfast or lunch, depending on the test time).** You'll be better able to think when you have some food in your stomach. However, don't eat too much. You don't want to be drowsy during the test. Also, don't drink too much water. The test proctors will allow you to use the restroom if you need to, but with certain rules. If you leave to use the restroom during the paper version of the test, you can't come back until the next subtest begins. You can't leave to use the restroom during the computer version unless you're between subtests, and you can only be absent for up to five minutes.

- ✔ **If possible, arrange to arrive at the test site a little early, find a quiet place (such as your recruiter's car), and do a ten-minute power-study to get your brain turned on and tuned up.**

- ✔ **Bring only the paperwork your recruiter gave you and a photo ID.** Don't bring a calculator, your MP3 player, a backpack, or a sack full of munchies to the testing site. You won't be allowed to have them with you. The same goes for your cellphone.

- ✔ **Keep in mind that the MEPS is owned and operated by the military, so it doesn't have much of a sense of humor when it comes to dress codes.** Dress conservatively. Don't wear clothes with holes in them or profanity written on them. The only people at the MEPS who want to see your underwear are the doctors during the physical exam. Leave your hat at home because, under the military civilian dress code, you can't wear hats indoors.

Read the directions

Although this instruction may seem obvious, you can sometimes *misread* the directions when you're in a hurry, and that won't help you get the right answer. Each subtest has a paragraph or two describing what the subtest covers and giving instructions on how to answer the questions.

Understand the question

Take special care to read the questions correctly. Most questions ask something like, "Which of the following equals 6?" But sometimes a question may ask, "Which of the following does *not* equal 6?" You can easily skip right over the *not* when you're reading and get the question wrong.

You also have to understand the terms being used. When a math problem asks you to find the product of two numbers, be sure you know what *finding the product* means. (It means you have to multiply the two numbers.) If you add the two numbers together, you arrive at the wrong answer (and that wrong answer will likely be one of the answer choices).

Review all the answer options

Often, people read a question, decide on the answer, glance at the answer options, choose the option that agrees with their answer, mark the answer, and then move on.

Although this approach usually works, it can sometimes lead you astray. On the ASVAB, you're usually supposed to choose the answer that's "most correct." (Now and then, you actually need to do the opposite and choose the answer that's "least correct.") Sometimes several answers are reasonably correct for the question at hand, but only one of them is "most correct." If you don't stop to read and review all the answers, you may not choose the one that's "most correct." Or, after reviewing all the answer options, you may realize that you hastily decided upon an incorrect answer because you misread it.

When in doubt, guess. On the paper ASVAB, guessing is okay. If you choose the correct answer, that's the equivalent of +1 (or more, depending on how the question is weighted). If you don't answer a question, that's the equivalent of 0. If you guess on a question and get the question wrong, that's also the equivalent of 0, not −1. (No penalties here!) But if you guess correctly, that's +1 (or more). So you have everything to gain and nothing to lose by guessing if you take the paper version.

However, if you are taking the CAT-ASVAB, keep in mind that choosing answers randomly toward the end of your subtests may increase the likelihood of a penalty. If time is running short, try to read and legitimately answer the questions instead of filling in random guesses for the remaining items. The CAT-ASVAB applies a relatively large penalty when you provide several incorrect answers toward the end of a subtest.

In each of the chapters on a particular subtest (Chapters 5, 7, 9, and 11), I give you hints for making educated guesses that are specific to that topic. But here are some general rules:

- ✔ **Often, an answer that includes the word** *always, all, everyone, never, none,* **or** *no one* **is incorrect.**

- ✔ **If two choices are very similar in meaning,** *neither of them* **is probably the correct choice.**

- ✔ **If two answer options contradict each other,** *one of them* **is usually correct.**

- ✔ **The longer the answer, the better the chances that it's the correct answer.** The test makers have to get all those qualifiers in there to make sure that it's the correct answer and you can't find an example to contradict it. If you see phrases like *in many cases* or *frequently,* that's usually a clue that the test makers are trying to make the answer "most correct."

- ✔ **Don't eliminate an answer based on how frequently it appears.** For example, if Choice (B) has been the correct answer for the last five questions, don't assume that it must be the wrong answer for the question you're on just because that would make it six in a row.

- ✔ **If all else fails, trust your instincts.** Often, your first instinct is the correct answer.

The Air Force Senior NCO Academy conducted an in-depth study of several Air Force multiple-choice test results taken over several years. It found that when students changed answers on their answer sheets, they changed from a right to a wrong answer more than 72 percent of the time! The students' first instinct was the correct one.

Part II
English as a First Language

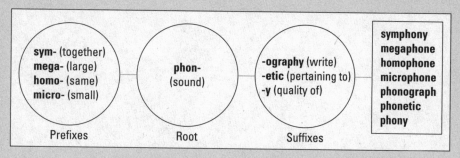

sym- (together)
mega- (large)
homo- (same)
micro- (small)

Prefixes

phon-
(sound)

Root

-ography (write)
-etic (pertaining to)
-y (quality of)

Suffixes

symphony
megaphone
homophone
microphone
phonograph
phonetic
phony

Illustration by Thomson Digital

Visit www.dummies.com/extras/asvabafqt for a free article that suggests ways to boost your vocabulary.

In this part . . .

- ✔ Discover how to build a strong vocabulary. You also review prefixes, suffixes, and roots to figure out the meaning of unfamiliar words.

- ✔ Understand how to find the main point and subpoints of a reading passage and analyze what you've read.

- ✔ Test yourself with Word Knowledge and Paragraph Comprehension practice questions.

Chapter 4

Developing a Solid Vocabulary

The military is in love with words. Military personnel write almost everything down in memos, manuals, regulations, standard operating procedures, and policy letters. They should hire a few *For Dummies* authors to write these items, because the current writers seem to love fancy words. A hammer isn't a hammer in the military; it's a "manually operated nail impact implement." The boss of your duty section isn't "the boss," or even "the supervisor"; she's the "noncommissioned officer in charge" (NCOIC for short).

If you're going to be successful in the military, you have to have a solid vocabulary, and that's why the military includes a Word Knowledge subtest as part of the AFQT score. How can you obey a regulation if you don't know what the words mean? And trust me, failure to obey a regulation is a big no-no in the military.

Your score on the Word Knowledge subtest, along with your score on the Paragraph Comprehension subtest (see Chapters 6 and 7), is used to compute what the military calls a *verbal expression* (VE) score. The VE score is then combined with your Arithmetic Reasoning score (see Chapters 10 and 11) and your Mathematics Knowledge score (see Chapters 8 and 9) to compute your AFQT score. (For more information on how these scores combine, turn to Chapter 2.)

The VE score is also used to determine qualification for many military jobs. If you're interested in which military jobs require a good VE score, you may want to consider picking up a copy of the bestselling *ASVAB For Dummies*, written by your friendly neighborhood ASVAB expert (me) and published by Wiley.

The good news is that anybody can improve his vocabulary. Ever since you first learned to talk, you've been learning new words and their meanings. In this chapter, I give you some hints, tips, and techniques you can use to speed up the process.

Growing Your Vocabulary

Your vocabulary naturally grows throughout your life. Even grumpy old writers like me learn a new word once in a while through everyday life experiences. But if the ASVAB is staring you in the face, you may not want to wait for life's natural process. In the following sections, you descry omnifarious contrivances to expedite progression of a comprehensive phraseology. I'm sorry; I got carried away. What I mean is you find some ways to improve your vocabulary.

Reading more to learn more

People who read a lot have larger vocabularies than people who don't read much. That sounds kind of obvious, but I'm sure the government has spent a few thousand dollars funding studies to confirm this.

It doesn't matter much what you read, as long as you make it a regular, daily practice. You don't have to read Homer or Keats. Leave that to the intellectuals in the Berkeley coffee shops. Your reading choices may be action-adventure or romance books for enjoyment, the daily newspaper, magazines, Internet articles and blogs, or even comic books. (If it weren't for Batman and Robin, I wouldn't know what "Zow!" means.)

When reading online, get into the habit of keeping an extra browser window open and pointed to an online dictionary site, such as www.dictionary.com. That way, if you run into a word you don't know, you can quickly copy and paste it to the online dictionary.

Talking to people

Other people have vocabularies that differ from yours. If you speak to a variety of people, and you do it often, you're exposed to a variety of different cultures and occupations, all of which expose you to new words.

Carry a small pocket notebook with you wherever you go. That way, when you come across a new word, you can write it down and look it up in a dictionary later.

Adding words to your vocabulary

Make a goal to learn at least one new word per day. A great way to meet that target is to visit or subscribe to one of the many Internet word-of-the-day websites. Here are a few suggestions:

- **Dictionary.com:** You can visit the site daily or subscribe to the word of the day via e-mail. Visit http://dictionary.reference.com/wordoftheday.

- **Merriam-Webster Online:** A new vocabulary word appears every single day. Point your browser to www.merriam-webster.com/cgi-bin/mwwod.pl.

- **A.Word.A.Day:** Provided by Wordsmith.org, this free service presents a new word for you to check out every day, or you can subscribe to its e-mail list. The site is www.wordsmith.org/words/today.html.

- **The New York Times Word of the Day:** *The New York Times* offers a new word every day, along with an example of how the word was used in a recent *New York Times* story. Visit http://learning.blogs.nytimes.com/category/word-of-the-day/.

- **The Oxford English Dictionary:** If you want more than just a word and definition, try the *Oxford English Dictionary* word of the day. In addition to definitions, the page also provides pronunciation, spelling, etymology, and a date chart that shows when the word was first used. The word of the day is also available by e-mail subscription and RSS feed. Check out www.oed.com.

Try to use your new word in conversation a couple of times to help you remember it. Writing a few example sentences with new vocabulary can help you remember the new words in context.

A crossword success story

My late father never finished high school. (That wasn't unusual in the 1940s, when many kids dropped out of school to work on family farms.) However, my dad had the most extensive vocabulary of anyone I've ever known. His secret? From the age of 20 on, my dad was hooked on the daily crossword puzzle that was published in the local newspaper. He did the crossword puzzle every single day of his life at the morning breakfast table, and if he didn't have time to finish, he would save it until he got home from work. Woe be to the family member who accidently threw away the paper if Dad hadn't finished the puzzle that morning.

Using puzzles and games to improve your vocabulary

A fun way to increase your word knowledge is to do crossword puzzles or play word games. Scrabble and Mad Libs, for example, are great ways to reinforce new vocabulary words. Many online games are available as well, such as Scrabble and Words With Friends. You can improve your vocabulary while having fun playing online games! It's a win-win.

You're on my list: Working with word lists

Learning a new word every day doesn't do you much good if you forget it a week later. Learning often requires repetition, and that's especially true when it comes to memorizing new words.

Keep a list of all the new words you learn and go over that list at least two or three times a week until you're sure the new words have become part of your vocabulary.

Just to get you started, I give you 50 free words in Table 4-1.

Table 4-1		50 Vocabulary Words
Word	*Part of Speech*	*Meaning*
Abrupt	Adjective	Beginning, ending, or changing suddenly
Acrid	Adjective	Harshly pungent or bitter
Becalm	Verb	To make quiet
Buffoon	Noun	A clown
Chaos	Noun	Utter disorder and confusion
Cognizant	Adjective	Taking notice of something
Defer	Verb	To put off or delay to a later time
Derision	Noun	The act of ridiculing or making fun of something
Effulgence	Noun	Great brightness
Enmity	Noun	Hatred
Famish	Verb	To cause extreme hunger or thirst
Fealty	Noun	Loyalty

continued

Table 4-1 *(continued)*

Word	Part of Speech	Meaning
Generalize	Verb	To draw general inferences
Grotto	Noun	A small cavern
Habitual	Adjective	According to usual practice
Hideous	Adjective	Extremely ugly or appalling
Ichthyic	Adjective	Fishlike
Icon	Noun	An image or likeness
Illusion	Noun	An unreal image
Irritate	Verb	To excite ill temper or impatience in something
Jovial	Adjective	Merry
Juxtapose	Verb	To place close together
Kernel	Noun	A grain or seed
Kinsfolk	Noun	Relatives
Laggard	Adjective or noun	Falling behind; one who lags behind
Laud	Verb	To praise
Maize	Noun	Native American corn
Malevolence	Noun	Ill will
Nestle	Verb	To adjust cozily in snug quarters
Novice	Noun	Beginner
Obese	Adjective	Exceedingly fat
Obtrude	Verb	To push or thrust oneself into undue prominence
Pare	Verb	To cut, shave, or remove the outside from anything
Pedagogue	Noun	Teacher; one who is fussily academic
Quadrate	Verb	To make square; to make conform or agree with
Quiescence	Noun	Quietness
Rancor	Noun	Malice
Raucous	Adjective	Loud and rowdy
Sanguine	Adjective	Cheerfully optimistic; having the color of blood
Sepulcher	Noun	A burial place
Teem	Verb	To be full to overflowing
Tenacious	Adjective	Unyielding
Umbrage	Noun	Injury or offense
Vacillate	Verb	To waver
Valid	Adjective	Founded on truth
Velocity	Noun	Speed
Wile	Noun	An act or a means of cunning deception
Wizen	Verb	To become or cause to become withered or dry
Yokel	Noun	Country bumpkin
Zealot	Noun	One who is enthusiastic to an extreme or excessive degree

Flashing yourself with flashcards

Flashcards have been around for a long time. They're still in wide use in these days of electronics and computers because they work. And they work especially well for subjects that just require simple memorization.

You can make flashcards out of any stiff paper material, like index cards, construction paper, or card stock. Write the words from your list on flashcards — words on the front and a short definition on the back. Use only one word per card.

As far back as 1885, a psychologist named Hermann Ebbinghaus, who specialized in memory research, published a study that detailed the effective use of flashcards. According to his rules, you should follow these steps:

1. **Review all the cards in the set, looking at each front and back.**

   Go through the set several times.

2. **Test and sort.**

   Read the front of the card. Try to say what's written on the back. If you're wrong, put the card in a "wrong" pile. Do the same for each card until the cards are sorted into "right" and "wrong" piles.

3. **Review the "wrong" pile.**

   Read each card in the "wrong" pile, front and back. Go through the "wrong" pile several times.

4. **Test and sort with the "wrong" pile.**

   Go through the cards of the "wrong" pile, testing yourself with them and sorting them into "right" and "wrong" piles just as you did with all the cards in Step 2. Keep working with the cards of the "wrong" pile until they're all in the "right" pile.

Building a Word from Scratch

Many English words are created from building blocks called roots, prefixes, and suffixes. Not every word has all three, but many have at least one. The *prefix* is the part that comes at the front of a word, the *suffix* is the part that comes at the end of a word, and the *root* is the part that comes in the middle of a word. Think of roots as the base of the word and prefixes and suffixes as word parts that are attached to the base.

If you don't know the meaning of a word, you can often break it down into smaller parts and analyze those parts. For instance, *introspect* is made up from the root *spect*, which means to look, and the prefix *intro*, which means within. Taken together, *introspect* means "to look within." Wasn't that fun?

If you memorize some of these word parts, you'll have a better chance of figuring out the meaning of an unfamiliar word when you see it on the Word Knowledge subtest — and that's a good thing. Figuring out the meaning of unfamiliar words is how people with large vocabularies make them even larger. (They look up words in the dictionary, too.)

Rooting around for roots

A root is a word part that serves as the base of a word. If you recognize a root, you can generally get an idea of what the word means, even if you're not familiar with it. As Mr. Miyagi said in *The Karate Kid,* "Root strong, tree grow strong." All right, Daniel-san, in terms of your vocabulary, think of it this way: If your knowledge of word roots is strong, your vocabulary will be much larger.

In Table 4-2, I list some common roots. Memorize them. When you sit down to take the ASVAB, you'll be glad you did.

Table 4-2	Roots	
Root	**Meaning**	**Sample Word**
anthro or anthrop	relating to humans	anthropology
bibli or biblio	relating to books	bibliography
brev	short	abbreviate
cede or ceed	go, yield	recede
chrom	color	monochrome
circum	around	circumnavigate
cogn or cogno	know	cognizant
corp	body	corporate
dic or dict	speak	diction
domin	rule	dominate
flu or flux	flow	influx
form	shape	formulate
frac or frag	break	fragment
graph	writing	biography
junct	join	juncture
liber	free	liberate
lum	light	illuminate
oper	work	cooperate
pat or path	suffer	pathology
port	carry	portable
press	squeeze	repress
scrib or script	write	describe
sens or sent	think, feel	sentient
tract	pull	traction
voc or vok	call	revoke

Attaching prefixes and suffixes

A prefix is a group of letters added before a word or base to alter the base's meaning and form a new word. In contrast, a suffix is a group of letters added after a word or base. Prefixes and suffixes are called *affixes* because they're attached to a root.

Tables 4-3 and 4-4 list some common prefixes and suffixes. Each list has the word part, its meaning, and one word that uses each word part. Writing down additional words that you know for each word part can help you memorize the list.

Table 4-3	Prefixes	
Prefix	**Meaning**	**Sample Word**
a-	no, not	atheist
ab- or abs-	away, from	absent
anti-	against	antibody
bi-	two	bilateral
con- or contra-	against	contradict
de-	away from	depart
dec-	ten	decathlon
extra-	outside, beyond	extracurricular
fore-	in front of	foreman
geo-	earth	geology
hyper-	excess, over	hyperactive
il-	not	illogical
mal- or male-	wrong, bad	malnutrition
multi-	many	multifamily
non-	not	nonfat
omni-	all	omnivore
ped-	foot	pedestrian
que-, quer-, or ques-	ask	question
re-	back, again	replay
semi-	half	semisweet
super-	over, more	superior
tele-	far	telephone
trans-	across	transplant
un-	not	uninformed

Table 4-4	Suffixes	
Suffix	**Meaning**	**Sample Word**
-able or -ible	capable of	agreeable
-age	action, result	breakage
-al	characterized by	functional
-ance	instance of an action	performance
-ation	action, process	liberation
-en	made of	silken
-ful	full of	helpful

continued

Table 4-4 *(continued)*

Suffix	Meaning	Sample Word
-ic	consisting of	acidic
-ical	possessing a quality of	statistical
-ion	result of act or process	legislation
-ish	relating to	childish
-ism	act, practice	Buddhism
-ist	characteristic of	elitist
-ity	quality of	specificity
-less	not having	childless
-let	small one	booklet
-man	relating to humans, manlike	gentleman
-ment	action, process	establishment
-ness	possessing a quality	goodness
-or	one who does something	orator
-ous	having	dangerous
-y	quality of	tasty

A Word by Any Other Name: Surveying Synonyms and Antonyms

English is a complicated language. You could probably learn Spanish, German, or even Korean from scratch more easily than you could English. How many other countries do you know that have to teach their own native language throughout all the school grades (and even college!)?

In the English language, you usually have more than one way to say the same thing, even by swapping just one word. These different words with the same meaning are called *synonyms*. Synonyms are different words that have the same or very similar meanings. *Funny, amusing,* and *comical* are synonyms; they all mean the same thing.

In fact, that's what the Word Knowledge subtest on the ASVAB really does: It tests your ability to select synonyms for the underlined words contained in the question stem. Look at the following example.

Perform most nearly means:

(A) eat

(B) dance

(C) execute

(D) sing

The correct answer is Choice (C). *Execute* (to carry out something) is a synonym of *perform*, which means the same thing. Although you can perform a dance or perform a song, *dance* and *sing* don't actually mean the same thing as *perform*.

When you look up a new word in the dictionary (see "Adding words to your vocabulary") and add it to your word list (see "You're on my list: Working with word lists"), you should include synonyms, because you're very likely to see them on the Word Knowledge subtest.

An *antonym* is a word that has the opposite or nearly opposite meaning of another word. *Smile* and *frown* are antonyms of one another. The test makers often use antonyms as wrong answers on the Word Knowledge subtest. Knowing antonyms for words not only improves your chances of narrowing your answer choices but also beefs up your vocabulary. For example, if you know that *fast* is an antonym of *slow* and you know what *slow* means, you also know what *fast* means.

How can you find the synonym of a word (or the antonym, for that matter)? A good place to start is the dictionary. Many dictionary entries include the abbreviation *syn,* which means *synonym.* The words that follow this abbreviation are synonyms of the entry word. You may also see the abbreviation *ant* in an entry. This abbreviation stands for *antonym,* and the word or words that follow it mean the opposite of the entry word.

Thesauruses are special dictionaries of synonyms and antonyms. We writers use them all the time to make us look smarter. Here are a couple of online thesauruses you can use to look up synonyms for words on your word list:

✔ **Thesaurus.com:** `http://thesaurus.com`

✔ **Merriam-Webster Online:** `www.merriam-webster.com`

Getting Homogeneous with Homonyms

Some words in the English language are spelled the same but have two or more meanings. For example, a *fluke* can mean a fish, the end parts of an anchor, the fins on a whale's tail, or a stroke of luck.

Some words are spelled the same but have different meanings and are often pronounced differently. The word *bow,* meaning a special kind of knot, is pronounced differently from *bow,* meaning to bend at the waist. *Bow,* meaning the front of a boat, is pronounced the same as *bow* (bend at the waist), but *bow,* meaning a weapon, is pronounced the same as *bow* (a special knot). See why foreigners trying to learn English get frustrated?

Other words are pronounced the same but are spelled differently and mean something different. *To, too,* and *two* and *there, their,* and *there* are examples. All these types of words are collectively known as *homonyms.*

The last type of homonym is especially important when it comes to the Word Knowledge subtest of the ASVAB. The test makers won't try to trick you by having two homonym answers for words that are spelled the same but have multiple possible answers, but they will use homonyms that are spelled differently and have different meanings.

Flue most nearly means:

(A) sickness

(B) fly

(C) chimney

(D) None of the above

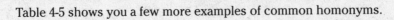

You may be tempted to choose Choice (A), but that would be correct if *flu* were the test word. The past tense of *fly* is *flew*. The word *flue* means a chimney pipe.

Table 4-5 shows you a few more examples of common homonyms.

You can see an extensive list of homonyms on Alan Cooper's Homonym Page at www.cooper.com/alan/homonym_list.html.

Table 4-5	Common Homonyms	
Word	**Definition**	**Example Sentence**
Allowed	Permitted	He <u>allowed</u> the audience to participate.
Aloud	Normal volume of speaking	They couldn't speak <u>aloud</u> in the library.
Cent	A bronze coin	I couldn't believe I got the comic book for just one <u>cent</u>.
Scent	Aroma	The <u>scent</u> coming from the kitchen made my mouth water.
Sent	Past tense of send	He <u>sent</u> the letter Monday.
Cue	Stimulus to action	A door slamming was his <u>cue</u> to exit the stage.
Queue	Line	There was a large <u>queue</u> of cars waiting to park.
Die	To cease living	I'll <u>die</u> if my parents find out!
Dye	To color or stain	She wants to <u>dye</u> her hair red.
Elicit	To draw or bring out	He vowed to <u>elicit</u> the truth from his friend.
Illicit	Unlawful	He used <u>illicit</u> means to avoid paying taxes.
Fairy	Supernatural being	The <u>fairy</u> was dancing in the night.
Ferry	A boat for crossing rivers or other small bodies of water	The <u>ferry</u> took us quickly across the river.
Gorilla	Large ape	I threw the <u>gorilla</u> a banana.
Guerrilla	Irregular soldier	The band of <u>guerrillas</u> attacked the convoy.
Hangar	Building for airplanes	Jack pulled the aircraft into the <u>hangar</u>.
Hanger	A device for hanging things	Mom said to put the shirt on a <u>hanger</u>.
It's	Contraction of *it is*	<u>It's</u> a very hot day.
Its	Possessive pronoun	The bank said <u>its</u> savings accounts were the best.
Know	To possess knowledge	I <u>know</u> you went to the store.
No	Zero or negative	I told John there was <u>no</u> way we would travel together.
Lessen	To make less	We gave him medicine to <u>lessen</u> his pain.
Lesson	Something to be learned	We must never forget the <u>lessons</u> of the past.

Word	Definition	Example Sentence
Mail	Postal delivery	I expected the check to be in the <u>mail</u>.
Male	A gender	The teacher asked all <u>males</u> to go to one room and all females to go to another.
Naval	Pertaining to ships	He wanted to become a <u>naval</u> officer.
Navel	Belly button	Mom always said not to play with my <u>navel</u>.
Ordinance	Decree or local law	Spitting on the sidewalk was against the town <u>ordinance</u>.
Ordnance	Military ammunition	We were running low, so we asked the sergeant for more <u>ordnance</u>.
Patience	The ability to suppress restlessness	I couldn't believe her <u>patience</u> with the students.
Patients	People under medical care	The nurse treated all her <u>patients</u> with respect.
Reek	Bad smell	The <u>reek</u> of the skunk invaded the living room.
Wreak	Inflict	Jack continued to <u>wreak</u> havoc every time he got upset.
Sleight	Dexterity	The magician's <u>sleight</u> of hand was amazing.
Slight	Small amount	There was only a <u>slight</u> increase in salaries this year.
Threw	Propelled by hand	He <u>threw</u> the ball to first base.
Through	In one side and out the other	Dad drove <u>through</u> the tunnel.
Vary	Change	The interest rate continues to <u>vary</u> up and down.
Very	Extreme	I am <u>very</u> happy with *ASVAB AFQT For Dummies*.
Weak	Not strong	After his illness, Paul was very <u>weak</u>.
Week	Seven days	It'll take at least a <u>week</u> to finish this report.
Your	Belongs to you	<u>Your</u> new car is really cool.
You're	Contraction of *you are*	<u>You're</u> going to be in trouble when Dad gets home.

Chapter 5

The Word Knowledge Subtest

A decent vocabulary is essential in the military if you want to get ahead. The military operates on paperwork, and whether you're trying to get more supplies (submit necessary logistical requisitions) or get the assignment you want (application for personnel career-enhancement programs), you need to develop a good vocabulary.

Word Knowledge is what the military calls the vocabulary subtest on the ASVAB. Because a strong vocabulary is essential to success in the military, the Department of Defense has made this vocabulary test a part of the all-important AFQT score — the score that determines whether you're qualified to join the military service of your choice (see Chapter 2). The military considers clear communication so important that this skill is taught and graded at all levels of leadership training and often required for promotion.

Word knowledge isn't part of the AFQT score just because the military likes to use big words. It's included because words stand for ideas, and the more words you understand, the more ideas you can understand (and the better you can communicate with others). So society (including people in the military) often equates a large vocabulary with intelligence and success.

Getting Acquainted with the Test Format

The Word Knowledge portion of the ASVAB measures your vocabulary knowledge. It consists of 35 questions on the paper version (but only 16 on the CAT-ASVAB), and the questions usually come in one of two flavors. The first type of question asks for a straight definition. Your task is to choose the answer closest in meaning to the underlined word. Look at the following example:

Abatement most nearly means:

(A) encourage

(B) relax

(C) obstruct

(D) terminate

In this case, the correct answer is Choice (D) because *abatement* means putting an end to something or subsiding.

In the second type of question, you see an underlined word used in the context of a sentence. Again, your goal is to choose the answer closest in meaning to the underlined word as it's used in the sentence. For example:

His painting was <u>garish</u>.

(A) offensive

(B) tacky

(C) pretty

(D) expensive

"Closest in meaning" doesn't mean "the exact same thing." You're looking for words most similar in meaning.

In case you're wondering, the answer is Choice (B).

Bumping Up Your Test Score

Usually, on the Word Knowledge subtest, you know the answer at first glance or you don't. Even with that restriction, however, you can pick up a few tricks to help you get the best score possible.

Keeping an eye on the clock

Like all the ASVAB subtests, the Word Knowledge subtest is timed. On the paper version, you have 11 minutes to answer the 35 questions, which means that you have slightly less than 20 seconds to answer each question. On the CAT-ASVAB, you have 16 questions in 8 minutes, giving you 30 seconds for each question. These amounts are plenty of time as long as you stay focused and don't waste time thinking about last night's date (sorry, I mean "social encounter").

If you're taking the computerized version of the ASVAB, your remaining time appears on the computer screen. If you're taking the paper version of the test, a clock is clearly visible in the room, and the test proctor posts the start and stop time for the subtest on a blackboard or whiteboard.

Watching out for the evil homonym

A *homonym* is a word with more than one meaning (see Chapter 4). The word may be spelled the same or it may be spelled differently. If it's spelled the same, it may have a different pronunciation. Some homonyms spelled differently can have the same pronunciation.

The ASVAB doesn't contain any trick questions. In other words, the test doesn't present you with two legitimate answers and ask you to try to decide which one is the "best." However, homonyms can still trip you up if you don't pay attention. Look at the following example:

<u>Bate</u> most nearly means:

(A) tease

(B) lessen

(C) treasure

(D) pregnant

Bate and *bait* are homonyms. They're two words that sound the same, but they're spelled differently and mean different things. *Bait* means to torment or tease (it's also used to entice fish), and *bate* means to make less.

Some homonyms are spelled the same but have different meanings. You won't see multiple correct definitions on the Word Knowledge subtest when you're doing a direct definition problem, but you may see such multiple correct definitions when the word is used in the context of a sentence. For example:

Jack tied a <u>bow</u> around his neck.

(A) knot

(B) weapon

(C) ship front

(D) triangle

All the answer choices are proper definitions for the word *bow*. However, only one choice makes sense for bow in the context of the sentence. It just wouldn't make sense for Jack to tie a weapon, front of a ship, or triangle around his neck.

Considering guessing

Sometimes on the Word Knowledge subtest, you just don't know the answer. In that case, don't leave it blank. (You can't leave answers blank on the computerized version of the test anyway.) The paper version of the ASVAB doesn't penalize you for wrong answers. If you leave the answer blank, you have a 0 percent chance of getting it right. But if you make a wild guess, you have a 25 percent chance of stumbling upon the right answer.

However, on the CAT-ASVAB, you may want to make sure your guesses are educated and spaced out. Those pesky test graders have programmed the grading software to issue a pretty hefty penalty for multiple wrong answers toward the end of your subtests. They figure this scenario implies you were running out of time and didn't read the questions; to do well on the ASVAB and AFQT, you need to be prepared with adequate time for each question.

Keep in mind that although you may know the word in the question, you may not know one or more of the words in the multiple-choice answers. In that case, use process of elimination to narrow your choices. Eliminate the words you know *aren't* correct, and guess which of the remaining words is most *likely* correct.

Before making a wild guess, take a few seconds and look at the word from a different perspective. You may find that you know the word after all — just in a different form. In English, one root word can be changed slightly to perform all sorts of roles — it can act as a noun, a verb, an adjective, or an adverb with just a little modification. So if you know what the root word *attach* means, you can figure out what the word *attachment* means. If you know *adherent*, you can deduce what *adherence* means. (You can find much more information on this topic in Chapter 4.)

You can use root word clues to identify unfamiliar words on the ASVAB. Say you run across the word *beneficent* on the Word Knowledge test:

<u>Beneficent</u> most nearly means:

(A) kind

(B) beautiful

(C) unhappy

(D) troubled

If you don't have a clue what the word *beneficent* means, all is not lost. Take a closer look. What other word starting with the letters *benefi-* do you know? How about the word *benefit*? A *benefit* is something that helps or aids, so the word *beneficent* is likely related to helping or aiding. So when you look over the possible choices, you can choose the one that has something to do with helping.

But wait. None of the answers says help or aid. Now what? Just use process of elimination. If something is helpful (beneficent), it probably isn't troubled or unhappy. It may be beautiful, but more likely, it's kind. So the best answer is Choice (A) — and it just so happens that that's correct!

Trying On Some Sample Questions

Now you're ready to pit your skills against the Word Knowledge section of the ASVAB. Try these sample questions to see how you do. They're similar to what you'll see on the ASVAB.

1. <u>Bestial</u> most nearly means:
   (A) playful
   (B) animal-like
   (C) tantalizing
   (D) pregnant

2. The enemy was <u>relentless</u> with negotiations.
   (A) overwhelmed
   (B) happy
   (C) strict
   (D) peaceful

3. <u>Malignant</u> most nearly means:
   (A) tumor
   (B) angry
   (C) kind
   (D) evil

4. Bernard wanted to ask a lawyer whether his friend's investment idea was <u>licit</u>.
   (A) legal
   (B) profitable
   (C) illegal
   (D) sensible

5. <u>Achromatic</u> most nearly means:
   (A) automatic
   (B) tasty
   (C) colorless
   (D) manual

6. The legal team was impressed with her <u>dynamic</u> ideas.
   (A) offensive
   (B) fun
   (C) powerful
   (D) cowering

7. <u>Wry</u> most nearly means:

    (A) smile

    (B) distorted

    (C) angry

    (D) happy

8. Melissa was justifiably proud of her recent <u>abstinence</u>.

    (A) grades

    (B) sobriety

    (C) trustworthiness

    (D) awards

9. <u>Tolerate</u> most nearly means:

    (A) accept

    (B) conserve

    (C) annoy

    (D) rush

10. Lyle's landlord instructed him to <u>vacate</u> the apartment.

    (A) paint

    (B) leave

    (C) clean

    (D) sell

Answers and Explanations

Use this answer key to score the practice Word Knowledge questions.

1. **B.** *Bestial* is an adjective that means having animal characteristics. Noting the similarity between the words *bestial* and *beast* can lead you in the right direction with this question.

2. **C.** Used as an adjective, *relentless* means unyieldingly severe, strict, or harsh. The other words don't fit the context of the sentence.

3. **D.** *Malignant* is an adjective that means evil or harmful. You may have been tempted to select Choice (A) because you may have heard of a malignant tumor, but *tumor* and *malignant* don't mean the same thing.

4. **A.** *Licit* is an adjective that means lawful. Although you may not have been familiar with the word *licit,* chances are good that you've come across the opposite-meaning word, *illicit,* and you probably know that it means illegal. So, you can deduce that *licit* means the opposite of illegal, or legal.

5. **C.** *Achromatic* is an adjective that means having no color. If you knew that the word root *chrom* refers to color and that the prefix *a-* means without, you could figure out that *achromatic* means without color.

6. **C.** Used as an adjective, *dynamic* means having a powerful personality with ambition and new ideas. You can use clues in the sentence to rule out Choices (A) and (D) because if the legal team is impressed, she's probably not offensive or cowering. Although *dynamic* can mean fun, the word closest in meaning is *powerful.*

7. **B.** *Wry* is an adjective that means crooked or twisted.

8. **B.** *Abstinence* is a noun that means the willful avoidance of something — for example, a substance such as alcohol or drugs.

9. **A.** *Tolerate* is a verb meaning to allow or accept without hindrance.

10. **B.** *Vacate* is a verb that means to give up occupancy of a location. Word roots are key here. A vacation involves leaving your normal place of residence. When people evacuate an area, they leave that area. A vacuum is created when matter leaves a given area.

Chapter 6

Reading for Comprehension

The military services want their members to not only be able to read but also understand what they're reading. This skill is known as *reading comprehension,* but the military calls its version *paragraph comprehension* and includes it as one of the ASVAB subtests that make up your AFQT score.

Why does the military place so much importance on reading comprehension? Quite simple: Miscommunication has been the leading cause of almost every major military accident or battlefield disaster in history.

The military runs on paperwork. A former Air Force vice chief of staff once commented that he had looked at 13,000 pieces of paper in a five-day period. Granted, you won't see quite so much correspondence as a newly enlisted member, but you'll have to read and understand your share of memos, policy letters, regulations, manuals, and forms. In fact, as an enlisted member, your promotions are based, in part, on how well you can read, comprehend, and retain information from written material. And the higher you get in rank, the more paperwork you'll see.

Reading comprehension involves several skills that anyone can develop with practice. To thoroughly understand what you read, you must develop the abilities to recognize the main idea, recall details, and make inferences. The information in this chapter helps you improve your reading comprehension skills, making it possible for you to nail the Paragraph Comprehension subtest of the ASVAB.

Taking Pointers about Points

When someone writes something, he's almost always trying to make a point. This message is called the *main point* or *principal idea* of the writing. The paragraph or passage may also contain information that supports or reinforces the main point; these little gems are called *subpoints*.

Picking out the main point

The main point is the most important part of a paragraph or passage. It's the primary theme that the writer wants you to understand. In many cases, the writer states the main point simply. In other cases, the writer may imply the main point rather than state it directly.

Quite often, the main point of a paragraph or passage is contained in the first sentence. You may recall from school that your English teacher referred to this sentence as the *topic sentence*. Sometimes a writer also rephrases or summarizes the main point in the passage's last sentence.

In the following passage, the main idea is stated in the first sentence:

> U.S. military forces will increasingly be called upon in the immediate future for peaceful military-to-military contacts, humanitarian intervention, peace support, and other nontraditional roles. The end of the Cold War transformed U.S. national security. The United States entered the 21st century with unprecedented prosperity and opportunities threatened by complex dangers. Problems associated with fostering a stable global system require the U.S. military to play an essential role in building coalitions and shaping the international environment in ways that protect and promote U.S. interests.

The main point is stated clearly in the very first sentence: "U.S. military forces will increasingly be called upon in the immediate future for peaceful military-to-military contacts, humanitarian intervention, peace support, and other nontraditional roles." The sentences that follow are subpoints that help clarify and emphasize the paragraph's main point.

Sometimes the main point isn't in the first sentence. Look at the passage again, slightly reworded:

> The end of the Cold War transformed U.S. national security. The United States entered the 21st century with unprecedented prosperity and opportunities threatened by complex dangers. Problems associated with fostering a stable global system require the U.S. military to play an essential role in building coalitions and shaping the international environment in ways that protect and promote U.S. interests. A key assumption is that U.S. military forces will increasingly be called upon for peaceful military-to-military contacts, humanitarian intervention, peace support, and other nontraditional roles.

The paragraph's main point remains the same, but it isn't stated until the last sentence.

Sometimes the main point isn't clearly stated but rather implied. Take a look at the following paragraph:

> The plane landed at 9 p.m. The children were disappointed that new security rules prevented them from meeting their father at the gate. They waited with their mother in the car outside the airport doors, amidst dozens of other people in vehicles, there for similar purposes. With each passing moment, their excitement grew. Finally, the automatic doors opened, and he walked out. "Dad! Hey, Dad!" the excited children yelled.

Though it's not directly stated, the main point of this paragraph is obviously that the children's father is coming home.

Take another look at the preceding passage. When trying to determine the main point of a paragraph, ask yourself the following:

- ✔ **Who or what is this paragraph about?** A father returning to his family.
- ✔ **What aspect of this subject is the author talking about?** The moments before and the moment of the father's appearing at the airport doors.
- ✔ **What is the author trying to get across about this aspect of the subject?** The drama of the father's reunion with his family.

Simplifying subpoints

Most writers don't stick to just one point. If they did, most paragraphs could be reduced to just one sentence. But it doesn't work that way. Writers usually try to reinforce their main points by providing details. These subpoints may include facts, statistics, or descriptions that support the passage's main point. Subpoints help you see what the author is saying. Take, for instance, the following passage:

> For the purposes of drill, Air Force organizations are divided into elements, flights, squadrons, groups, and wings. The "rule of two" applies (that is, an element must consist of at least two people, a flight must consist of at least two elements, and so on). Usually, an element consists of between eight and ten people, and a flight has six or eight elements. Drill consists of certain movements by which the flight or squadron is moved in an orderly manner from one formation to another or from one place to another.

Notice how the writer uses the second, third, and fourth sentences to explain in detail how Air Force organizations are divided for the purposes of drill. These supporting details are subpoints.

Look for signal words in the passage — words like *again, also, as well as, furthermore, moreover,* and *significantly.* These signal words may call your attention to supporting facts.

Analyzing What You've Read

Understanding what you read involves more than just picking out main points and subpoints. To analyze a paragraph, you need to examine the passage carefully to identify causes, key factors, and possible results. Analyzing a passage requires you to draw conclusions from what you've read and understand relationships among the ideas in the text.

Say what? What does that passage mean?

By drawing conclusions about a passage's meaning, you reach new ideas that the author implies but doesn't come right out and state. You must analyze the information the author presents to make inferences from what you've read. What conclusions can you infer from the following paragraph?

> The local school district is facing a serious budgetary crisis. The state, suffering a revenue shortfall of more than $600 million, has cut funding to the district by $18.7 million. Already, 65 teachers have been laid off, and more layoffs are expected.

Can you conclude that the local school district really stinks? Possibly, but that's not the point I'm trying to make. Although the author doesn't come straight out and say so, you can draw the conclusion that if the state revenue shortfall could somehow be corrected — by increasing state sales tax or income tax, for example — the local school district's budgetary crisis could be resolved. The author never actually makes this point, but you can draw this conclusion from the facts presented by using reason and logic.

When analyzing a passage, leave your baggage at the door. For example, you may not like the current governor, but nothing in the passage suggests that the writer supports electing a new governor to solve the budget problem.

Say it again, Sam: Paraphrasing

Paraphrasing means to rewrite a passage using your own words. This strategy is often useful when you're trying to understand a complex idea. Putting the passage in your own words can help you understand the main idea, which can in turn help you discover information that may not be stated directly. Paraphrasing can also be helpful in making inferences and drawing conclusions from the information provided. Look at the following short passage:

> On-the-job training (OJT) is often the most effective method of training because the employer tailors the training to meet the specific job requirements. OJT can be as casual as giving a few pointers to a new worker or as formal as a fully structured training program with timetables and specified subjects.

How would you paraphrase this passage? If you wrote something like the following, you'd be on the right track:

> Some OJT programs involve a formal lesson plan, while others simply tell a new employee what to do and how to do it. OJT works well because new employees can be taught what they need to do the specific job.

 Paraphrasing is just saying the same thing using different words. In basic training, your drill instructor may say, "You really need to work on your running time," or he may say, "Get the %$@* lead out of your pants and run faster!" Both mean the same thing.

Improving Your Reading Comprehension Skills

Some people read and comprehend better than others, but one thing is for certain: You're not born with the ability to read. It's something you learn. Like almost anything that is learned, you can use proven techniques to help you do it better:

- ✔ Read more and watch TV less.
- ✔ Practice skimming and scanning.
- ✔ Learn to identify the main ideas and the all-important subpoints.
- ✔ Work on the meanings of strange or difficult words.
- ✔ Practice paraphrasing.
- ✔ Reflect on what you've read.

Taking the time to read

Joseph Addison once noted that "Reading is to the mind what exercise is to the body." My first tae kwon do instructor has been practicing his art for 52 years. He is very, very good at it. I have a good friend who has spent every day of his working life for the past 30 years working on air-conditioning systems. He can take your air conditioner apart and put it back together blindfolded in less time than it takes you to say, "I'm hot."

The point is that anything gets better with practice. If you don't read well, the chances are good that you don't read much. You don't need a $4-million government-funded study (although I'm sure there are a few) to know that people who read a lot are more likely to be better readers than people who don't read so much.

If you learn to read for fun, you'll automatically read more, and I guarantee that your reading skills will improve immeasurably after a relatively short time. So how do you learn to read for fun? Simple: Choose reading material in subject areas that interest you.

You don't have to pick up *A Tale of Two Cities* or *War and Peace.* You can start with the newspaper, a biography of a person you admire, or magazines you find at the library. Personally, I like *For Dummies* books. If you devote at least one hour a day to improving your reading comprehension, you'll see results fast — maybe within a month or so.

Skimming and scanning

Different situations call for different styles of reading. The technique you choose depends on your purpose for reading. For example, you may be reading for enjoyment, to find information, or to complete a task. If you're reading for enjoyment, you usually read and savor every word. However, in other situations — such as when you're just trying to find the main ideas or look up specific information — you may not want to read every single word.

Skimming

You can skim to quickly identify the main ideas of a text. For example, most people don't read a newspaper word for word. Instead, they skim through the text to see whether they want to read an article in more depth. Most people can skim three to four times faster than normal reading. Skimming is especially useful if you have lots of material to read in a limited amount of time.

Here are some points to keep in mind when you practice skimming:

- ✔ **If the article or passage has a title, read it.** It's often the shortest possible summary of the content.
- ✔ **Read the first sentence or paragraph.** This introductory text often consists of the main point(s).
- ✔ **If the text has subheadings, read each one, looking for relationships among them.**
- ✔ **Look for clue words that answer who, what, where, how, why, and when.**
- ✔ **Pay attention to qualifying adjectives, such as** *best, worst, most,* **and so on.**
- ✔ **Look for typographical clues such as boldface, italics, underlining, or asterisks.**

Scanning

Scanning involves moving your eyes quickly down the page seeking specific words and phrases. When you scan, you must be willing to skip over several lines of text without actually reading and understanding them.

Scanning is a useful technique when you're looking for keywords or specific ideas. For example, when you look up a word in the dictionary, you probably use the scanning technique. In most cases, you know what you're looking for, so you concentrate on finding a particular answer.

When scanning a document:

- ✔ **Keep in mind what you're scanning for.** If you keep a picture in your mind, the information is more likely to jump out at you from among all the other printed words.
- ✔ **Anticipate what form the information is likely to appear in.** Will it be numbers? Proper nouns?
- ✔ **Let your eyes run over several lines of print at a time.**
- ✔ **When you find the information you're looking for, read the entire sentence.**

Skimming and scanning are useful techniques for many of the Paragraph Comprehension problems. I talk more about this subtest in Chapter 7.

Looking for the main ideas and subpoints

Reading wouldn't have much purpose if you just let your eyes wander over the words without walking away with some sense of what the author is talking about. The author's ideas are included in the main point and subpoints of the writing. You need to practice extracting this information from your reading material. See the "Taking Pointers about Points" section earlier in this chapter.

Building your vocabulary

It's hard to understand what you're reading if you don't understand the individual words. Effective reading comprehension involves developing a solid vocabulary. Use the techniques in Chapter 4 to strengthen your vocabulary, and you'll simultaneously improve your reading comprehension skills. The two skills go hand in hand.

When practicing reading, try not to look up new words in a dictionary right away. Stopping to look up words often impairs your concentration and lessens your ability to comprehend what you've read.

Instead, start by trying to puzzle out the meaning of a new word by looking at the context in which the word is used in the sentence or phrase. For example, take the following passage:

> It had been three days since the shipwreck, and Tammy was unable to find food or much drinkable water. At that point, she would have done anything to get off that wretched island.

You can derive several important clues about the meaning of the word *wretched* based on its context in the passage. Obviously, Tammy isn't having a very good time, nor does she find the island to be a pleasant environment. Therefore, you can surmise that *wretched* has something to do with unpleasantness.

Paraphrasing

Putting the text in your own words can help you understand what the writer is talking about. I talk more extensively about this in the "Say it again, Sam: Paraphrasing" section earlier in this chapter.

You probably won't have time on the Paragraph Comprehension subtest to rewrite passages on your scratch paper. But by practicing the technique while you hone your reading comprehension skills, you'll develop the ability to paraphrase in your mind.

Remembering by reflecting

Reflecting simply means thinking about what you've read. If you take a few minutes to think about it, you're more likely to remember it. Did you enjoy the passage or article? Did you find it interesting? Do you agree or disagree with the author's views? *Warning:* Thinking about what you've read may cause you to learn something!

Speaking about Speed

Dozens of speed-reading courses, software, and online programs absolutely guarantee, without qualification, to turn you into a speed-reading wizard. However, if your goal is to score well on the Paragraph Comprehension subtest, I recommend you save your money.

The Paragraph Comprehension subtest isn't a speed-reading test. On the paper version, you have 13 minutes to read between 8 and 10 short paragraphs and answer 15 questions. On the CAT-ASVAB, you must complete 11 questions in 22 minutes. Either way, this is plenty of time for most people. You don't get extra points on this test for finishing early. If you blaze through the test in six minutes and get all the questions right, your score is the same as if you take the entire allotted time. Instead, concentrate on improving your comprehension skills. That's what this subtest is all about: How well do you understand what you've read?

If you're still worried about your reading speed, just remember: The more you read, the better (and faster) you'll get at it. Read to comprehend by using the information in this chapter, and your speed will automatically get faster as you practice.

Chapter 7

The Paragraph Comprehension Subtest

In This Chapter
▶ Trying out types of questions
▶ Looking at proven techniques for a better score
▶ Getting a handle on practice questions

The Paragraph Comprehension subtest has the fewest questions of any of the ASVAB subtests. However, it's one of the most important subtests of the ASVAB. The military uses this test (along with the Word Knowledge subtest; see Chapters 4 and 5) to compute your verbal expression (VE) score, which in turn is an important part of your AFQT score. (If you want to see how these scores combine, turn to Chapter 2.)

This subtest is nothing more than a reading comprehension test, much like many of the reading tests you took in school. You're asked to read a short passage (a paragraph), and then answer one to four questions about information contained in that paragraph. Unfortunately, you probably won't find the reading to be very interesting. No passages from Harry Potter or spacemen shooting ray guns here. You're more likely to read about the corn crop harvest rates in Nebraska or the principles of time management. The key is to stay focused. After all, you have to answer only 11 or 15 questions, depending on your test, and the paragraphs aren't that long.

A large percentage of military jobs require a solid score on this subtest. If you're interested in which military jobs require you to score well on the Paragraph Comprehension subtest, I humbly recommend you head to your favorite book retailer and buy a copy of my best-selling *ASVAB For Dummies* (Wiley). You'll be glad you did.

Tackling the Test Format: Types of Questions

The Paragraph Comprehension subtest requires you to read a short paragraph and then answer one or more multiple-choice questions about what you've read. These questions can generally be broken down into one of four types, which I like to call the treasure hunt, getting the point, dictionary, and deep thinking.

The treasure hunt

Treasure hunt questions require you to find specific information within the paragraph. The good thing about this type of question is that by employing the scanning techniques in Chapter 6, you can often find the answer without having to read the entire paragraph. Try the following example:

A new study has found that 21 percent of people arrested in the United States for driving under the influence were arrested again for the same crime within five years. The study, commissioned by the U.S. Department of Justice, analyzed recidivism rates for DUI between 2002 and 2007. During this period, there were more than 930,000 arrests for DUI. Of these, 195,300 — or 21 percent — were arrested again for violating DUI laws a second time within the established time frame. The study found that 34 percent of the repeat offenses occurred within six months of the original arrest.

How many people were arrested for DUI more than once between 2002 and 2007?

(A) 930,000

(B) 195,300

(C) 210,000

(D) None of the above

By using the scanning technique and letting your eyes quickly scan through the paragraph, you notice that all the large numbers are contained in the middle. If you stop and read the two sentences that include large numbers, you quickly find the answer to the question: Choice (B).

Sometimes the answer isn't so obvious, and you have to dig a little deeper to find the treasure. Take the following question, for example:

George Armstrong Custer (December 5, 1839–June 25, 1876) was a U.S. Army officer and cavalry commander in the Civil War and the American Indian Wars. At the start of the Civil War, Custer was a cadet at the U.S. Military Academy at West Point, and his class's graduation was accelerated so that they could enter the war. Early in the Gettysburg Campaign, Custer's association with cavalry commander Major General Alfred Pleasonton earned him a promotion at the age of 23 from first lieutenant to brigadier general of volunteers. By the end of the Civil War (April 9, 1865), Custer had achieved the rank of major general of volunteers but was reduced to his permanent grade of captain in the regular army when the troops were sent home.

How old was George Custer at the end of the Civil War?

(A) 24

(B) 25

(C) 26

(D) 34

The answer is still right there in the paragraph, but you have to use a little judgment (and math) to find it. General Custer was born on December 5, 1839 (which you can find in the first sentence) and the Civil War ended on April 9, 1865 (which the last sentence tells you). Therefore, Custer was 25 years old, Choice (B), at the end of the war. (He didn't turn 26 until December of that year.)

Getting the point

This type of question asks you to discern the main topic, point, or idea of the paragraph (see Chapter 6 for more information). When you look for the main point, skimming the paragraph rather than reading it in its entirety is often helpful (see Chapter 6). Try this one on for size:

> The farmers' market reopened the second weekend of May. Amid the asparagus and flowers, shoppers chatted about the return of temperatures in the seventies. Across the street, children (and their dogs) were playing Frisbee in the park. Finally, spring had come to town.

What is the main point of the passage?

(A) The farmers' market has reopened.

(B) Children like playing Frisbee.

(C) Spring had come to town.

(D) Shoppers were chatting.

In this paragraph, you may think that the farmers' market reopening is the main point, but the other information about the temperature and the kids playing Frisbee tells you that the main idea is something a bit broader than the market opening. The main idea is stated in the last sentence: "Finally, spring had come to town." Therefore, Choice (C) is the correct answer.

When skimming for the main point of a paragraph, start with the first sentence, and then read the last sentence. The main idea is often contained in one of these sentences.

Dictionary

Much like the Word Knowledge subtest (covered in Chapters 4 and 5), this type of question requires you to define a word as used in the context of the passage. The correct definition that the question is looking for can be the most common meaning of the word, or it can be a less well-known meaning of the word.

In either case, you have to read the passage, make sure you understand how the word is being used, and select the answer option that is closest in meaning to the word as it's used in the passage. Consider this example:

In the 18th century, it was common for sailors to be pressed into service in Britain. Young men found near seaports could be kidnapped, drugged, or otherwise hauled aboard a ship and made to work doing menial chores. They were not paid for their service, and they were given just enough food to keep them alive.

In this passage, pressed means:

(A) hired

(B) ironed

(C) enticed

(D) forced

The correct answer is Choice (D). The descriptions of the conditions these sailors found themselves in should help you decide that they weren't hired or enticed; ironed is one meaning of the word *pressed,* but it isn't correct in this context.

Deep thinking

If the paragraph comprehension questions on the ASVAB simply asked you to scan a passage and find the main point or supporting details, it would be a pretty simple test. But the subtest goes beyond that. In order to properly answer some of the questions on the test, you have to analyze what you've read and draw conclusions.

The *conclusion* — which may be called an *inference* or *implication* — must be reasonably based on what the passage says. You have to use good judgment when deciding what conclusions you can logically draw from what you've read. Be careful not to confuse passage content with your opinion.

Try this example:

One of the main reasons motorcyclists are killed in crashes is that the motorcycle itself provides virtually no protection in a crash. For example, approximately 80 percent of reported motorcycle crashes result in injury or death; a comparable figure for automobiles is about 20 percent.

Safe motorcycle riding means:

(A) always wearing a helmet

(B) using premium gas

(C) selecting the most expensive motorcycle

(D) always riding with a buddy

The correct answer is Choice (A). The author didn't specifically state in the passage that wearing a helmet is important, but you can infer the correct answer because the author gives the reason for fatalities: Motorcycles themselves offer virtually no protection in a crash. Based on the information provided in the passage, you can logically conclude that even the small degree of protection offered by a helmet increases the safety of riding motorcycles. None of the other choices is as closely connected to the idea of safety.

Planning Your Attack

The best way to score well on the Paragraph Comprehension subtest is to improve your reading comprehension skills by following the advice I give in Chapter 6. However, you can also do a few things on test day to make sure you score as high as possible:

✔ **Watch the time.** As with all the ASVAB subtests, this test is timed. You have 13 minutes to read through approximately 9 paragraphs and answer 15 questions on the paper version, or 11 questions in 22 minutes if you take the computer version. This period is plenty of time, so you shouldn't feel rushed. Although you don't have time for day-dreaming, either.

✔ **If you don't know the answer, you may take an educated guess by using the process of elimination.** On the paper version, you may guess freely at your discretion (hopefully, you won't have to after reading this book). However, on the computerized test, you risk receiving a penalty for too many wrong answers at the end of the subtest. (Those pesky test graders have figured out that means you've run out of time and have become desperate to finish). If you need to guess, make sure to eliminate as many choices as possible before choosing your answer.

✔ **Question first, read later.** Your first instinct may be to read the entire paragraph first, before looking at the questions. However, many reading comprehension test experts recommend the opposite. If the question asks you to find specific information or discern the main idea of the paragraph, skimming or scanning (see Chapter 6) can save loads of time. Read the question first so that you can best decide what reading technique to use.

✔ **Take it one question at a time.** Some passages have more than one question associated with them, but you should look at only one question at a time.

✔ **Understand each question.** What is the question asking you to do? Are you supposed to find the main point? Draw a conclusion? Find a word that is nearest in meaning? Make sure you know what the question is asking before you choose among the answer options. This tip may seem obvious, but when you're in a hurry, you can make mistakes by misunderstanding the questions.

✔ **Read each answer option carefully.** Don't just select the first answer that seems right. *Remember:* On the Paragraph Comprehension subtest, one answer is often "most right" while others are "almost right." You want to choose the "most right" answer, not the "almost right" answer. And to do that, you have to read *all* the answers.

✔ **Check your baggage at the door.** Answer each question based on the passage, not your own opinions or views on the topic.

✔ **Don't choose ambiguous answer options.** They're incorrect 99.99 times out of 100. (Oh, heck, call it 100 times out of 100.) If an answer strikes you as not quite true but not totally false, that answer is incorrect. Those nasty ASVAB test makers have put it there to throw you off. Don't give them the satisfaction of falling for their trap!

✔ **Always be cautious about never.** For the most part, answer options that are absolutes are incorrect. *Never, always,* and related words are often a sign that you should select a different answer. Words like *generally* and *usually* are more likely to be correct.

Surveying Sample Test Questions

Time for you to put all the great advice I provide in this chapter and Chapter 6 to good use. (You can see that I'm not usually accused of being too modest.) Quiz yourself on the following sample test questions to see whether your reading comprehension is up to speed. Read each short paragraph, which is followed by one or more questions regarding information contained in that passage. Make sure to read the paragraph carefully before selecting the choice that most correctly answers the question.

First, stick to one excuse. Thus, if a tradesman, with whom your social relations are slight, should chance to find you taking coppers from his till, you may possibly explain that you are interested in Numismatics and are a Collector of Coins; and he may possibly believe you. But if you tell him afterwards that you pitied him for being overloaded with unwieldy copper discs, and were in the act of replacing them by a silver sixpence of your own, this further explanation, so far from increasing his confidence in your motives, will (strangely enough) actually decrease it. And if you are so unwise as to be struck by yet another brilliant idea, and tell him that the pennies were all bad pennies, which you were concealing to save him from a police prosecution for coining, the tradesman may even be so wayward as to institute a police prosecution himself.

—G. K. Chesterton

1. The author is giving the reader advice about:

   (A) collecting coins

   (B) stealing

   (C) dealing with tradesmen

   (D) becoming a police officer

Ethics are standards by which one should act based on values. Values are core beliefs such as duty, honor, and integrity that motivate attitudes and actions. Not all values are ethical values (integrity is — happiness is not). Ethical values relate to what is right and wrong and, thus, take precedence over nonethical values when making ethical decisions.

2. According to the paragraph, values can best be defined as:

   (A) ethics

   (B) stealing

   (C) core beliefs

   (D) right and wrong

Although the average consumer replaces the tires on his or her automobile every 50,000 miles, steel-belted radials can last for 60,000 miles. However, they must be properly maintained. The tires must be inflated to the correct air pressure at all times, and tires must be rotated and balanced according to a routine maintenance schedule. The tread should be checked for correct depth regularly.

3. How long can steel-belted radials last?

   (A) 25,000 miles

   (B) 50,000 miles

   (C) 60,000 miles

   (D) No one knows.

4. According to the passage, proper tire maintenance does *not* include:

   (A) keeping tires properly inflated

   (B) balancing and rotating tires

   (C) checking the tread

   (D) checking the lug nuts

   Some people argue that baking is an art, but Chef Debra Dearborn says that baking is a science. She says that if you follow a recipe carefully, assembling the ingredients accurately, cooking at the specified temperature for the specified period of time, your cookies will always turn out right. Chef Dearborn says the best baking is like the best experiment; anyone can duplicate it.

5. In this passage, the word *assembling* most nearly means:

   (A) measuring

   (B) putting together

   (C) buying

   (D) storing

6. According to the passage, a person who can't make a decent batch of cookies:

   (A) should get out of the kitchen

   (B) is an artist

   (C) isn't following the recipe carefully

   (D) is Chef Dearborn

   Boiler technicians operate main and auxiliary boilers. They maintain and repair all parts, including pressure fittings, valves, pumps, and forced-air blowers. Technicians may have to lift or move heavy equipment. They may have to stoop and kneel and work in awkward positions.

7. According to this job description, a good candidate for this job would be

   (A) a person with management experience

   (B) an individual with keen eyesight

   (C) a person who isn't mechanically minded

   (D) a person who is physically fit

   In June 2004, the city council passed a resolution requiring all residents to paint their address numbers on their homes using a bright color. This was done to assist firemen, police, and paramedics in finding an address during an emergency. In August, 300 residences were randomly sampled and it was found that 150 had complied with the new ordinance.

8. According to the above passage, what percentage of the randomly sampled residences had complied with the new ordinance?

   (A) 10 percent

   (B) 20 percent

   (C) 50 percent

   (D) 60 percent

The younger the child, the trickier using medicine is. Children under 2 years shouldn't be given any over-the-counter (OTC) drug without a doctor's approval. Your pediatrician can tell you how much of a common drug, like acetaminophen (Tylenol), is safe for babies. Prescription drugs also can work differently in children than adults. Some barbiturates, for example, which make adults feel sluggish, will make a child hyperactive. Amphetamines, which stimulate adults, can calm children. When giving any drug to a child, watch closely for side effects. If you're not happy with what's happening with your child, don't assume that everything's okay. Always be suspicious. It's better to make the extra calls to the doctor or nurse practitioner than to have a bad reaction to a drug. And before parents dole out OTC drugs, they should consider whether they're truly necessary. Americans love to medicate — perhaps too much. A study published in the October 1994 issue of the *Journal of the American Medical Association* found that more than half of all mothers surveyed had given their 3-year-olds an OTC medication in the previous month. Not every cold needs medicine. Common viruses run their course in seven to ten days with or without medication. Although some OTC medications can sometimes make children more comfortable and help them eat and rest better, others may trigger allergic reactions or changes for the worse in sleeping, eating, and behavior. Antibiotics, available by prescription, don't work at all on cold viruses.

9. A common problem in America is:

   (A) over-medication

   (B) parents not heeding the advice of their doctors

   (C) OTC drugs not requiring a prescription

   (D) the cost of prescription medication

10. When a parent is in doubt about giving a child medication, it's best to:

    (A) speak with a pharmacist

    (B) call a doctor or nurse practitioner

    (C) read the label closely

    (D) research the side effects

Answers and Explanations

Use this answer key to score the practice Paragraph Comprehension questions.

1. **B.** Mr. Chesterton is expounding on how sticking to one excuse may help you if you're caught taking coins from the tradesman's till.

2. **C.** The second sentence defines the word *values*.

3. **C.** If you used the scanning technique explained in Chapter 6, you would've found this answer quickly.

4. **D.** This example is a negative question that requires extra care in answering. A negative question asks you for something that is not true or not included in the paragraph. If you're rushed or in a hurry, you can easily misread the question.

5. **B.** Although measuring is something you do when baking, it doesn't "most nearly" mean the same thing as assembling. *Putting together* does.

6. **C.** The passage states that if you follow a recipe carefully, your cookies will always turn out right.

7. **D.** Although the passage doesn't say, "This job requires a physically fit person," the duties listed imply that conclusion. A person with management experience or keen eyesight may make a good candidate, but the passage doesn't list these traits as requirements for the job. A person who isn't mechanically minded may not have the knowledge necessary to maintain and repair boilers and all their parts. This leaves Choice (D), and it's true that a person who is physically fit would be a good choice for the job.

8. **C.** The author didn't specifically say that 50 percent hadn't complied, but she included enough information in the passage so you can calculate it on your own.

9. **A.** The 11th and 12th sentences in the passage suggest that Americans probably medicate too much.

10. **B.** The passage states that making the extra calls is better than having a bad reaction to a drug. Although the other choices may be good advice, they aren't stated or implied in the paragraph.

Part III
Calculating Better Math Knowledge

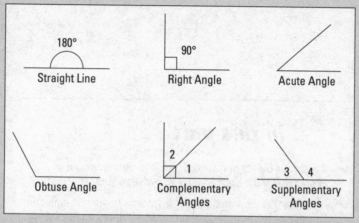

© John Wiley & Sons, Inc.

web extras

When you take the ASVAB math subtests, you should check your work before you choose your answer and move onto the next question. Visit www.dummies.com/extras/asvabafqt for a free article that explains how to check an answer to an algebra problem.

In this part . . .

✔ Review the basics of fractions, decimals, algebra, and geometry to prepare for the Mathematics Knowledge subtest.

✔ Figure out how to translate words into mathematical equations so you can solve word problems on the Arithmetic Reasoning subtest.

✔ Test yourself with Mathematics Knowledge and Arithmetic Reasoning practice questions.

Chapter 8

Knowing Your Math

• •

In This Chapter

▶ Understanding math-talk and basic concepts

▶ Finagling fractions and decimals

▶ Brushing up on positive and negative numbers

▶ Getting into roots, exponents, and quadratics

▶ Digging into algebra and geometry

• •

Lazarus Long, a fictional character created by Robert A. Heinlein, once said, "Anyone who cannot cope with mathematics isn't fully human. At best, he is a tolerable subhuman who has learned to wear shoes, bathe, and not make messes in the house."

Perhaps Mr. Long's observation is a little harsh. Some people seem to be born mathematicians, while others struggle with it. The fact remains, however, that the military seems to agree with him. You can't join the military without proving that you know the fundamentals of math. Fully 50 percent of your AFQT score is based on your ability to solve math problems. And as I indicate in Chapter 2, your AFQT score determines whether you can join the military.

The good news is that although the military wants you well grounded in math, it's not looking for rocket scientists. That's NASA's job. The two math subtests of the AFQT test your math ability only at the high-school level, so you don't have to break out any advanced calculus or plot the orbit of subatomic particles.

While I was deciding what to cover in this chapter, I quickly realized that I can't give you an entire high-school math education in one chapter. Heck, I couldn't do that in one whole book. Then I realized that I don't have to try to cram all the math you learned in 13 years of school into one chapter. If you're reading this book, you're obviously interested in joining the military. And to join the military, you must be either a high-school graduate or a GED holder, or you must have at least 15 college credits. That means you've already learned this stuff. All I need to do is provide you a bit of a refresher — remind you of all those rules of math you may have forgotten or put into the back of your mind. And that's what you find here: a refresher course, designed to draw out all the math you should already know!

So look at it this way: You already know what you need to know in order to ace the AFQT. Your job is just to remind yourself of what you know. In this chapter, I help you do exactly that.

Making the Most of Math Terminology

Some people are intimidated by math in part because it has its own language. In Chapter 10, I explain how to use keywords in math word problems to translate English into mathematical equations. But that's not enough. You need to know basic math terminology to solve many of the problems you see on the two math subtests that make up the AFQT.

I just looked in my handy-dandy pocket math dictionary. There are more than 700 mathematical terms listed there. Wait a minute! Sit back down. You don't need to memorize 700 terms. You won't see the math term *brachistochrone* on any of the subtests, for example.

Brachistochrone is a term from Greek meaning "shortest time." The special property of a brachistochrone is the fact that a bead sliding down a brachistochrone-shaped frictionless wire will take a shorter time to reach the bottom than with a wire curved into any other shape. Just in case you were curious.

Although you don't need to know 700 math terms, you should memorize the most common terms because you're likely to see them used in one way or another on the Mathematics Knowledge subtest or the Arithmetic Reasoning subtest. Here's some of what you need to know:

- **Average:** The *average* usually refers to the *arithmetic mean* or just the mean average. To find the mean of a set of *n* numbers, add the numbers in the set and divide the sum by *n*. For example, the average (or arithmetic mean) of 3, 7, 10, and 12 is $\frac{3+7+10+12}{4}$, or 8.

- **Coefficient:** The number multiplied times a variable or a product of variables or powers of variables in a term. For example, 123 is the coefficient in the term $123x^3y$.

- **Evaluate:** *Evaluate* means to figure out or calculate. If you're asked to evaluate 5 + 3, that means to simplify the term to 8.

- **Integer:** An *integer* is a whole number that can be expressed without a decimal or fraction component. Examples of integers include 1, 70, and –583.

- **Pi:** In mathematic equations and terms, pi is usually expressed by its Greek letter, π. *Pi* represents the ratio of the circumference of a circle to its diameter, and it's used in several formulas, especially formulas involving geometry. Pi's value is 3.141592653589793 . . . (on and on forever), but using the value 3.14 or $\frac{22}{7}$ is traditional in common math problems.

- **Prime/composite numbers:** A *prime number* is a positive integer that can only be divided evenly by itself and 1. For example, 2, 3, 5, 7, 11, 13 are the first six primes. One afternoon, all the famous mathematicians got together over a beer and agreed among themselves that 1 isn't a prime number.

   Positive numbers that have factors other than themselves and 1 as factors are called *composite numbers.* Again, by convention, 1 isn't considered a composite number.

- **Product:** The result of multiplication. The product of 2 and 9 is 18.

- **Quotient/remainder:** The *quotient* is the result of division. 40 divided by 5 has a quotient of 8.

   But what if one number doesn't divide evenly into the other? The *remainder* is what's left over in that scenario. 43 divided by 5 has a quotient of 8 and a remainder of 3.

- **Reciprocal:** A fraction flipped upside down. The reciprocal of *x* is $\frac{1}{x}$. The reciprocal of $\frac{1}{x}$ is *x*, and $x \neq 0$.

- **Sum:** The result of addition. The sum of 3 and 6 is 9.

You're not done with math vocabulary yet. You still need to know many more math words and terms. I explain them throughout the rest of the chapter.

The Heart of Math: Exploring Expressions and Equations

Math without expressions and equations is like a fire hydrant without a dog; they just go together. So what's the difference between a mathematical *expression* and an *equation?*

✔ An *expression* is any mathematical calculation or formula combining numbers and/or variables. Expressions don't include equal signs (=). For example, 3 + 2 is an expression, and so is $x(x + 2) - 3$.

✔ An *equation,* on the other hand, is a mathematical sentence built from expressions that use one or more equal signs (=). For example, 3 + 2 = 5 is an equation, and $x(x + 2) - 3 = 30$ is also an equation.

Obeying the order of operations

In math, you must solve equations by following steps in a proper order. If you don't, you won't get the right answer. Many of the most frequent math errors occur when people don't follow the *order of operations* when solving mathematical problems.

Keep in mind the following order of operations:

1. **Start with any calculations in brackets or parentheses.**

   When you have *nested* parentheses or brackets (parentheses or brackets inside other parentheses or brackets), do the inner ones first and work your way outward.

2. **Do any terms with exponents and roots.**

3. **Complete any multiplication and division, in order from left to right.**

4. **Do any addition and subtraction, in order from left to right.**

An easy way to remember this order is to think of the phrase "**P**lease **E**xcuse **M**y **D**ear **A**unt **S**ally" (**P**arentheses, **E**xponents, **M**ultiply, **D**ivide, **A**dd, **S**ubtract).

Take the following expression out for a ride.

Solve: $3 \times (5 + 2) + 5^2 \div 2$.

Do the calculations in the parentheses first:

$$3 \times (5 + 2) + 5^2 \div 2 = 3 \times 7 + 5^2 \div 2$$

Next, simplify the exponents:

$$3 \times 7 + 25 \div 2$$

Do multiplication and division from left to right:

$$21 + 12.5$$

Finally, perform addition and subtraction from left to right:

$$33.5$$

Keeping equations balanced

One of the coolest things about equations is that you can do almost anything you want to them as long as you remember to do the exact same thing to both sides of the equation. This rule is called keeping the equation *balanced*. For example, if you have the equation $4 + 1 = 3 + 2$, you can add 3 to both sides of the equation, and it still balances out: $4 + 1 + 3 = 3 + 2 + 3$. You can divide both sides by 3, and it still balances: $(4 + 1) \div 3 = (3 + 2) \div 3$.

Equation balancing becomes especially handy in algebra (see the later "Alphabet Soup: Tackling Algebra Review" section).

Mental Math: Dealing with the Distributive Property

Have you ever envied those people who can perform calculations on large numbers in their heads? What if I told you that you can be one of those people? That's right. All you have to do is practice the distributive property of math.

The *distributive property,* often referred to as the *distributive law of math,* lets you separate or break larger numbers into parts for simpler arithmetic. It basically says that $a(b + c)$ is the same as $(a \times b) + (a \times c)$.

Suppose you want to mentally multiply 4 by 53.

4×53 is the same as $(4 \times 50) + (4 \times 3)$. Four times 50 is easy; it's 200. Four times 3 is also easy. It's 12. Two hundred plus 12 is 212.

Try another one with a bit of a twist.

Mentally perform the calculation 12×19.

12×19 is equivalent to $12(20 - 1) = (12 \times 20) - (12 \times 1)$.

You can quickly mentally calculate that 12 times 20 is 240, and that 12 times 1 is 12. Subtract 12 from 240, and you have 228.

Figure 8-1 illustrates how this process works.

If 12×20 is still too large for mental calculation, you can break it down to $(12 \times 10) + (12 \times 10)$, or $120 + 120$.

You can also use the distributive property for division, although that takes a bit more practice: $340 \div 4$ is the same as $(340 \div 2) \div 2$. You can quickly calculate that 340 divided by 2 is 170, and 170 divided by 2 is 85.

And you can express $340 \div 4$ as $(100 \div 4) + (100 \div 4) + (100 \div 4) + (40 \div 4)$. You can mentally calculate 100 divided by 4 as 25. Forty divided by 4 is also easy — it's 10. So $25 + 25 + 25 + 10 = 85$. Keep practicing, and you'll be known as the neighborhood lightning calculator.

You're not allowed to use calculators on the math subtests of the ASVAB, so practicing the distributive property can be a big timesaver.

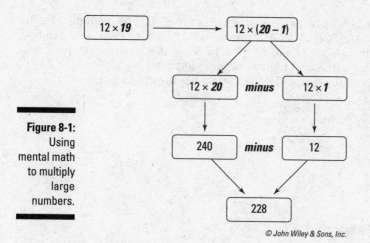

Figure 8-1:
Using mental math to multiply large numbers.

© John Wiley & Sons, Inc.

Having Fun with Factors

A *factor* is simply a number that is multiplied to get a product. *Factoring* a number means taking the number apart. It's kind of like multiplying in reverse. For example, the factors of 12 are 1, 2, 3, 4, 6, and 12 because all these numbers can be divided evenly into 12.

Here are some other factors:

- ✔ **2:** 1, 2
- ✔ **3:** 1, 3
- ✔ **4:** 1, 2, 4
- ✔ **5:** 1, 5
- ✔ **6:** 1, 2, 3, 6
- ✔ **16:** 1, 2, 4, 8, 16
- ✔ **20:** 1, 2, 4, 5, 10, 20
- ✔ **45:** 1, 3, 5, 9, 15, 45

Understanding types of factors

A factor can be either a prime number or a composite number (except that 1 and 0 are nei-ther prime nor composite). As I mention in the "Making the Most of Math Terminology" sec-tion earlier in this chapter, prime numbers have only themselves and 1 as a factor, while composite numbers can be divided evenly by other numbers.

The prime numbers up to 100 are 2, 3, 5, 7, 11, 13, 17, 19, 23, 29, 31, 37, 41, 43, 47, 53, 59, 61, 67, 71, 73, 79, 83, 89, and 97.

Finding prime factors

Any composite number can be written as a product of prime factors. Mathematicians call this process *prime factorization*. To find the prime factors of a number, you divide the number by the smallest possible prime number and work up the list of prime numbers until the result is itself a prime number.

Say you want to find the prime factors of 240. Because 240 is even, start by dividing it by the smallest prime number, which is 2: $240 \div 2 = 120$. The number 120 is also even, so it can be divided by 2: $120 \div 2 = 60$. Then $60 \div 2 = 30$ and $30 \div 2 = 15$. Now, 15 isn't even, so check to see whether you can divide it by 3 (the next highest prime number); $15 \div 3 = 5$, which itself is a prime number, so 240 is now fully factored. Now, simply list the divisors to write the prime factors of 240:

$$240 \div 2 = 120$$
$$120 \div 2 = 60$$
$$60 \div 2 = 30$$
$$30 \div 2 = 15$$
$$15 \div 3 = 5$$

The prime factors of 240 are $2 \times 2 \times 2 \times 2 \times 3 \times 5$.

Looking at Least Common Multiples

A *common multiple* is a number that is a multiple of two or more numbers. For example, 20, 30, and 40, are common multiples of the numbers 5 and 10. The *least common multiple* (LCM) of two or more numbers is the smallest number (not zero) that's a multiple of both or all the numbers. The LCM is useful in solving many math problems — especially those involving fractions (check out the following section for info on working with fractions).

One way to find the LCM is to list the multiples of each number, one at a time, until you find the smallest multiple that's common to all the numbers.

Find the LCM of 45 and 50.

- ✔ **Multiples of 45:** 45, 90, 135, 180, 225, 270, 315, 360, 405, 450
- ✔ **Multiples of 50:** 50, 100, 150, 200, 250, 300, 350, 400, 450

The LCM of 45 and 50 is 450.

That's rather cumbersome, isn't it? Wouldn't it be great if you had an easier way? You do, and I'm here to let you in on the secret: The easiest way to find the LCM is first to list the prime factors of each number as explained in the preceding section:

- ✔ The prime factors for 45 are $3 \times 3 \times 5$.
- ✔ The prime factors for 50 are $2 \times 5 \times 5$.

Then multiply each factor the greatest number of times it occurs in either number. If the same factor occurs more than once in both numbers, you multiply the factor the greatest number of times it occurs. For example, 5 occurs as a prime factor of both 45 (where it occurs once) and 50 (where it occurs twice); the two occurrences in the factorization of 50 trump the single occurrence in the factorization of 45. The number 3 occurs two times, 5 occurs two times, and 2 occurs once, so you have $3 \times 3 \times 5 \times 5 \times 2 = 450$.

Checking your answer to see whether the original numbers divide evenly into the LCM you calculate is always a great idea. You can in fact divide 45 and 50 evenly into 450, so you're good to go in this example.

Now that you're getting the hang of it, try another one:

What is the least common multiple of 5, 27, and 30?

List the prime factors of each number:

✔ **Prime factors of 5:** 5

✔ **Prime factors of 27:** $3 \times 3 \times 3$

✔ **Prime factors of 30:** $2 \times 3 \times 5$

The number 3 occurs a maximum of three times, 5 occurs a maximum of one time, and 2 occurs a maximum of one time: $3 \times 3 \times 3 \times 5 \times 2 = 270$. Check your answer by seeing whether 5, 27, and 30 can all divide evenly into 270.

Conquering the Fear of Fractions

I don't know why, but most people I know don't like to do math with fractions. Maybe it's because teachers always used pies as examples, and that just makes you hungry. The pies were all imaginary, too, so you didn't even get a piece after all the figuring was done. I'm going to break convention and use squares of cardboard instead. Sure, they're harder to cut than pies, but they don't smell as enticing.

A *fraction* is nothing more than part of a whole. Take a look at Figure 8-2.

1/4	1/4
1/4	1/4

1/4

1/4	1/4
1/4	1/4

2/4 or 1/2

1/4	1/4
1/4	1/4

3/4

Figure 8-2: Fractions are part of a whole.

1/4	1/4
1/4	1/4

4/4 or 1

1/4	1/4
1/4	1/8 / 1/8

1/2 of 1/4, or 1/8

© John Wiley & Sons, Inc.

Each shaded area represents part of a whole, or a fraction of the whole. It doesn't have to be fourths. If I had divided the cardboard into two equal pieces, each shaded area would represent one-half. If the cardboard were cut into three equal pieces, each piece would be one-third of the whole.

Fractions aren't difficult to work into your mathematical skills as long as you remember a few rules and techniques.

Defining parts and types of fractions

The top number of a fraction is called the *numerator*. The bottom number is known as the *denominator*. For example, in the fraction $\frac{7}{16}$, 7 is the numerator, and 16 is the denominator.

You may also see numerators and denominators separated by a / sign rather than one on top of the other. $\frac{1}{4}$ is the same as $\frac{1}{4}$.

If the numerator is smaller than the denominator, the fraction is less than a whole (smaller than 1). This kind of fraction is called a *proper fraction*. The fraction $\frac{3}{16}$ is a proper fraction, as is $\frac{1}{3}$.

If the numerator is larger than the denominator, the fraction is larger than a whole (larger than 1), and the fraction is called an *improper fraction*. The fraction $\frac{17}{16}$ is an improper fraction.

Converting improper fractions to mixed numbers is customary in math, especially after all mathematical operations are complete. A *mixed number* is a whole number plus a fraction. The easiest way to convert an improper fraction to a mixed number is to divide the numerator by the denominator. You convert $\frac{17}{16}$ to a mixed number by dividing 17 by 16: $17 \div 16 = 1$, with a remainder of 1, so the improper fraction converts to $1\frac{1}{16}$.

Simplifying fractions

Simplifying (or *reducing*) fractions means to make the fraction as simple as possible. You're usually required to simplify fractions on the ASVAB math subtests before you can select the correct answer. For example, if you worked out a problem and the answer were $\frac{4}{8}$, the correct answer choice on the math subtest would probably be $\frac{1}{2}$, which is the simplest equivalent to $\frac{4}{8}$.

Many methods of simplifying fractions are available. In this section, I give you the two that I think are the easiest; you can decide which is best for you.

Method 1: Dividing by the lowest prime numbers

Try dividing the numerator and denominator by the lowest prime numbers until you can't go any farther. (The earlier section "Understanding types of factors" has details on this process.)

Simplify $\frac{24}{108}$.

Both the numerator and denominator are even numbers, so they can be divided by the lowest prime number, which is 2. Then $24 \div 2 = 12$, and $108 \div 2 = 54$. The result is $\frac{12}{54}$.

The numerator and denominator are both still even numbers, so divide by 2 again: $12 \div 2 = 6$ and $54 \div 2 = 27$. The result is $\frac{6}{27}$.

This time the denominator is an odd number, so you know it isn't divisible by 2. Try the next highest prime number, which is 3: $6 \div 3 = 2$, and $27 \div 3 = 9$. The result is $\frac{2}{9}$.

Because no common prime numbers divide evenly into both 2 and 9, the fraction is fully simplified.

Method 2: Listing prime factors

This method of simplification is my favorite. Simply list the prime factors of both the numerator and the denominator as explained in the earlier "Finding prime factors" section and then see whether any cancel out (are the same).

Simplify $\frac{24}{108}$.

The prime factors of 24 are $2 \times 2 \times 2 \times 3$.

The prime factors of 108 are $2 \times 2 \times 3 \times 3 \times 3$.

You can now write the fraction as $\frac{2 \times 2 \times 2 \times 3}{2 \times 2 \times 3 \times 3 \times 3}$.

Two of the 2s and one of the 3s cancel out, so you can remove them from both the numerator and the denominator. What's left is $\frac{2}{3 \times 3}$, or $\frac{2}{9}$.

Multiplying fractions

Multiplying fractions is very easy. All you have to do is multiply the numerators by each other, multiply the denominators by each other, and then simplify the result, as shown in the following equation:

$$\frac{4}{5} \times \frac{3}{7} \times \frac{9}{15} = \frac{4 \times 3 \times 9}{5 \times 7 \times 15} = \frac{108}{525}$$

The fraction $\frac{108}{525}$ can be simplified to $\frac{36}{175}$ (see the earlier section "Simplifying fractions").

Before multiplying mixed numbers, change them to improper fractions by multiplying the denominator by the integer and adding it to the numerator. For example, $2\frac{5}{8}$ is a mixed number. To convert it to an improper fraction, multiply 8 by 2 and add 5 to the result:

$$2 \times 8 = 16$$
$$16 + 5 = 21$$

The end result is $\frac{21}{8}$.

Dividing fractions

Dividing fractions is almost the same as multiplying, with one important difference: You have to convert the second fraction (the *divisor*) to the reciprocal and then multiply. As I explain in the earlier "Making the Most of Math Terminology" section, the reciprocal is simply a fraction flipped over.

Solve: $\frac{3}{5} \div \frac{2}{5}$.

Take the reciprocal of the second fraction and multiply it with the other fraction:

$$\frac{3}{5} \div \frac{2}{5} = \frac{3}{5} \times \frac{5}{2} = \frac{3 \times 5}{2 \times 5} = \frac{15}{10}$$

The fraction $\frac{15}{10}$ is an improper fraction, which you can convert to $1\frac{5}{10}$ (see the earlier "Defining parts and types of fractions" section). Then you can simplify $1\frac{5}{10}$ to $1\frac{1}{2}$ (see the earlier "Simplifying fractions" section).

Adding and subtracting fractions

Adding and subtracting fractions can be as simple as multiplying and dividing them, or it can be more difficult. As the following sections show, it all depends on whether the fractions have the same denominator.

Adding and subtracting fractions with like denominators

To add or subtract two fractions with the same denominator, add (or subtract) the numerators and place that sum (or difference) over the common denominator:

$$\frac{2}{9} + \frac{3}{9} = \frac{2+3}{9} = \frac{5}{9}$$

$$\frac{3}{9} - \frac{2}{9} = \frac{3-2}{9} = \frac{1}{9}$$

Adding and subtracting fractions with different denominators

You can't add or subtract fractions with different denominators. You have to convert the fractions so they all have the same denominator, and then you perform addition or subtraction as I explain in the preceding section.

Converting fractions so they share the same denominator involves finding a *common denominator*. A common denominator is nothing more than a common multiple of all the denominators, as I describe in the earlier section "Looking at Least Common Multiples."

Find a common denominator for the fractions $\frac{3}{5}$ and $\frac{1}{8}$.

The multiples of 5 are 5, 10, 15, 20, 25, 30, 35, and 40.

The multiples of 8 are 8, 16, 24, 32, and 40.

A common denominator for the fractions $\frac{3}{5}$ and $\frac{1}{8}$ is 40.

The next step in the addition/subtraction process is to convert the fractions so they share the common denominator. In order to do this, divide the original denominator into the new common denominator and then multiply the result by the original numerator.

Start with $\frac{3}{5}$. Divide the original denominator (5) into the new common denominator (40): $40 \div 5 = 8$. Next multiply the result (8) by the original numerator (3): $8 \times 3 = 24$. The equivalent fraction is $\frac{24}{40}$.

Perform the same operation with the second fraction, $\frac{1}{8}$. Divide the original denominator (8) into the new common denominator (40): $40 \div 8 = 5$. Next multiply this (5) by the original numerator (1): $5 \times 1 = 5$. The equivalent fraction is $\frac{5}{40}$.

Now that the fractions have the same denominator, you can add or subtract them as shown in the previous section:

$$\frac{3}{5} + \frac{1}{8} = \frac{24}{40} + \frac{5}{40} = \frac{29}{40}$$

Performing multiple operations

Sometimes you have do more than one operation on a set of fractions. Give this one a try:

$$\left(\frac{\left(\frac{1}{8}+\frac{3}{4}\right)}{\left(\frac{3}{5}-\frac{2}{10}\right)}\right)\times\frac{4}{5}$$

On the surface, this problem looks complicated. But if you remember the *order of operations* (see the "Obeying the order of operations" section) and take the problem one step at a time, it's really easy.

Under the order of operations, you do the work in the inner sets of parentheses first:

$$\frac{1}{8}+\frac{3}{4}=\frac{1}{8}+\frac{6}{8}=\frac{7}{8}\text{ and }\frac{3}{5}-\frac{2}{10}=\frac{6}{10}-\frac{2}{10}=\frac{4}{10}=\frac{2}{5}$$

The problem now reads $\left(\frac{7}{8}\div\frac{2}{5}\right)\times\frac{4}{5}$.

Continue by performing the next operation in the parentheses:

$$\frac{7}{8}\div\frac{2}{5}=\frac{7}{8}\times\frac{5}{2}=\frac{35}{16}$$

The problem is now much simpler: $\frac{35}{16}\times\frac{4}{5}$.

$$\frac{35}{16}\times\frac{4}{5}=\frac{35\times4}{16\times5}=\frac{140}{80}=\frac{70}{40}=\frac{35}{20}=1\frac{15}{20}=1\frac{3}{4}$$

Converting fractions to decimals

Some math problems require you to perform operations on both decimal numbers (see the later "Dealing with Decimals" section) and fractions. To properly perform such calculations, you must either convert the fraction to a decimal number or convert the decimal to a fraction.

Converting a fraction to a decimal number is easy. You simply divide the numerator by the denominator:

$$\frac{3}{4}=3\div4=0.75$$

What could be easier than that? Try the following:

Solve: $\frac{1}{2}+0.34$.

Convert the fraction to a decimal by dividing the numerator by the denominator:

$$\frac{1}{2}=1\div2=0.5$$

Now you can easily perform the operation: $0.5 + 0.34 = 0.84$.

Comparing fractions

The two math subtests of the ASVAB often ask you to compare fractions to determine which one is the largest or smallest. If the fractions all have the same denominator, it's easy. The fraction with the largest numerator is the largest, and the one with the smallest numerator is the smallest.

But how do you compare fractions that have different denominators? I'll leave it up to you to determine which of the following proven methods you like the best.

Method 1: Finding a common denominator

The first method is to convert the fractions so they all have a common denominator (see the "Adding and subtracting fractions with different denominators" section). After conversion, the fraction with the largest numerator is the largest fraction, and the one with the smallest numerator is the smallest. This method is what you probably learned in school.

Which of the following fractions is the largest: $\frac{5}{12}$, $\frac{3}{4}$, $\frac{9}{15}$, or $\frac{13}{16}$?

First, find a common multiple for each denominator:

- ✔ **The multiples of 12:** 12, 24, 36, 48, 60, 72, 84, 96, 108, 120, 132, 144, 156, 168, 180, 192, 204, 216, 228, 240.

- ✔ **The multiples of 4:** 4, 8, 12, 16, 20, 24, 28, 32, 36, 40, 44, 48, 52, 56, 60, 64, 68, 72, 76, 80, 84, 88, 92, 100, 104, 108, 112, 116, 122 . . . 240.

- ✔ **The multiples of 15:** 15, 30, 45, 60, 75, 90, 105, 120, 135, 150, 165, 180, 195, 210, 225, 240.

- ✔ **The multiples of 16:** 16, 32, 48, 64, 80, 96, 112, 128, 144, 160, 176, 192, 208, 224, 240.

The lowest common denominator for all four fractions is 240.

Next, convert all the fractions so they have a denominator of 240 by dividing the new common denominator by the original denominator of the fraction and then multiplying the result by the original numerator:

- ✔ $\frac{5}{12} = \frac{100}{240}$
- ✔ $\frac{3}{4} = \frac{180}{240}$
- ✔ $\frac{9}{15} = \frac{144}{240}$
- ✔ $\frac{13}{16} = \frac{195}{240}$

The largest fraction is the one with the largest numerator: $\frac{195}{240}$, or $\frac{13}{16}$.

Method 2: The cross-product method

You may find Method 1 to be a bit time-consuming. If so, I think you'll enjoy this method. I certainly wish my teachers had heard of it when I was in high school. Maybe they explained it and I was sleeping that day.

The second method is called the *cross-product method.* To use it, you compare the cross-products of two fractions. The first cross-product is the product of the first numerator and the second denominator. The second cross-product is the product of the second numerator and the first denominator. If the cross-products are equal, the fractions are equivalent. If the first cross-product is larger, the first fraction is larger. If the second cross-product is larger, the second fraction is larger.

Which of the following fractions is the largest: $\frac{5}{12}$, $\frac{3}{4}$, $\frac{9}{15}$, or $\frac{13}{16}$?

Compare the first two fractions, $\frac{5}{12}$ and $\frac{3}{4}$: $5 \times 4 = 20$ and $12 \times 3 = 36$. The second fraction is larger.

Compare the larger fraction, $\frac{3}{4}$, with the third fraction, $\frac{9}{15}$: $3 \times 15 = 45$ and $4 \times 9 = 36$, so $\frac{3}{4}$ is still the largest fraction.

Now compare $\frac{3}{4}$ to the final fraction, $\frac{13}{16}$: $3 \times 16 = 48$, and $4 \times 13 = 52$.

The final fraction, $\frac{13}{16}$, is the largest.

Getting rational about ratios

Ratios represent how one quantity is related to another quantity. A ratio may be written as $A{:}B$ or $\frac{A}{B}$ or by the phrase "*A* to *B*."

A ratio of 1:3 says that the second quantity is three times as large as the first. A ratio of 2:3 means that the second quantity is three times larger than one-half of the first quantity. A ratio of 5:4 means the second quantity is four times larger than one-fifth of the first quantity.

A ratio is actually a fraction. For example, the fraction $\frac{3}{4}$ is also a ratio of 3 to 4. Solve problems including ratios the same way you solve problems that include fractions.

Dealing with Decimals

Decimals are a method of writing fractional numbers without using a numerator and denominator. You can write the fraction $\frac{7}{10}$ as the decimal 0.7; you pronounce it "seven-tenths" or "zero point seven." The period or decimal point indicates that the number is a decimal.

Other decimals exist, such as hundredths or thousandths. They're all based on the number ten, just like our number system:

- 0.7: Seven-tenths $\left(\frac{7}{10} \right)$
- 0.07: Seven-hundredths $\left(\frac{7}{100} \right)$
- 0.007: Seven-thousandths $\left(\frac{7}{1,000} \right)$
- 0.0007: Seven-ten-thousandths $\left(\frac{7}{10,000} \right)$
- 0.00007: Seven-hundred-thousandths $\left(\frac{7}{100,000} \right)$

If a decimal is less than 1, it's traditional in mathematics to place a zero before the decimal point. Write "0.7" not ".7"

A decimal may be greater than one. The decimal 3.7 would be pronounced as "three and seven-tenths" $\left(3\frac{7}{10} \right)$.

Converting decimals to fractions

To convert a decimal to a fraction, write all the digits following the decimal point in the numerator. If you see zeros before any nonzero digits, you can ignore them.

The denominator is always a one followed by zeros. The number of zeros in the denominator is determined by the total number of digits to the right of the decimal point (including the leading zeros):

- ✓ **One digit:** Denominator = 10. Example: $0.7 = \dfrac{7}{10}$

- ✓ **Two digits:** Denominator = 100. Example: $0.25 = \dfrac{25}{100}$

- ✓ **Three digits:** Denominator = 1,000. Example: $0.351 = \dfrac{351}{1,000}$

- ✓ **Four digits:** Denominator = 10,000. Example: $0.0041 = \dfrac{41}{10,000}$

Of course, you can also convert fractions to decimals (see the "Converting fractions to decimals" section earlier in this chapter).

Adding and subtracting decimals

You add and subtract decimals just as you do regular numbers (integers), except that before you perform your operation, you arrange the numbers in a column with the decimals lined up one over the other.

Add the numbers 3.147, 148.392, and 0.074.

Put the numbers in an addition column with the decimals lined up and perform the addition:

$$
\begin{array}{r}
3.147 \\
148.392 \\
+\ 0.074 \\
\hline
151.613
\end{array}
$$

Multiplying decimals

Multiplying decimals requires three steps:

1. **Convert the decimals to whole numbers by moving the decimal points to the right, remembering to count how many spaces you move each decimal point.**

2. **Multiply the whole numbers just as you'd perform any other multiplication.**

3. **Place the decimal point in the product by moving the decimal point to the left the same number of total spaces you moved the decimal points to the right at the beginning.**

Multiply: $3.724 \times 0.0004 \times 9.42$.

First convert the decimals to whole numbers by moving the decimal points to the right (remember to count).

3.724 becomes 3,724 (decimal moved three spaces).

0.0004 becomes 4 (decimal moved four spaces).

9.42 becomes 942 (decimal moved two spaces).

Next, perform the multiplication on the whole numbers:

$3,724 \times 4 \times 942 = 14,032,032$

Finally, replace the decimal point in the correct position by moving it to the left the same number of places you moved the points to the right. You moved the decimal points a total of nine spaces to the right at the beginning, so now place the decimal point nine spaces to the left:

14,032,032 becomes 0.014032032

If you run out of numbers before you're finished counting spaces to the left, add zeros (as shown in the example) until you're finished counting.

Dividing decimals

Dividing decimals can be a challenge. You have to use both subtraction and multiplication. You also need to be pretty good at rounding (see the later "Rounding" section) and estimating numbers.

You're not allowed to use a calculator on the ASVAB math subtests.

You can divide decimals in two ways: long division and conversion.

Method 1: Long division

To do long division with decimals, follow these steps:

1. **If the divisor isn't a whole number, move the decimal point in the divisor all the way to the right (to make it a whole number), and move the decimal point in the dividend the same number of places to the right.**

2. **Position the decimal point in the result directly above the decimal point in the dividend.**

3. **Divide as usual.**

   If the divisor doesn't go into the dividend evenly, add zeros to the right of the last digit in the dividend and keep dividing until it comes out evenly or a repeating pattern shows up.

Try the following division problem:

$7.42 \div 0.7$

Write the problem on your scratch paper in long-division form:

$$0.7\overline{)7.42}$$

Now move the decimal point one place to the right, which makes the divisor a whole number. Also move the decimal point in the dividend one place to the right:

$$7\overline{)74.2}$$

Position the decimal point in the result directly above the decimal point in the dividend:

$$7\overline{)74.2}^{\;.}$$

Divide as usual. Seven goes into 70 ten times with 4 leftover; then drop the 2 down:

$$
\begin{array}{r}
10. \\
7\overline{)74.2} \\
\underline{70} \\
04\,2
\end{array}
$$

Seven goes into 42 six times:

$$
\begin{array}{r}
10.6 \\
7\overline{)74.2} \\
\underline{70} \\
042 \\
\underline{42} \\
0
\end{array}
$$

When you're finished dividing decimals, you're finished. You don't have to move the decimal around like you do after you've multiplied decimals.

Method 2: Conversion

The other way to divide decimals is to convert the decimals to fractions, and then divide the fractions (see the earlier sections "Converting decimals to fractions" and "Dividing fractions," respectively).

Try the problem from the preceding section, using the conversion method.

$7.42 \div 0.7$

First, convert the decimals to fractions:

$$7.42 = 7\frac{42}{100} = \frac{742}{100}$$

$$0.7 = \frac{7}{10}$$

$$7.42 \div 0.7 = \frac{742}{100} \div \frac{7}{10}$$

Take the reciprocal of the divisor (flip the second fraction upside down) and then multiply:

$$\frac{742}{100} \times \frac{10}{7} = \frac{742 \times 10}{100 \times 7} = \frac{7,420}{700}$$

The fraction $\frac{7,420}{700}$ can be simplified (see "Simplifying fractions") to $10\frac{3}{5}$. Convert $\frac{3}{5}$ to a decimal (see "Converting fractions to decimals"), and the answer is 10.6.

Rounding

Rounding a number means limiting a number to a few (or no) decimal places. For example, if you have a $1.97 in change in your pocket, you may say, "I have about $2." The rounding process simplifies mathematical operations.

To round a number, you first determine what place you're rounding to. For example, the math subtests that make up the AFQT may ask you to round to the nearest tenth. Then look at the number immediately to the right of that place. If the number is 5 or greater, round the digit to the left up; for any number under five, round the digit to the left down. Thus, you'd round 1.55 up to 1.6 and 1.34 down to 1.3.

You can also round other numbers, such as whole numbers. For example, 1,427 becomes 1,400 when you round to the nearest 100. However, most of the rounding operations you encounter on the Mathematics Knowledge subtest involve rounding decimals to the nearest tenth or nearest hundredth.

Perusing percents

Percent literally means "part of 100." That means, for example, that 25 percent is equal to $\frac{25}{100}$, which is equal to 0.25.

If a problem asks you to find 25 percent of 250, it's asking you to multiply 250 by 0.25.

To convert a percent to a decimal number, remove the percentage sign and move the decimal point two places to the left: 15 percent is 0.15, and 15.32 percent is 0.1532. Conversely, to change a decimal number to percent, add the percentage sign and move the decimal point two places to the right: 4.321 is equal to 432.1 percent.

Playing with Positive and Negative Numbers

Numbers can be positive or negative. A *positive* number is any number greater than zero. So 4; 3.2; 793; $\frac{3}{4}$, $\frac{1}{2}$; and 430,932,843,784 are all positive numbers.

Numbers smaller than zero are *negative* numbers. Every positive number has a negative number equivalent. You express negative numbers by putting a negative (minus) sign (–) in front of the number. –7, –18, $-\frac{3}{4}$, and –743.42 are all negative numbers.

In the math subtests of the ASVAB, you'll often be asked to perform mathematical operations on positive and negative numbers. Just remember the following rules:

- ✔ **Adding two positive numbers always results in a positive number:** $3 + 3 = 6$
- ✔ **Adding two negative numbers always results in a negative number:** $-3 + -3 = -6$
- ✔ **Adding a negative number is the same as subtracting a positive number:** $3 + (-3) = 3 - 3 = 0$
- ✔ **Subtracting a negative number is the same as adding a positive number:** $3 - (-3) = 3 + 3 = 6$
- ✔ **Multiplying or dividing two positive numbers always results in a positive number:** $3 \div 3 = 1$
- ✔ **Multiplying or dividing two negative numbers always results in a positive number:** $-3 \times -3 = 9$
- ✔ **Multiplying or dividing a negative number with a positive number always results in a negative number:** $-3 \times 3 = -9$

When you multiply a series of positive and negative numbers, count the number of negative numbers. If the number is even, the result will be positive. If the number is odd, the result will be negative.

Everyone knows that 10 is larger than 5 and that 20 is larger than 15. With negative numbers, however, it works just the opposite: –10 is smaller than –5, and –20 is smaller than –15.

As you'll recall from your math in school, any number multiplied by zero is zero.

Rooting for Roots and Powers

Many of the problems you see on the ASVAB math subtests require you to perform calculation involving roots, such as square roots and cube roots, and numbers raised by exponents. If that sounds confusing, don't worry; it's really not. Read on.

Advice about exponents

Exponents are an easy way to show that a number is to be multiplied by itself a certain number of times. For example, 5^2 is the same as 5×5, and 4^3 is the same as $4 \times 4 \times 4$. The number or variable that is to be multiplied by itself is called the *base,* and the number or variable showing how many times it's to be multiplied by itself is called the *exponent.*

Here are important rules when working with exponents:

- ✔ **Any base raised to the power of one equals itself.** For example, $6^1 = 6$.

- ✔ **Any base raised to the zero power (except 0) equals 1.** For example, $3^0 = 1$.

   In case you were wondering, according to most calculus textbooks, 0^0 is an "indeterminate form." What mathematicians mean by "indeterminate form" is that in some cases it has one value, and in other cases it has another. This stuff is advanced calculus, however, and you don't have to worry about it on the ASVAB math subtests.

- ✔ **To multiply terms with the same base, you add the exponents.** For example, $7^2 \times 7^3 = 7^5$.

- ✔ **To divide terms with the same base, you subtract the exponents.** For example, $4^5 \div 4^3 = 4^2$.

- ✔ **If a base has a negative exponent, it's equal to its reciprocal with a positive exponent.** For example, $3^{-4} = \dfrac{1}{3^4}$.

- ✔ **When a product has an exponent, each factor is raised to that power.** For example, $(5 \times 3)^3 = 5^3 \times 3^3$.

Roots

A root is the opposite of a power or an exponent. There are infinite kinds of roots. You have the *square root,* which means "undoing" a base to the second power; the cube root, which means "undoing" a base raised to the third power; a fourth root, for numbers raised to the fourth power; and so on. However, on the ASVAB math subtests, the only questions you're likely to see will involve square roots, and possibly a couple of cube roots.

Square roots

A math operation requiring you to find a square root is designated by the *radical symbol* $\left(\sqrt{}\right)$. The number underneath the radical line is called the *radicand.* For example, in the operation $\sqrt{36}$, the number 36 is the radicand.

A square root is a number that, when multiplied by itself, produces the radicand. Take the square root of $36\left(\sqrt{36}\right)$ for example. If you multiply 6 by itself (6×6), you come up with 36, so 6 is the square root of 36.

However, as I mention in the earlier "Playing with Positive and Negative Numbers" section, when you multiply two negative numbers together, you get a positive number. For example, -6×-6 also equals 36, so -6 is also the square root of 36.

That brings me to an important rule: When you take a square root, the results include two square roots — one positive and one negative.

Computing the square roots of negative numbers, such as $\sqrt{-36}$, is also possible, but it involves concepts such as imaginary numbers that are more advanced than what you're asked to do on the ASVAB.

Square roots come in two flavors:

- **Perfect squares:** Only a few numbers, called *perfect squares,* have exact square roots.

- **Irrational numbers:** All the rest of the numbers have square roots that include decimals that go on forever and have no pattern that repeats (non-repeating, non-terminating decimals), so they're called *irrational numbers.*

Perfect squares

Finding a square root can be difficult without a calculator, but because you can't use a calculator during the test, you're going to have to use your mind and some guessing methods. To find the square root of a number without a calculator, make an educated guess and then verify your results.

The radical symbol indicates that you're to find the principal square root of the number under the radical. The principal square root is a positive number. But if you're solving an equation such as $x^2 = 36$, then you give both the positive and negative roots: 6 and –6.

To use the educated-guess method, you have to know the square roots of a few perfect squares. One good way to do so is to study the squares of the numbers 1 through 12:

- 1 and –1 are both square roots of 1.

- 2 and –2 are both square roots of 4.

- 3 and –3 are both square roots of 9.

- 4 and –4 are both square roots of 16.

- 5 and –5 are both square roots of 25.

- 6 and –6 are both square roots of 36.

- 7 and –7 are both square roots of 49.

- 8 and –8 are both square roots of 64.

- 9 and –9 are both square roots of 81.

- 10 and –10 are both square roots of 100.

- 11 and –11 are both square roots of 121.

- 12 and –12 are both square roots of 144.

Irrational numbers

When the ASVAB asks you to figure square roots of numbers that don't have perfect squares, the task gets a bit more difficult. If you have to find the square root of a number that isn't a perfect square, the ASVAB usually asks you to find the square root to the nearest tenth.

Suppose you run across this problem:

$$\sqrt{54} =$$

Think about what you know:

- The square root of 49 is 7, and 54 is slightly greater than 49. You also know that the square root of 64 is 8, and 54 is slightly less than 64. (If you didn't know that, check out the preceding section.)

- So if the number 54 is somewhere between 49 and 64, the square root of 54 is somewhere between 7 and 8.

✔ Because 54 is closer to 49 than to 64, the square root will be closer to 7 than to 8, so you can try 7.3 as the square root of 54:

   1. Multiply 7.3 by itself.

   $7.3 \times 7.3 = 53.29$, which is very close to 54.

   2. Try multiplying 7.4 by itself to see whether it's any closer to 54.

   $7.4 \times 7.4 = 54.76$, which isn't as close to 54 as 53.29.

   3. So 7.3 is the square root of 54 to the nearest tenth.

Cube roots

A *cube root* is a number that when multiplied by itself three times equals the number under the radical. For example, the cube root of 27 is 3 because $3 \times 3 \times 3 = 27$. A cube root is expressed by the radical sign with a 3 written on the left of the radical. For example, the cube root of 27 would be expressed as $\sqrt[3]{27}$.

You may see one or two cube-root problems on the math subtests of the ASVAB, but probably not more than that. Plus, the problems you encounter are perfect cubes and won't involve irrational numbers.

Unlike square roots, numbers only have one possible cube root. If the radicand is positive, the cube root will be a positive number.

Also, unlike square roots, finding the cube root of a negative number without involving advanced mathematics is possible. If the radicand is negative, the cube root will also be negative. For example, $\sqrt[3]{-27} = -3$.

Just like square roots, you should memorize a few common cube roots:

✔ 1 is the cube root of 1, and –1 is the cube root of –1.

✔ 2 is the cube root of 8, and –2 is the cube root of –8.

✔ 3 is the cube root of 27, and –3 is the cube root of –27.

✔ 4 is the cube root of 64, and –4 is the cube root of –64.

✔ 5 is the cube root of 125, and –5 is the cube root of –125.

✔ 6 is the cube root of 216, and –6 is the cube root of –216.

✔ 7 is the cube root of 343, and –7 is the cube root of –343.

✔ 8 is the cube root of 512, and –8 is the cube root of –512.

✔ 9 is the cube root of 729, and –9 is the cube root of –729.

✔ 10 is the cube root of 1,000, and –10 is the cube root of –1,000.

Scientific notation

Scientific notation is a compact format for writing very large or very small numbers. Although it's most often used in scientific fields, you may find a question or two on the Mathematics Knowledge subtest of the ASVAB asking you to convert a number to scientific notation, or vice versa.

Scientific notation separates a number into two parts: a *characteristic,* always greater than or equal to 1 and less than 10, and a *power of ten.* Thus, 1.25×10^4 means 1.25 times 10 to the fourth power, or 12,500; 5.79×10^{-8} means 5.79 times 10 to the negative eighth power. (Remember that a negative exponent is equal to its reciprocal with a positive exponent, so 10^{-8} means $\frac{1}{100,000,000}$). In this case, the scientific notation comes out to 0.0000000579.

Alphabet Soup: Tackling Algebra Review

Algebra problems are equations, which means that the quantities on both sides of the equal sign are equal — they're the same: $2 = 2$, $1 + 1 = 2$, and $3 - 1 = 2$. In all these cases, the quantities are the same on both sides of the equal sign. So, if $x = 2$, then x is 2 because the equal sign says so.

Visiting variables

Most algebraic equations involve using one or more variables. A *variable* is a symbol that represents a number. Usually, algebra problems use letters such as n, t, or x for variables. In most algebra problems, your goal is to find the value of the variable. For example, in the equation, $x + 4 = 60$, you'd try to find the value of x by using several different useful rules of algebra.

Following the rules of algebra

Algebra has several rules or properties that — when combined — allow you to simplify equations. Some (but not all) equations can be simplified to a complete solution:

- **You may combine like terms.** This rule means adding or subtracting terms with variables of the same kind. The expression $4x + 4x$ simplifies to $8x$. $2y + y$ is equal to $3y$. The expression $13 - 7 + 3$ simplifies to 9.

- **You may use the distributive property to remove parentheses around unlike terms (see "Mental Math: Dealing with the Distributive Property" earlier in this chapter).**

- **You may add or subtract any value as long as you do it to both sides of the equation.**

- **You may multiply or divide by any number (except 0) as long as you do it to both sides of the equation.**

Combining like terms

One of the most common ways to simplify an expression is to combine like terms. Numeric terms may be combined, and any terms with the same variable part may be combined.

Take, for instance, the expression $5x + 3 + 3x - 6y + 4 + 7y$.

In algebra, when two or more variables are multiplied, it's traditional to place the variables next to each other and omit the multiplication sign ($\times$): $a \times b = ab$. The same rule applies to variables multiplied by numbers: $4 \times y = 4y$.

$5x$ and $3x$ are like terms. So are $-6y$ and $7y$. 3 and 4 are also like terms because they're numbers without variables. So combining the like terms, you have

$$5x + 3x = 8x$$

$$-6y + 7y = 1y \text{ (or just } y)$$

$$3 + 4 = 7$$

By combining the like terms, the expression $5x + 3 + 3x - 6y + 4 + 7y$ simplifies to $8x + y + 7$.

Using the distributive property

I know what you're thinking: You're thinking that combining like terms is pretty cool, but what if you have unlike terms contained within parentheses? Doesn't the order of operations require you to deal with terms in parentheses first? Indeed, it does, and that's where the distributive property comes in.

As I explain earlier in the chapter, $a(b + c) = ab + ac$. For example, $6(4 + 3)$ is mathematically the same as $(6 \times 4) + (6 \times 3)$.

Applying the same principle to algebra, the distributive property can be very useful in getting rid of those pesky parentheses:

$$4(x + y) = 4x + 4y$$

Using addition and subtraction

You can use addition and subtraction to get all the terms with variables on one side of an equation and all the numeric terms on the other. That's an important step in finding the value for the variable.

The equation $3x = 21$ has only the variable on one side and only a number on the other. The equation $3x + 4 = 25$ doesn't.

You can add and subtract any number as long as you do it to both sides of the equation. In this case, you want to get rid of the number 4 on the left side of the equation. How do you make the 4 disappear? Simply subtract 4 from it:

$$3x + 4 - 4 = 25 - 4$$

The equation simplifies to $3x = 21$.

Using multiplication and division

The rules of algebra also allow you to multiply and divide both sides of an equation by any number except zero. Say you have an equation that reads $3x = 21$, or 3 times x equals 21. You want to find the value of x, not three times x.

What happens if you divide a number by itself? The result is 1. Therefore, to change $3x$ to $1x$ (or x), divide both sides of the equation by 3:

$$3x = 21$$

$$\frac{3x}{3} = \frac{21}{3}$$

$$1x = 7$$

$$x = 7$$

But what if the equation were $\frac{2}{3}x = 21$? What would you do then?

I'll give you a hint: If you multiply any fraction by its reciprocal, the result is 1. Remember, a reciprocal is a fraction flipped upside down.

$$\frac{2}{3}x = 21$$

$$\frac{3}{2} \times \frac{2}{3}x = 21 \times \frac{3}{2}$$

Remember to multiply both sides of the equation by $\frac{3}{2}$.

$$1x = \frac{21}{1} \times \frac{3}{2}$$

$$x = \frac{21 \times 3}{1 \times 2}$$

$$x = \frac{63}{2}$$

$$x = 31\frac{1}{2}$$

All Is Not Equal: Examining Inequalities

Earlier in the chapter, I say that all equations include one or more equal signs (=), and I stand by that statement. After all, I wouldn't lie to you. However, some math problems look very much like equations, but they use signs other than the equal sign.

These problems are called *inequalities*. An equation states that each side of the equation separated by the equal sign is equal to the other. An inequality, on the other hand, says that the two sides separated by an inequality sign are *not* equal to each other.

Just as with equations, the solution to an inequality is all the values that make the inequality true. For the most part, you solve inequalities the same as you'd solve a normal equation. You need to keep some facts of inequality life need to keep in mind, however. Short and sweet, here they are:

- **Negative numbers** are less than zero and less than positive numbers.
- **Zero** is less than positive numbers but greater than negative numbers.
- **Positive numbers** are greater than negative numbers and greater than zero.

Although there's only one equal sign (=), several signs are associated with inequalities:

- $\neq$ means *does not equal* in the way that 3 *does not equal* 4, or $3 \neq 4$.
- $>$ means *greater than* in the way that 4 *is greater than* 3, or $4 > 3$.
- $<$ means *less than* in the way the 3 *is less than* 4, or $3 < 4$.
- $\leq$ means *less than or equal to* in the way that x may be less than or equal to 4, or $x \leq 4$.
- $\geq$ means *greater than or equal to* in the way that x may be greater than or equal to 3, or $x \geq 3$.

You solve inequalities by using the same principles of algebra used to solve equations, with the exception of multiplying or dividing each side by a negative number (check out the earlier "Following the rules of algebra" section). Take the following example:

Solve: $3x + 4 < 25$.

The inequality says that $3x$ plus 4 is less than 25. You solve it in the same way as you would the equation $3x + 4 = 25$:

$$3x + 4 < 25$$
$$3x + 4 - 4 < 25 - 4$$
$$3x < 21$$
$$\frac{3x}{3} < \frac{21}{3}$$
$$x < 7$$

Although you solve inequalities the same way you solve equations, keep two important rules in mind when working with inequalities:

- In algebra, if $a = b$, then $b = a$. In other words, you can swap the data on each side of the equal sign, and the equation means the same thing. So $2x + 4 = 18$ and $18 = 2x + 4$ are the same thing. This interchangeability doesn't work with inequalities. In other words, $2x + 4 > 18$ isn't the same as $18 > 2x + 4$. When you swap the data in an inequality, you have to change the inequality sign to balance the inequality (keep the inequity true). So $2x + 4 > 18$ is the same as $18 < 2x + 4$.

- When you multiply or divide both sides of the inequality by a negative number, the inequality sign is reversed. So if you multiply both sides of the inequality $3 < 4$ by -4, your answer is $-12 > -16$.

Solving Quadratics

A *quadratic equation* is an algebraic equation in which the unknown is raised to an exponent no higher than 2, as in x^2. They can be very simple or very complex (or several degrees of difficulty in between). Here are some examples:

- $x^2 = 36$
- $x^2 + 4 = 72$
- $x^2 + 3x - 33 = 0$

The exponent in quadratics is never higher than 2 (because it would then no longer be the *square* of an unknown, but a cube or something else). An equation that includes the variable x^3 or x^4 is *not* a quadratic.

You can solve quadratics in three primary ways: the square-root method, factoring, or the quadratic formula. Which method you choose depends on the difficulty of the equation.

Method 1: The square-root method

Simple quadratic equations (those that consist of just one squared term and a number) can be solved by using the *square-root rule*:

If $x^2 = k$, then $x = \pm\sqrt{k}$, as long as k isn't a negative number.

Remember to include the ± sign, which indicates that the answer is a positive or negative number. Take the following simple quadratic equation:

Solve: $3x^2 + 4 = 31$.

1. **First, isolate the variable by subtracting 4 from each side.**

   The result is $3x^2 = 27$.

2. **Next, get rid of the 3 by dividing both sides of the equation by 3.**

   The result is $x^2 = 9$.

3. **You can now solve by using the square root rule.**

$$x^2 = 9$$
$$x = \pm\sqrt{9}$$
$$x = 3 \text{ and } x = -3$$

Method 2: The factoring method

Most quadratic equations you encounter on the ASVAB math subtests can be solved by putting the equation into the quadratic form and then factoring.

The *quadratic form* is $ax^2 + bx + c = 0$, where a, b, and c are just numbers. All quadratic equations can be expressed in this form. Want to see some examples?

- ✔ **$2x^2 - 4x = 32$:** This equation can be expressed in the quadratic form as $2x^2 + (-4x) + (-32) = 0$. So $a = 2$, $b = -4$, and $c = -32$.

- ✔ **$x^2 = 36$:** You can express this equation as $1x^2 + 0x + (-36) = 0$. So $a = 1$, $b = 0$, and $c = -36$.

- ✔ **$3x^2 + 6x + 4 = -33$:** Expressed in quadratic form, this equation reads $3x + 6x + 37 = 0$. So $a = 3$, $b = 6$, and $c = 37$.

Ready to factor? How about trying the following equation?

Solve: $x^2 + 5x + 6 = 0$.

Because I like you, I've already expressed the equation in quadratic form, saving you a little time.

You can use the factoring method for most quadratic equations where $a = 1$ and c is a positive number.

The first step in factoring a quadratic equation is to draw two sets of parentheses on your scratch paper, and then place an x at the front of each, leaving some extra space after it. As with the original quadratic, the equation should equal zero:

$$(x\ )(x\ ) = 0$$

The next step is to find two numbers that equal c when multiplied together and equal b when added together. In the example equation, $b = 5$ and $c = 6$, so you need to hunt for two numbers that multiply to 6 and add up to 5. For example, $2 \times 3 = 6$ and $2 + 3 = 5$. In this case, the two numbers you're seeking are positive 2 and positive 3.

Finally, put these two numbers into your set of parentheses:

$$(x + 2)(x + 3) = 0$$

This means that $x + 2 = 0$, and/or $x + 3 = 0$. The solution to this quadratic equation is $x = -2$ and/or $x = -3$.

When choosing your factors, remember that they can be either positive or negative numbers. You can use clues from the signs of b and c to help you find the numbers (factors) you need:

✔ If c is positive, then the factors you're looking for are either both positive or both negative:

- If b is positive, then the factors are positive.
- If b is negative, then the factors are negative.
- b is the sum of the two factors that give you c.

✔ If c is negative, then the factors you're looking for are of alternating signs; that is, one is negative and one is positive:

- If b is positive, then the larger factor is positive.
- If b is negative, then the larger factor is negative.
- b is the difference between the two factors that give you c.

Try another one, just for giggles:

Solve: $x^2 - 7x + 6 = 0$.

Start by writing your parentheses:

$$(x\ )(x\ ) = 0$$

In this equation, $b = -7$ and $c = +6$. Because b is negative and c is positive, both factors will be negative.

You're looking for two negative numbers that multiply to 6 and add to -7. Those numbers are -1 and -6. Plugging the numbers into your parentheses, you get $(x - 1)(x - 6) = 0$. So $x = 1$ and/or $x = 6$.

Method 3: The quadratic formula

The square-root method can be used for simple quadratics, and the factoring method can easily be used for many other quadratics, as long as $a = 1$. (See the two preceding sections.) But what if a doesn't equal 1, or you can't easily find two numbers that multiply to c and add up to b?

You can use the quadratic formula to solve any quadratic equation. So why not just use the quadratic formula and forget about the square-root and factoring methods? Because the quadratic formula is kind of complex:

$$x = \frac{-b \pm \sqrt{b^2 - 4ac}}{2a}$$

The quadratic formula uses the a, b, and c from $ax^2 + bx + c = 0$, just like the factoring method.

Armed with this knowledge, you can apply your skills to a complex quadratic equation:

Solve: $2x^2 - 4x - 3 = 0$.

In this equation, $a = 2$, $b = -4$, and $c = -3$. Plug the known values into the quadratic formula:

$$x = \frac{-b \pm \sqrt{b^2 - 4ac}}{2a}$$

$$x = \frac{-(-4) \pm \sqrt{(-4)^2 - 4(2)(-3)}}{2(2)}$$

$$x = \frac{4 \pm \sqrt{16 + 24}}{4}$$

$$x = \frac{4 \pm \sqrt{40}}{4}$$

$$x = \frac{4 \pm 6.3}{4}$$

$$x = \frac{4 + 6.3}{4} \text{ and } x = \frac{4 - 6.3}{4}$$

$$x = 2.58 \text{ and } x = -0.58$$

Rounded to the nearest tenth, $x = 2.6$ and $x = -0.6$.

Knowing All the Angles: Geometry Review

According to my handy pocket dictionary, *geometry* is "the branch of mathematics that deals with the deduction of the properties, measurement, and relationships of points, lines, angles, and figures in space from their defining conditions by means of certain assumed properties of space." Sounds interesting!

Really, geometry is simply the branch of mathematics that's concerned with shapes, lines, and angles. From the perspective of the ASVAB math subtests, you should be able to identify basic geometric shapes and know certain properties about them so you can determine their angles and measurements. You see a lot of geometry-related questions on both the Mathematics Knowledge and the Arithmetic Reasoning subtests of the ASVAB.

Knowing all the angles

Angles are formed when two lines intersect at a point. Many geometric shapes are formed by intersecting lines, which form angles. Angles can be measured in degrees. The greater the number of degrees, the wider the angle is:

- ✔ A straight line is exactly 180°.
- ✔ A *right angle* is exactly 90°.
- ✔ An *acute angle* is more than 0° and less than 90°.

✔ An *obtuse angle* is more than 90° but less than 180°.

✔ *Complementary angles* are two angles that equal 90° when added together.

✔ *Supplementary angles* are two angles that equal 180° when added together.

Take a look at the different types of angles in Figure 8-3.

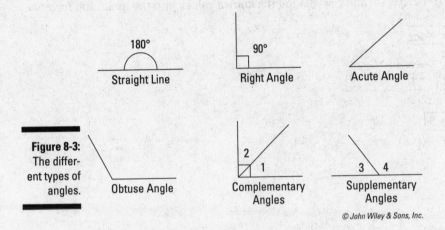

Figure 8-3: The different types of angles.

© John Wiley & Sons, Inc.

Common geometric shapes

I'm not going to explain all the possible geometric shapes for two reasons: Doing so would take this entire book, and you don't need to know them all to solve the math problems you find on the ASVAB. However, you should recognize the most common shapes associated with geometry.

Getting square with quadrilaterals

A *quadrilateral* is a geometric shape with four sides. All quadrilaterals contain interior angles totaling 360°. Here are the five most common types of quadrilaterals:

✔ **Squares** have four sides of equal length, and all the angles are right angles.

✔ **Rectangles** have all right angles.

✔ **Rhombuses** have four sides of equal length, but the angles don't have to be right angles.

✔ **Trapezoids** have at least two sides that are parallel.

✔ **Parallelograms** have opposite sides that are parallel, and their opposite sides and angles are equal.

Figure 8-4 gives you an idea of what these five quadrilaterals look like.

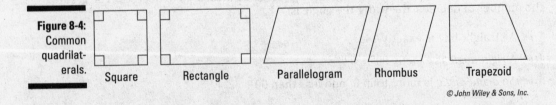

Figure 8-4: Common quadrilaterals.

Square   Rectangle   Parallelogram   Rhombus   Trapezoid

© John Wiley & Sons, Inc.

Trying out triangles

A *triangle* consists of three straight lines whose three interior angles always add up to 180°. The sides of a triangle are called *legs*. Triangles can be classified according to the relationship between their angles, the relationship between their sides, or some combination of these relationships. You should know the three most common types of triangles:

- **Isosceles triangle:** Has two equal sides, and the angles opposite the equal sides are also equal.

- **Equilateral triangle:** Has three equal sides, and all the angles measure 60°.

- **Right triangle:** Has one right angle (90°); therefore, the remaining two angles are *complementary* (add up to 90°). The side opposite the right angle is called the *hypotenuse*, which is the longest side of a right triangle.

Check out Figure 8-5 to see what these triangles look like.

Figure 8-5:
The three most common types of triangles.

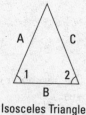

Isosceles Triangle

If sides A and C are equal, then angles 1 and 2 are equal.

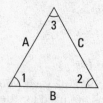

Equilateral Triangle

Sides A, B, C are equal.
Angles 1, 2, 3 are equal.

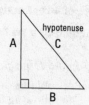

Right Triangle

$$A^2 + B^2 = C^2$$

© John Wiley & Sons, Inc.

Settling on circles

A *circle* is formed when the points of a closed line are all located equal distances from a point called the *center* of the circle. A circle always has 360°. The closed line of a circle is called its perimeter or *circumference*. The *radius* of a circle is the measurement from the center of the circle to any point on the circumference of the circle. The *diameter* of the circle is measured as a line passing through the center of the circle, from a point on one side of the circle to a point on the other side of the circle. The diameter of a circle is always twice as long as the radius. Figure 8-6 shows these relationships.

Figure 8-6:
The parts of a circle.

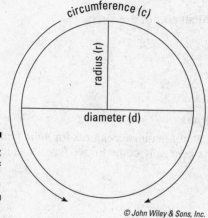

© John Wiley & Sons, Inc.

Famous geometry formulas

The math subtests of the ASVAB often ask you to use basic geometry formulas to calculate geometric measurements. You should commit these simple formulas to memory.

Quadrilateral formulas you should know

You may be asked to calculate the length of the perimeter, the area, or the diagonal of a square or rectangle. Use the following formulas:

- ✔ **Perimeter of a square:** $p = 4s$, where s = one side of the square

- ✔ **Area of a square:** $a = s^2$

- ✔ **Diagonal of a square:** $d = s\sqrt{2}$

- ✔ **Perimeter of a rectangle:** $p = 2l + 2w$, where l = the length and w = the width of the rectangle

- ✔ **Area of a rectangle:** $a = lw$

- ✔ **Diagonal of a rectangle:** $d = \sqrt{l^2 + w^2}$

Good-to-know triangle formulas

Some math problems on the ASVAB may ask you to calculate the perimeter or area of a triangle. The following formulas are used for these two purposes:

- ✔ **Perimeter of a triangle:** $p = s_1 + s_2 + s_3$, where s = the length of each leg of the triangle

- ✔ **Area of a triangle:** $a = \frac{1}{2}bh$, where b = the length of the triangle's base (bottom) and h = the height of the triangle

A special formula called the *Pythagorean theorem* says that if you know the length of any two sides of a right triangle, you can find the length of the third side. It only works on right triangles, however. The formula is $a^2 + b^2 = c^2$, where c equals the length of the triangle's hypotenuse and a and b equal the lengths of the remaining two sides.

Circle formulas

Circles are a bit more complex than squares, rectangles, and triangles and often involve invoking the value of π. In the "Making the Most of Math Terminology" section earlier in this chapter, I tell you that π is approximately equal to 3.14.

- ✔ **Radius of a circle:** $r = \frac{1}{2}d$, where d = the diameter of the circle

- ✔ **Diameter of a circle:** $d = 2r$

- ✔ **Circumference of a circle:** $c = 2\pi r$

- ✔ **Area of a circle:** $a = \pi r^2$

Handy formulas for three-dimensional shapes

Sometimes the math subtests require you to calculate measurements for solid (three-dimensional) shapes. These types of questions generally come in two flavors: calculating volume or calculating surface area.

Volume is the space a shape takes up. You can think of volume as how much a shape would hold if you poured water into it. *Surface area* is the area of the outside of the shape — for example, the amount of area you'd have to cover if you were to paint the outside of the solid shape.

- **Volume of a cube:** $v = s^3$, where s = the length of one side of the cube

- **Volume of a rectangular box:** $v = lwh$, where l = the length, w = the width, and h = the height of the box

- **Volume of a cylinder:** $v = \pi r^2 h$, where r = the radius of the cylinder and h = the height of the cylinder

- **Surface area of a cube:** $SA = 6s^2$

- **Surface area of a rectangular box:** $SA = 2lw + 2wh + 2lh$

Chapter 9

The Mathematics Knowledge Subtest

The Mathematics Knowledge subtest is one of two math subtests given to help determine your AFQT score. This chapter and Chapter 8 prepare you for the type of questions and knowledge you need in order to feel confident and score competitively on the Mathematics Knowledge portion of the ASVAB. Chapters 10 and 11 review your ability to correctly answer word problems for the Arithmetic Reasoning subtests.

Most of the time, the Mathematics Knowledge subtest contains only one or two questions testing each specific mathematical concept. For example, one question may ask you to multiply fractions, the next question may ask you to solve a mathematical inequality, and the question after that may ask you to find the value of an exponent. (If you've suddenly become nervous after reading the previous sentence, don't worry. I cover all this stuff in Chapter 8.)

All this variety forces you to constantly shift your mental gears to quickly deal with different concepts. You can look at this situation from two perspectives: These mental gymnastics can be difficult and frustrating, especially if you know everything about solving for x but nothing about deriving a square root. But variety can also be the spice of life, as your grandma may have said. If you don't know how to solve a specific type of problem, this oversight may cause you to get only one question wrong (or maybe two — but think positive). On the flip side, having trouble in a specific area helps you home in on what you need to focus your study on so you can improve your weaker areas.

Taking Stock of the Test Structure

On the CAT-ASVAB, the Mathematics Knowledge subtest consists of 16 questions covering the entire array of high-school math, and you have 20 minutes to complete the subtest. (If you're taking the paper version of the ASVAB, you have to answer 25 questions in 24 minutes.) You don't necessarily have to rush through each calculation, but the pace you need to set (about a minute per question) doesn't exactly give you time to daydream about what you're having for dinner. You have to focus and concentrate to solve each problem quickly and accurately.

The lovely people who make up the rules have dictated you can't use a calculator for any of the math questions on the ASVAB. When you enter the testing room, you get a pencil and a sheet of scratch paper. (I guess their thinking is that if you're in the middle of a combat zone and find a sudden need to solve for *x*, you may find your calculator full of sand and worthless.) The good news is that all the questions on the math subtests of the ASVAB are designed so that you can solve them without electronic calculation.

The Mathematics Knowledge subtest features three types of questions:

- ✔ **Direct math:** This type of question presents you with a mathematical equation and asks you to solve it.

- ✔ **Math law:** This type of question asks you a about a mathematical law, rule, term, or concept.

- ✔ **Combined:** This type of question asks you to use a mathematical law, rule, term, or concept to solve a problem.

Direct math questions

The direct math question is the most common type of question on the Mathematics Knowledge subtest. In a direct math question, you're presented with an equation and asked to solve it. You see a lot of these.

Solve for *x*: $2x + 4(2x + 7) = 3(2x + 4)$.

(A) 0.75

(B) −4

(C) 1.25

(D) −1.25

The correct answer is Choice (B), −4. This is an algebraic equation that you can solve using the rules of algebra (see Chapter 8):

$$2x + 4(2x + 7) = 3(2x + 4)$$
$$2x + 8x + 28 = 6x + 12$$
$$10x + 28 = 6x + 12$$
$$4x + 28 = 12$$
$$4x = -16$$
$$x = -4$$

Math law questions

Sometimes the Mathematics Knowledge subtest asks you a question that doesn't involve solving a mathematical problem. Instead, you're expected to answer a question concerning a mathematical concept, math term, rule, or law. You're not likely to see more than two or three of these kinds of questions on the test, however.

In the expression $432xy + 124xy$, the "432" is called the

(A) multiplier

(B) coefficient

(C) matrix

(D) prime

The correct answer is Choice (B), coefficient. A *coefficient* is the number multiplied times a variable or a product of variables or powers of variables in a term. (You can find more useful math terms in Chapter 8.)

Combined questions

You may see eight or nine combined questions on the Mathematics Knowledge subtest. These questions require you to use a particular math term, rule, or concept to solve a mathematical problem.

What is the quotient of 4 and 4?

(A) 8

(B) 16

(C) 0

(D) 1

The right answer is Choice (D), 1. To solve this problem, you need to know that a *quotient* is the result of a division operation. When you've figured that out, you have to perform the operation:

$$4 \div 4 = 1$$

Planning Your Test Attack

For most people, scoring well on the Mathematics Knowledge subtest requires more than just showing up on time and borrowing a No. 2 pencil and piece of scratch paper. Maybe everything on the test will go perfectly, and you'll breeze through without a problem. On the other hand, maybe you'll get stuck on a question or run into other roadblocks. When this happens, having a plan of attack is helpful.

Keeping an eye on the all-important clock

Like all subtests of the ASVAB, the Mathematics Knowledge subtest is timed. If you're taking the paper test, you have just 24 minutes to try to correctly answer 25 questions. That's 57.6 seconds per question. (Do you like the way I used math to figure that out?) The room will have a clock in it, and the start time and stop time will be posted somewhere in the room, easily visible to you and the other test takers.

If you're taking the computerized version of the ASVAB, you get 16 questions in 20 minutes, and your remaining time will be shown in the upper corner of your computer screen.

Keep an eye on the clock. You want to try to finish the test before time runs out. Try to average about 45 or 50 seconds per question. If you get stuck on a question, try the "Playing the guessing game" techniques later in this chapter.

Doubling your chances by double-checking

If you have time, double-check your answers. Those crafty test makers often provide wrong answer choices that work if you made a common error, so don't assume that your answer is the right one just because it matches one of the possible answer choices. Look at the following example:

Solve: $\frac{1}{4} \div \frac{1}{2} =$

(A) $\frac{1}{8}$

(B) 2

(C) 17

(D) $\frac{1}{2}$

To correctly solve this problem, you multiply the first fraction by the *reciprocal* (flipped over) value of the second fraction:

$$\frac{1}{4} \div \frac{1}{2} = \frac{1}{4} \times \frac{2}{1} = \frac{2}{4} = \frac{1}{2}$$

So the correct answer is Choice (D), $\frac{1}{2}$. If you multiplied the fractions instead of dividing, you would've gotten Choice (A). If you took the reciprocal of the first fraction rather than the second, you would've gotten Choice (B). If you took a wild guess, you might've gotten Choice (C).

Although double-checking your answers is always a good idea, remember to keep an eye on the clock. You don't want to run out of time with only half the questions answered because you've spent too much time double-checking all your answers.

Using the answer choices to your advantage

If you're stuck on a particular problem, sometimes plugging the possible answer choices into the equation can help you find the right answer.

Solve: $\frac{1}{2}x - 45 = 5$.

(A) 25

(B) 50

(C) 100

(D) 75

The right answer is Choice (C), 100. Suppose you experience a complete brain-freeze and can't remember how to handle a variable multiplied by a fraction. You don't have to jump straight to random guessing at this point. You can replace x in the equation with the known possible answer choices and see whether any of them work.

First, recognize that you can simplify the equation to $\frac{1}{2}x = 50$ by adding 45 to both sides. Now start substituting the answer choices for x:

- ✔ **$x = 25$:** $\frac{1}{2} \times 25 = 50 \rightarrow 12.5 = 50$. That doesn't work.

- ✔ **$x = 50$:** $\frac{1}{2} \times 50 = 50 \rightarrow 25 = 50$. That certainly doesn't work.

- ✔ **$x = 100$:** $\frac{1}{2} \times 100 = 50 \rightarrow 50 = 50$. You can stop here because Choice (C) is the correct answer.

Don't forget that plugging in all the answers is time-consuming, so save this procedure until you've answered all the problems you can answer. If you're taking the computer version, you can't skip a question, so remember to budget your time wisely; if you don't have much time, just make a guess and move on. You may be able to solve the next question easily.

Playing the guessing game

Guessing incorrectly on any of the paper ASVAB subtests doesn't count against you. So fill in an answer — any answer — on your answer sheet because if you don't, your chances of getting that answer right are zero. But if you take a shot at it, your chances increase to 25 percent, or one in four. If time is running short on the CAT-ASVAB, try to read and legitimately answer the questions rather than filling in random guesses for the remaining items. The CAT-ASVAB applies a relatively large penalty when you provide several incorrect answers toward the end of the subtest.

If you're taking the paper version of the ASVAB, you can always skip the tough questions and come back to them after you've finished the easier ones. If you're taking the computerized version of the ASVAB, the software doesn't let you skip questions.

If you're taking the paper version of the test and elect to skip questions until later, make sure you mark the next answer in the correct space on the answer sheet. Otherwise, you may wind up wearing out the eraser on your pencil when you discover your error at the end of the test. Or, even worse, you may not notice the error, and you may wind up getting several answers wrong because you mismarked your answer sheet.

The process of elimination

Guessing doesn't always mean "pick an answer, any answer." You can increase your chances of picking the right answer by eliminating answers that can't be right.

Solve: $\frac{1}{8} \times \frac{4}{5} =$

(A) $1\frac{1}{8}$

(B) $1\frac{1}{4}$

(C) $\frac{1}{10}$

(D) $\frac{1}{5}$

Any fraction that is less than 1 that is multiplied by another fraction that is less than 1 is going to result in an answer that is less than 1. That means Choices (A) and (B) can't be correct. Your odds of guessing the right answer have just improved from one in four to one in two, or a 50/50 chance. (By the way, the correct answer is Choice (C).)

Solving what you can and guessing the rest

Sometimes you may know how to solve part of a problem but not all of it. If you don't know how to do all the operations, don't give up. You can still narrow your choices by doing what you can. Suppose this question confronts you:

What is the value of $(-0.4)^3$?

(A) -0.0027

(B) -0.000064

(C) 0.000064

(D) 0.0009

What if you don't remember how to multiply decimals? All is not lost! If you remember how to use exponents, you'll remember that you have to multiply −0.04×−0.04×−0.04. So if you simplify the problem and just multiply −4×−4×−4 without worrying about those pesky zeros, you know that your answer will be negative and will end in the digits 64. With this pearl of wisdom in mind, you can see that Choices (A), (C), and (D) are all wrong. You logically guessed your way to the correct answer, Choice (B)!

Practice Makes Perfect: Sampling Some Practice Questions

How about putting all the knowledge you've gained about the Mathematics Knowledge subtest to the test? Here are ten questions that are very similar to those you're likely to see when you take the actual test.

1. Which of the following fractions is the smallest?

(A) $\frac{3}{4}$

(B) $\frac{14}{17}$

(C) $\frac{4}{7}$

(D) $\frac{5}{8}$

2. What is the product of $\sqrt{36}$ and $\sqrt{49}$?

(A) 1,764

(B) 42

(C) 13

(D) 6

3. Solve: $2x - 3 = x + 7$.

(A) 10

(B) 6

(C) 21

(D) −10

4. A circle has a radius of 15 feet. What is most nearly its circumference?

(A) 30 feet

(B) 225 feet

(C) 94 feet

(D) 150 feet

5. At 3 p.m., the angle between the hands of the clock is

(A) 90 degrees

(B) 180 degrees

(C) 120 degrees

(D) 360 degrees

6. If $3 + y \geq 13$, what is the value of y?

(A) Greater than or equal to 10

(B) Less than or equal to 10

(C) 10

(D) 6

7. $y^3 \times y^2 \times y^3 =$

(A) y^2

(B) y^{-18}

(C) y^8

(D) x^{23}

8. 14 yards + 14 feet =

(A) 16 yards

(B) 15 yards

(C) 28 feet

(D) 56 feet

9. What is 35 percent of 85?

(A) 33.2

(B) 65.32

(C) 21.3

(D) 29.75

10. What is most nearly the average of 37, 22, 72, and 44?

(A) 43.8

(B) 55.2

(C) 175

(D) 77.1

Answers and Explanations

Use this answer key to score the practice Mathematics Knowledge questions.

1. **C.** One method of comparing fractions is called the *cross-product method* (see Chapter 8).

   The cross-products of the first fraction and the second fraction are $3 \times 17 = 51$ and $14 \times 4 = 56$. The first fraction is smaller.

   The cross-products of the first fraction and the third fraction are $3 \times 7 = 21$ and $4 \times 4 = 16$. The third fraction is smaller.

   The cross-products of the third fraction and the fourth fraction are $4 \times 8 = 32$ and $5 \times 7 = 35$. The third fraction, Choice (C), is still smaller, so it's the smallest of all the fractions.

2. **B.** The square root of 36 is 6, and the square root of 49 is 7. The product of those two numbers is $6 \times 7 = 42$.

3. **A.** Rearrange the equation and solve as follows:

   $$2x - 3 = x + 7$$
   $$2x - x = 7 + 3$$
   $$x = 10$$

4. **C.** The circumference of a circle is $\pi \times$ diameter; the diameter equals two times the radius; and π is approximately 3.14. Therefore, $30 \times 3.14 \approx 94$.

   The $\approx$ sign means *approximately equals*. It's used here because the answer, 94, is a rounded number.

5. **A.** At 3 p.m., one hand is on the 12, and the other is on the 3. This setup creates a *right angle* — a 90-degree angle.

6. **A.** Solve the inequality the same way you'd solve an algebraic equation:

   $$3 + y \geq 13$$
   $$y \geq 13 - 3$$
   $$y \geq 10$$

7. **A.** When you multiply powers with the same base, add the exponents: $y^3 \times y^2 \times y^{-3} = y^{3 + 2 + (-3)} = y^2$.

8. **D.** Convert the yards to feet by multiplying by 3: $14 \times 3 = 42$ feet. Add this to 14 feet: $42 + 14 = 56$ feet.

9. **D.** Multiply 85 by the decimal equivalent of 35 percent, or 0.35: $0.35 \times 85 = 29.75$.

10. **A.** Add the numbers and then divide by the number of terms: $37 + 22 + 72 + 44 = 175$, and $175 \div 4 = 43.75$. Round this number up to 43.8.

Chapter 10

Working with Word Problems

*T*wo types of mathematics tests are part of the AFQT. The first type is the Mathematics Knowledge subtest that I discuss in Chapters 8 and 9. The second type is the Arithmetic Reasoning subtest, which is the topic of this chapter and Chapter 11.

In the Mathematics Knowledge subtest, you have it pretty easy. You see a mathematical equation, and you do your best to solve it. The Arithmetic Reasoning subtest is more involved. You have to set up your own equations to solve the problem. Ouch! How unfair! Those test makers are asking you not only to solve the problem but also to write the equation in the first place!

Lots of people have difficulty with translating a math word problem into a mathematical equation that can be solved. If you feel yourself starting to sweat at the mere thought of math word problems, you're not alone. Just take a deep breath, relax, and don't worry. I'm here to guide you through the process.

Making Sense of Word Problems

The purpose of math word problems is to test your ability to use general mathematics to solve everyday, real-world problems. That's what all the textbooks say. However, in my "real world," I've never once wondered how old Anna is if she's three years older than Chuck, and in five years, her age and Chuck's age would equal 54. I'd just ask Anna how old she is. If she didn't answer, I wouldn't buy her a birthday present.

In all fairness, arithmetic reasoning can actually be quite helpful in sharpening your ability to figure out dimensions of spaces, construction information, travel time, and the probability of being late if you decide to go shopping at the BX before your important meeting with your First Sergeant. You may even want to understand how much interest you've acquired in your bank account, how much cash you have left over after lunch, and how much that badminton set really costs after you take 20 percent off.

When you realize that math word problems are designed to measure your ability to use basic math to solve *fictional* problems, they can be kind of fun — sort of like solving a puzzle.

Setting Up the Problem

Word problems are nothing more than a series of expressions that fit into an equation. An equation is a combination of math expressions. (If that sounds like Greek to you, check out Chapter 8.) The expressions in math word problems are generally stated in English. Your job is to dig out the relevant facts and state them in mathematical terms. You do so by

- Getting organized
- Understanding the problem
- Identifying the information you need
- Translating the problem into one or more solvable mathematic equations

I cover all these tasks in greater detail in the following sections.

Getting organized

Getting organized isn't really a step as much as it is a method. You need to be organized throughout the problem-solving process. Working clearly helps you think clearly and ensures you don't get lost while trying to define and solve the problem.

When using your scratch paper, draw and label your pictures and graphs clearly. And be sure to mark your calculations with the question number. If you go back to your notes and can't remember what you were thinking about when you drew that picture, you'll be frustrated and will waste valuable time — and you don't have any time to waste on the Arithmetic Reasoning subtest. (For more on pictures, see the sidebar "A picture can be worth a thousand equations.")

A picture can be worth a thousand equations

When you walk in to take the ASVAB, the kindly test proctors are going to give you a piece of blank scratch paper. If you want more, they'll gladly give you more; they'll even give you more if you run out during the exam. Sure, the scratch sheet is handy for figuring out equations, but it's also useful for drawing diagrams and pictures to help you clarify the problem in your mind.

Sometimes, drawing a simple diagram can save you loads of time when you're trying to get a quick grasp on how to solve a math word problem. Here's one of my favorite examples:

A ladybug walks 5 inches directly south. She then turns and walks 10 inches directly east. If she then sprouts her wings and flies directly back to her starting point, how far will she have to fly?

This problem becomes instantly clear with a quick diagram on your scratch paper, like the sketch shown here.

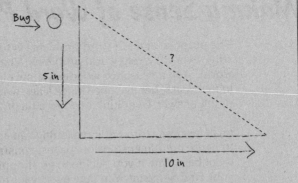

The crudely drawn diagram on your scratch paper makes it instantly clear that you need to find the length of the hypotenuse of a right triangle. If you read Chapter 8, you know that you can use the Pythagorean theorem ($a^2 + b^2 = c^2$) to quickly figure this problem out. Without that sketch, you may not realize how simple this problem really is.

Understanding the problem

Make sure you read the entire problem, but be careful: Don't try too hard to understand the problem on the first read-through. I know that doesn't seem to make any sense, but bear with me.

Math word problems can be broken down into two parts:

- ✔ **The problem statement:** The problem statement isn't really an object to be understood. It's simply a source of information, much like a dictionary or telephone book that has information you can look up, as needed, to solve the equation.

  The information included in the problem statement is often confusing or disorganized. Sometimes *distracters* (information that has nothing to do with solving the problem) are mixed in, leading to confusion and making the problem difficult to solve. (See the "Dealing with distracters" sidebar for more information.)

- ✔ **The problem question:** The problem question is the meat of the matter. Exactly what is the questioner asking you to find? This part of the problem is the one you really need to understand.

Identifying the information you need

After you've separated the question from the statement (see the preceding section), list the facts in a clear, concise list. Identify exactly what the question is asking of you. Figure out what you need but don't have, and name things. Pick variables (a, x, b, and so on) to stand for the unknowns, clearly labeling these variables with what they stand for.

Be as clear as possible when you identify the information you need. You don't want to spend five minutes on a word problem solving for x, only to reach the end and forget what x is supposed to stand for.

Dealing with distracters

If math word problems were all straightforward questions, such as "What is 10 multiplied by 10?", you could skip this chapter. However, those wascally wabbits who write the questions stay awake at night to think up ways to complicate things. The use of distracters is one such way.

A *distracter* is any piece of information included in the problem statement that has absolutely nothing to do with solving the problem. Consider the following example:

In November, the National Weather Service recorded 1 inch of snow and 3 inches of rain in Grand Forks, North Dakota. In December, these numbers were reversed, with 3 inches of snow and only 1 inch of rain. How much snow did Grand Forks Receive in total?

You don't need to know how much rain fell in Grand Forks in order to solve this problem. The amount of rain has absolutely nothing to do with the problem question. It's a distracter; its purpose is to distract you from focusing on the real question. The problem mentions rain, so it has to figure into the problem in some way, doesn't it? Wrong! Be sure to read the question carefully and ignore any information that's just there to trip you up.

Pay particular attention to include units of measure, such as feet, miles, inches, pounds, dollars, and so on. One of the fastest ways to mess up on a math word problem is by forgetting the apples-and-oranges rule. You generally can't perform mathematical operations on different units of measurement. Ten apples plus ten oranges equals 20 pieces of fruit; it does *not* equal 20 apples, nor does it equal 20 oranges. Look at the following example:

> A carpenter buys 44 feet of wood. If she adds the wood to the 720 inches of wood she already owns, how many feet of wood will she have?

If you add 44 to 720, you're going to get the wrong answer. Before you can add the numbers, you have to either convert 44 feet of wood to inches ($44 \cdot 12 = 528$ inches) or convert 720 inches to feet ($720 \div 12 = 60$ feet).

Make sure when you select your answer, it has the correct unit of measurement. Those tricky test writers often give several options with different units in order to make sure you're paying attention and can correctly identify what unit to use.

Translating the problem

Now you're at the tough part. The hardest thing about doing word problems is taking the English words and translating them into mathematics. Luckily, math word problems often contain certain *keywords* that can help.

Although the following keywords *often* indicate a mathematical operation in a word problem, that's not always the case. You have to use a little common sense. "*A man was walking down the street*" doesn't mean a division operation. "Matt and Paul were working *together*" doesn't necessarily mean you're going to perform a math addition problem regarding Matt and Paul.

Addition keywords

Several words and phrases used in math word problems indicate an addition operation:

- Increased by
- More than
- Combined
- Together
- Total of
- Sum
- Added to

"The drill sergeant can do 100 pushups more than Private Jones" is equivalent to Private Jones + 100 = drill sergeant. "Together, they can do 300 pushups" can be mathematically stated as drill sergeant + Private Jones = 300.

Try the following example, just to see if you're getting the hang of things:

The drill sergeant can do 100 pushups more than Private Jones. Together, they can do 300 pushups. How many pushups can Private Jones do?

The question is asking you how many pushups Private Jones can do. You're not really interested in how many the drill sergeant can do, and the problem statement tells you that they can do 300 total pushups together. You also know that the drill sergeant can do 100 more than Private Jones.

List the important information:

- Let j = the number of pushups that Private Jones can do. This figure is what you really want to find out, so you need to define it first.

- Let d = the number of pushups that the drill sergeant can do. You don't really want to know this information, but it's a necessary fact in order to solve the problem.

- You know another definition of d. The problem statement tells you that the drill sergeant can do 100 more pushups than Private Jones, which means that $d = j + 100$, which is the same (mathematically) as saying $j = d - 100$.

- You know that together they can do 300 pushups, which tells you that $d + j = 300$.

All you need to do now is to solve that final equation in terms of j. First, subtract d from both sides to express the equation in terms of j: $d + j = 300$ is the same as $j = 300 - d$. (I cover algebraic properties in Chapter 8.)

You already have a definition for d from above ($d = j + 100$). Substitute this value for d in the equation you're now working to solve:

$$j = 300 - d$$
$$j = 300 - (j + 100)$$
$$j = 300 - j - 100$$
$$2j = 200$$
$$j = 100$$

Private Jones can do 100 pushups.

As an alternative, you can also substitute "$j + 100$" for d in the equation $d + j = 100$. The answer will be the same.

Even if you can do this particular problem in your head (300 total – 100 more = 200, divide by two to get 100), try to avoid doing so. You want to get in the practice of setting up and solving equations for each question. Often, you'll stumble on a word problem that can only be solved by using an equation, and you want to be an expert at the proper procedures.

Because math can be a tricky thing (I've been known to believe 2 + 2 = 3 before my morning coffee), it's always a good idea to check your answer to make sure it makes sense. Plug your answer into the original problem and see whether it works out: The drill sergeant can do 100 pushups more than Private Jones: 100 + 100 = 200. The drill sergeant can do 200 pushups. Together, they can do 300 pushups: 100 + 200 = 300. Makes sense.

Subtraction keywords

If you see any of the following words and phrases in a math word problem, it generally indicates a subtraction operation:

- Decreased by

- Minus

- Less

- Difference between/of

- Less than

- Fewer than

"Becky's pay decreased by $10" can be stated mathematically as Becky – 10. This phrasing is also the same as "Becky's pay minus $10," or "Becky's pay less $10."

"The difference between Bob's pay and Becky's pay" can be expressed as Bob – Becky.

The *less than* and *fewer than* terms work backward in English from what they are in the math. Although "Becky's pay minus $10" is Becky – 10, "Becky's pay less than x" is *not* Becky – x; it's x – Becky.

Multiplication keywords

The following words and phrases usually mean a mathematical multiplication operation when included in a math word problem:

- ✔ Of
- ✔ Times
- ✔ Multiplied by
- ✔ Product of
- ✔ Increased/decreased by a factor of

"15 percent of x" is mathematically expressed as $x \cdot 0.15$. "x times y" and "x multiplied by y" mean $x \cdot y$. The product of x and y is the same as $x \cdot y$.

Increased by a factor of and *decreased by a factor of* can involve addition and subtraction in combination with multiplication. "x increased by a factor of 10 percent" is expressed as $x + (x \cdot 0.10)$.

Division keywords

If you see the following words/phrases in a math word problem, "division operation" should pop into your mind:

- ✔ A
- ✔ Per
- ✔ Average
- ✔ Ratio of
- ✔ Quotient of

The first two terms in this list mean "divided by" — for example, "I bought 2 gallons of milk at the grocery store and paid $3, so milk was $1.50 a gallon," or "Milk was $1.50 per gallon."

To find the average of a group of numbers, you add the numbers, and then divide by the number of terms. "The average of a, b, and c" is $(a + b + c) \div 3$.

Mathematically, *ratios* are expressed as fractions. A ratio of five to three is written as $\frac{5}{3}$, which is the same as saying $5 \div 3$. Chapter 8 has more detail about how to work with ratios.

The "quotient of x and y" is the same as $x \div y$.

Practicing keywords

Learning how to recognize keywords is essential in translating English into mathematical expressions. Try a few examples, just to see if you're getting the hang of it:

- ✔ **Translate "the sum of 13 and *y*" into an equation.** This phrase translates to 13 + *y*. The keyword *sum* indicates an addition operation.

- ✔ **How do you write "the quotient of *a* and 6" as an equation?** The keyword *quotient* means division, so this example translates to *a* ÷ 6.

- ✔ **How do you write "7 less than *y*" as a mathematical equation?** It's *y* − 7. If you answered 7 − *y*, you forgot that "less than" is backward in math from how it's used in English.

- ✔ **Translate "the ratio of *x* plus 6 to 8" into an equation.** "*x* plus 6" is an addition operation, while the keyword *ratio* indicates division. This problem translates to $\frac{x+6}{8}$.

Are you ready to try a couple of longer ones? I knew you were!

- ✔ **The length of a rectangle is 45 inches more than its width. Let the width = *w*; express the length in mathematical terms.** *More than* is a keyword that means addition. Because the width = *w*, you write the length mathematically as *w* + 45.

- ✔ **Paul is three years older than Marsha, who is four times the age of Brian. Express Marsha's age as an algebraic expression.** You can express Paul's age, Marsha's age, and Brian's age with any variables you choose, but using the first letters of their names just makes sense. That way, you have less chance of forgetting what variable stands for what factor. "Four *times*" indicates multiplication. Marsha's age can be written as 4 · *b*, or 4*b*. Paul's age can be expressed as *m* + 3, so Marsha's age can also be written as *p* − 3.

Confused? Check out Chapter 8 for the properties of algebraic equations.

Trying Out Typical Word Problems

When you can recognize common keywords and translate them into mathematical expressions as I describe earlier in the chapter, you're ready to take on a few math word problems.

Because math word problems generally represent fictional real-life situations, the test writers can theoretically come up with an infinite number of possible problems. However, math word problem test writers must have limited imaginations because certain types of questions seem to pop up more often than others. This observation is true whether you're taking the SAT or the Arithmetic Reasoning subtest of the ASVAB.

Age problems

Age problems involve figuring out how old someone is, was, or will be. You generally do solve them by comparing their ages to the ages of other people.

Sometimes you can solve an age problem by using a one-variable solution, and sometimes it takes several variables. In the following sections, I show you how to solve the same problem by using either a one-variable solution or a two-variable solution.

One-variable solution

Sid is twice as old as Mary. In three years, the sum of their ages will be 66. How old are they now?

Let Mary's age = x. Because Sid is twice as old as Mary, his age can be represented as $2x$.

In three years, Mary's age will be $x + 3$, and Sid's age will be $2x + 3$. The sum of their ages will be 66.

You now have an equation you can work with:

$$(x+3)+(2x+3)=66$$
$$3x+6=66$$
$$3x=60$$
$$x=\frac{60}{3}$$
$$x=20$$

What did x stand for again? Was it Mary's age or Sid's age? Be sure to clearly label variables on your scratch paper, so you don't get frustrated and tear your hair out in front of everyone else. That causes talk.

x represents Mary's age, so Mary is 20 years old. Because Sid is twice Mary's age, Sid is 40 ($2 \cdot 20 = 40$).

If you have time, check your answer to see that it makes sense: Sid (age 40) is twice as old as Mary (age 20). In three years, the sum of their ages will be $(40 + 3) + (20 + 3) = 43 + 23 = 66$. It fits! Isn't math fun?

Two-variable solution

Sid is twice as old as Mary. In three years, the sum of their ages will be 66. How old are they now?

Let m = Mary's age and s = Sid's age. You know that Sid is twice as old as Mary, so $s = 2m$. That gives you your first equation.

You also know that in three years, the sum of their ages will be 66. Stated mathematically:

$$(m + 3) + (s + 3) = 66$$

You can simplify this equation:

$$m+s+6=66$$
$$m+s=60$$

You now have two equations, with two variables that you can use to solve the problem:

$$s=2m$$
$$m+s=60$$

Replace s in the second equation with the definition of s in the first equation:

$$m+2m=60$$
$$3m=60$$
$$m=\frac{60}{3}$$
$$m=20$$

Mary is 20 years old. That's the same answer you get when you use the one-variable solution in the preceding section.

Geometric problems

These problems require you to compute the volume, perimeter, area, circumference, diameter, and so on of various geometric shapes.

You're painting a fence that is 20 feet long and 6 feet high. How much square footage of fence are you covering with paint?

The area formula for a rectangle is $a = lw$, so the answer to this simple problem is $a = 6 \cdot 20 = 120$ square feet.

Generally, the Arithmetic Reasoning test makers don't let you off so easy, though. The problem is more likely to be written something like the following.

You're painting a fence that is 20 feet long and 6 feet high. Paint costs $7.23 per gallon, and 1 gallon of paint covers 60 square feet of fence. How much do you need to spend on paint to complete the project?

The problem now requires a couple of extra steps to answer. First, you have to compute the area of the fence. You already did that: 120 square feet.

Now you have to determine how many gallons of paint you need to buy to cover 120 square feet. Because 1 gallon of paint covers 60 square feet, you need $120 \div 60 = 2$ gallons of paint.

Finally, you need to figure how much 2 gallons of paint cost. Paint is $7.23 per gallon, and you need 2 gallons, so $7.23 \cdot 2 = \$14.46$.

You get quite a few geometric problems on the Arithmetic Reasoning subtest. To make sure you're ready for them, memorize the basic geometric formulas in Table 10-1. You can find more information about using these formulas in Chapter 8.

Table 10-1	Basic Geometric Formulas	
Shape	*Function*	*Formula*
Square	Area	$a = s^2$
	Perimeter	$p = 4s$
	Diagonal	$d = s\sqrt{2}$
Rectangle	Area	$a = lw$
	Perimeter	$p = 2l + 2w$
	Diagonal	$d = \sqrt{l^2 + w^2}$
Triangle	Perimeter	$p = s_1 + s_2 + s_3$
	Area	$a = \frac{1}{2}bh$
Right Triangle	Pythagorean theorem	$a^2 + b^2 = c^2$
Circle	Radius	$r = \frac{1}{2}d$
	Diameter	$d = 2r$
	Circumference	$c = 2\pi r$
	Area	$a = \pi r^2$

continued

Table 10-1 *(continued)*

Shape	Function	Formula
Cube	Volume	$v = s^3$
	Surface Area	$SA = 6s^2$
Rectangular Box	Volume	$v = lwh$
	Surface Area	$SA = 2lw + 2wh + 2lh$
Cylinder	Volume	$v = \pi r^2 h$

Coin problems

I think mathematicians must have big piggy banks. Many math word problems ask you to figure out how many coins of various types a person has.

Jeremy has 12 more nickels than quarters. How many coins does he have if the total value of his coins is $2.70?

Let q = quarters. Because Jeremy has 12 more nickels than quarters, you can represent the number of nickels as $q + 12$. Jeremy has $2.70 worth of coins, which is equal to 270¢. A quarter is 25¢, and a nickel is 5¢. Jeremy's total coins together must equal 270¢. Therefore,

(25¢ · number of quarters) + (5¢ · number of nickels) = 270¢

Or, writing it another way:

$$25q + 5(q + 12) = 270$$
$$25q + 5q + 60 = 270$$
$$30q = 210$$
$$q = \frac{210}{30}$$
$$q = 7$$

Jeremy has 7 quarters. Because he has 12 more nickels than quarters, he has 7 + 12 = 19 nickels, for a total of 19 + 7 = 26 coins.

Does this answer make sense? Always remember to check your answer. Jeremy has 12 more nickels (19 nickels) than quarters (7 quarters). How many coins does he have if the total value of his coins is $2.70? So, 19 nickels = 95¢ and 7 quarters = 175¢, so 95¢ + 175¢ = 270¢ = $2.70. It looks good to me.

Travel problems

I wish I could travel as much as word problem test writers seem to. They come up with a lot of travel problems. They especially seem to like trains and planes.

Travel problems involve using the distance formula, $d = rt$, where d is the distance, r is the rate, and t is the time. Generally, the problems come in three basic flavors: traveling away from each other, traveling in the same direction, and traveling at 90-degree angles.

Traveling away from each other

When two planes (or trains, cars, people, or even bugs) travel in opposite directions, they increase the distance between them in direct proportion. To solve these types of problems, you compute the distance traveled from the starting point for each plane (or train, car, person, or bug).

Train A travels north at 60 mph. Train B travels south at 70 mph. If both trains leave the station at the same time, how far apart will they be at the end of two hours?

To solve this problem, you compute the distance traveled by train A and then the distance traveled by train B and add the results together.

The distance formula is $d = rt$. The rate of travel for train A is 60 mph, and it travels for two hours:

$$d = 60 \times 2$$
$$d = 120$$

Train A travels 120 miles during the two-hour period.

When using the distance formula, you have to pay attention to the units of measurement. Remember the apples-and-oranges rule (see "Identifying the information you need" earlier in this chapter). If rate (r) is expressed in kilometers per hour, your result (d) will be kilometers. If rate (r) is expressed as miles per second, you must either convert it to mph or convert time (t) to seconds.

The rate of travel for train B is 70 mph, and it also travels for two hours:

$$d = 70 \times 2$$
$$d = 140$$

Train B travels 140 miles during the two-hour period.

Train A is 120 miles from the station and train B is 140 miles from the station, in the opposite direction. The two trains are 120 + 140 = 260 miles apart.

Traveling in the same direction

If two trains are traveling in the same direction as each other but at different rates of speed, one train travels farther in the same time than the other travels. The distance between the two trains is the difference between the distance traveled by train A and the distance traveled by train B.

You know what they say about assuming . . .

Math word problems require you to make basic assumptions. In the train problem in the "Traveling away from each other" section, you're to assume that both trains travel at a constant rate of speed. You're supposed to ignore the fact that they may slow down for a curve, or that they'll probably need a little time to get up to cruising speed.

If a question gives you the average daily output of a factory and asks you what the output will be in a year, you're supposed to assume that the year is 365 days long.

If you're asked how high the kite is flying 300 feet away from you, you must assume that the ground is perfectly level.

If . . . well, you get the point.

Train A travels north at 60 mph. Train B also travels north, on a parallel track, at 70 mph. If both trains leave the station at the same time, how far apart will they be at the end of two hours?

Train A traveled 120 miles, and train B traveled 140 miles. (If you're wondering why I didn't show my work here, check out the calculations in the preceding section.) Because they're traveling in the same direction, you subtract to find the distance between them: $140 - 120 = 20$. The two trains are 20 miles apart.

Traveling at 90-degree angles

Some travel problems involve two people or things moving at 90-degree angles and then stopping; the problem then asks you what the distance is (as the crow flies) between the two people or things, which means you need to use the distance formula and a little basic geometry.

Train A travels north at 60 mph. Train B travels east at 70 mph. Both trains travel for two hours. Then a bee flies from train A and lands on train B. Assuming the bee flew in a straight line, how far did the bee travel between the two trains?

Train A travels 120 miles, and Train B travels a distance of 140 miles. (Head to the earlier section "Traveling away from each other" for the math that gets you those distances.)

Because the trains are traveling at 90-degree angles (one north and one east), the lines of travel form two sides of a right triangle. Figure 10-1 should make this setup easy to visualize.

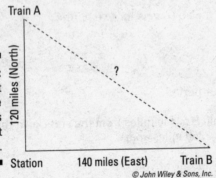

Figure 10-1:
Traveling at
90-degree
angles
forms a right
triangle.

© John Wiley & Sons, Inc.

The Pythagorean theorem says that if you know the length of two sides of a right triangle, you can find the length of the third side by using the formula $a^2 + b^2 = c^2$:

$$120^2 + 140^2 = c^2$$
$$14,400 + 19,600 = c^2$$
$$c = \sqrt{34,000}$$
$$c = 184.39$$

The bee flies 184.39 miles.

Finding the square root of a very large number can be a daunting task, especially because you don't have a calculator available during the ASVAB. When you reach this point of the equation, just squaring the possible answers to see which one works is often easier.

Investment/loan problems

These problems are primarily focused on simple interest rates for investments and loans, using the formula $I = prt$, where I is the interest, p is the principal, r is the rate of interest (in percentage), and t is the time.

The investment/loan problems you see on the Arithmetic Reasoning subtest are pretty simple. They're nowhere near as difficult as similar situations in real life, where interest is compounded.

To solve these problems, replace what's known in the interest formula and then solve for anything else.

John invests $1,500 for three years at an annual interest rate of 7 percent. How much will John have at the end of the three-year period?

Plug the known information into the interest formula, $I = prt$:

$$I = \$1,500 \times 0.07 \times 3$$
$$I = \$315$$

Percent means "part of 100." To convert percentage into a decimal, divide the percentage by 100.

So 7 percent $= \dfrac{7}{100} = 0.07$. To convert a decimal into percentage, multiply by 100. You get $0.07 = 0.07 \cdot 100 = 7$ percent. (Flip to Chapter 8 for more information about working with percentages and decimals.)

John will make $315 in interest. Adding this amount to his original investment of $1,500, John will have a total of $1,500 + $315 = $1,815.

That was pretty easy, so let me throw another one at you.

You invest $700, and after five years you receive a total of $900. What was the annual interest rate?

On the surface, this one looks a bit more complicated, but you solve it the same way: Plug what's known into the interest formula, $I = prt$, and solve for the rest.

You invested $700 and received $900. Therefore, you made $900 – $700 = $200 in interest.

$$\$200 = \$700 \times r \times 5$$
$$\$200 = \$3,500r$$
$$r = \frac{\$200}{\$3,500}$$
$$r = 0.057$$

Expressed as a percentage, this amount is $0.057 \cdot 100 = 5.7$ percent.

Mixture problems

Mixture problems often involve mixing different items at different costs and determining the final cost of the mixture. They can also involve mixing various solutions and determining percentages of the solution mixture. This concept sounds difficult, but it's really pretty easy when you know how. Are you ready to try a couple?

How many quarts of a 70-percent alcohol solution must be added to 50 quarts of a 40-percent alcohol solution to produce a 50-percent alcohol solution?

Let x = the number of quarts of 70-percent solution needed. The amount of alcohol contained in x quarts of the 70-percent solution is represented by $0.7x$. (I explain how to convert a percentage into a decimal in the preceding section.)

You have 50 quarts of the 40-percent solution, so the amount of alcohol contained in those 50 quarts is represented by $50 \cdot 0.4 = 20$ quarts.

The total number of quarts of solution can be represented as $50 + x$ (the number of quarts of 40-percent solution plus the unknown number of quarts of 70-percent solution). Half (50 percent) of that solution will be alcohol, so $0.5(50 + x)$.

Maybe Table 10-2 can make this scenario a bit clearer:

Table 10-2		Alcohol Mixtures	
	Quarts of Solution	Percent Alcohol (as Decimal)	Total Quarts of Alcohol
70% solution	x	0.7	$0.7x$
40% solution	50	0.4	$0.4 \times 50 = 20$
50% solution	$50 + x$	0.5	$0.5(50 + x)$

The fourth column of the table gives you your equation: $0.7x + 20 = 0.5(50 + x)$. First, distribute the 0.5 to the terms in parentheses. Then work the equation as follows:

$$0.7x + 20 = 25 + 0.5x$$
$$0.7x = 5 + 0.5x$$
$$0.7x - 0.5x = 5$$
$$0.2x = 5$$
$$x = \frac{5}{0.2}$$
$$x = 25$$

The final mixture will require 25 quarts of 70-percent solution.

A grocery store wants to offer a mixture of green and red grapes to sell for $4.20 per pound. If green grapes cost $3 per pound and red grapes retail for $6 per pound, how many pounds of red grapes should the grocer add to 12 pounds of green grapes to produce the desired mixture?

Let x = the pounds of red grapes. The total amount of grapes will be the pounds of green grapes (12) plus the unknown pounds of red grapes (x), or $12 + x$. The total cost of green grapes at $3 per pound is $12 \cdot 3 = \$36$.

Red grapes sell for $6 per pound, so their total cost is represented as $6x$.

The total cost of the mixture is to be $4.20 per pound, so you can represent it as $4.2(12 + x)$.

Table 10-2 works so well for the last problem that I want to use one again. Check out Table 10-3.

Table 10-3	Grape Mixtures		
Type	*Cost per Pound*	*Pounds*	*Total Cost*
Green	$3	12	$3 \cdot 12 = \$36$
Red	$6	x	$6x$
Mixture	$4.20	$12 + x$	$4.20(12 + x)$

Again, the last column gives you your equation: $36 + 6x = 4.2(12 + x)$. First, distribute the 4.2 to the terms in parentheses. Then work the equation as follows:

$$36 + 6x = 50.4 + 4.2x$$
$$6x - 4.2x = 50.4 - 36$$
$$1.8x = 14.4$$
$$x = \frac{14.4}{1.8}$$
$$x = 8$$

The mixture will require 8 pounds of red grapes.

Percent problems

Percent problems involve working with percentages, such as discount savings, pay raises, and so on. You often see them on the Arithmetic Reasoning subtest. They're relatively simple to solve.

Leroy makes $8.95 per hour. He's such a good worker that his boss gives him a 25-percent raise. How much per hour does Leroy make now?

To find the dollar amount of the raise, multiply Leroy's previous salary by the decimal equivalent of 25 percent: $\$8.95 \cdot 0.25 = 2.237$. Round this number up to $2.24, just to make Leroy smile. (You can read about rounding decimals in Chapter 8.) Now add the raise to Leroy's original salary: $\$8.95 + \$2.24 = \$11.19$.

Katie is very excited. For only $45, she bought a blouse that usually sells for $60. What was the percentage of her discount?

Divide the new price by the original price: $45 \div 60 = 0.75$. The new price is 75 percent of the original price, which means Katie's discount was 25 percent.

Work problems

These problems involve two or more people or things working together. You're expected to figure out how long they'll take to complete a task together.

Patrick can build a wall in five hours. Dennis can build the same wall in seven hours. How long will they take to build the wall together?

You can use a general formula to solve such work problems. It's $\frac{a \times b}{a+b}$, where a is the time the first person or thing takes to do the job and b is the time it takes the second person or thing takes to do the job.

Patrick needs five hours to build the wall, and Dennis seven hours. Plugging the data into the work formula gets you the following:

$$\frac{5 \times 7}{5+7} = \frac{35}{12} = 2\frac{11}{12}$$

It will take them $2\frac{11}{12}$ hours to build the wall together.

Wasn't that fun? I bet you're eager to try another one.

One hose can fill an aboveground pool in three hours. Another hose will fill it in six hours. How long will filling the pool take using both hoses?

Just plug the numbers into your handy-dandy work equation:

$$\frac{3 \times 6}{3+6} = \frac{18}{9} = 2$$

It will take two hours to fill the pool when using both hoses.

Number problems

Number problems are pretty straightforward. The questions ask you to manipulate numbers with basic addition, subtraction, multiplication, or division. Most people find these types of word problems to be pretty easy.

Do you want to try a few, just to get your feet wet? Sure you do.

Jesse is a bartender at a local pub. On Friday, he made $27.40 in tips; on Saturday, he made $34.70 in tips; and on Sunday, he made $7 less than he made on Friday. How much did Jesse earn in tips during the three days?

See what I mean? Pretty straightforward. Jesse made $27.40 + $34.70 + ($27.40 – $7) = $82.50 in tips.

Rob "Speedy Gonzalez" Barton ran 1.5 miles in 9:57. The next day, he ran it in 10:02. On the third day, he ran it in 10:07. What is his average time for the 1.5-mile run?

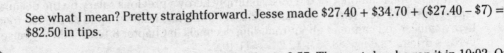

First, convert all the times into seconds, just to make the math a little easier:

$$9:57 = (9 \cdot 60) + 57 = 597 \text{ seconds}$$
$$10:02 = (10 \cdot 60) + 2 = 602 \text{ seconds}$$
$$10:07 = (10 \cdot 60) + 7 = 607 \text{ seconds}$$

Add the seconds together: $597 + 602 + 607 = 1,806$ seconds. Now, divide by the number of times Rob ran the 1.5-mile run (three times) to discover that his average speed is $1,806 \div 3 = 602$ seconds. Finally, convert the seconds to minutes by dividing by 60: $602 \div 60 = 10$ minutes, with 2 seconds left over. Rob's average time for the 1.5-mile run is 10:02.

The sum of two consecutive odd positive numbers is 112. What are the numbers?

As I note in the "Addition keywords" section earlier in this chapter, *sum* means addition. Let n = the first number. That means that $n + 2$ = the second number (because they're consecutive *odd* numbers). Here's your equation:

$$n + (n + 2) = 112$$

Solve for n:

$$2n + 2 = 112$$
$$2n = 110$$
$$n = \frac{110}{2}$$
$$n = 55$$

The first number is 55. The second number is $55 + 2 = 57$.

Chapter 11

The Arithmetic Reasoning Subtest

The ASVAB has two math subtests — Mathematics Knowledge and Arithmetic Reasoning — and both are used for computing your AFQT score. Of the two, the Arithmetic Reasoning subtest may be considered the more difficult for most people, probably because you first have to decide what the problem is before you can solve it.

Among other things, math word problems measure your reasoning skills. That's why the military services put so much emphasis on this particular subtest. They want recruits who can figure things out — recruits who can solve problems.

If you're starting to get nervous, don't. You've been doing arithmetic word problems since the third grade. Sure, they're a little more difficult now than when Mrs. Grundy was telling you that you had three apples and gave one to Tammy, but the fact is, this material isn't new for you. You've done it before. The military is just asking you to do it again, that's all.

I'm here to help you get ready. In this chapter, I tell you what you can expect on the Arithmetic Reasoning subtest, give you a few methods that may help improve your score and get you through those rough spots, and then — just for fun — toss a few practice questions at you. For help on the Mathematics Knowledge subtest, check out Chapters 8 and 9.

Looking at the Test Structure

The Arithmetic Reasoning subtest is the second subtest on the ASVAB, right after the General Science subtest. Therefore, it's the first subtest you encounter on the ASVAB that affects your AFQT score.

The Arithmetic Reasoning subtest asks you to read a word problem, determine what the question is asking, solve the problem with mathematics, and select the correct answer. (Then you have to repeat the process numerous times.) Most of the problems look like this:

Jane walks 5 miles to work each morning and 5 miles home each evening. How many miles does Jane walk in a day?

(A) 6 miles

(B) 8 miles

(C) 7 miles

(D) 10 miles

I hope you picked Choice (D), 10 miles! That was an easy question just to get you warmed up. Unfortunately, the questions the military writes are a bit tougher.

You have 39 minutes to answer 16 questions for the CAT-ASVAB (computerized version); if you happen to take the paper test, you must answer 30 questions in 36 minutes (makes sense, doesn't it?).

You see a mixture of hard questions, medium questions, and easy questions on this subtest. The hard ones are worth more points than the medium ones, which are worth more points than the easy ones. If you're taking the CAT-ASVAB (see Chapter 2), the computer automatically selects the question difficulty based on how you answered the previous question. If you're really good at math word problems, you may only see hard questions!

The test administrator supplies you with scratch paper so you can work out some of the problems on paper, if necessary. Those dirty rats who make up the rules don't allow the use of calculators on the ASVAB. All you're allowed is your brain, your trusty No. 2 pencil, and a piece of scratch paper. If you're lucky, they may let you sneak in your thinking cap.

Developing a Test Strategy

The U.S. military doesn't win wars without a strategy, and you should have a set strategy for conquering the Arithmetic Reasoning subtest. A strategy is more than "I'll try to solve all the problems quickly and correctly." That works fine if everything goes right and you know how to solve the questions instantly when you see them, but the test probably won't go that way. Your strategy needs to include plans to keep things going smoothly, as well as ideas of what to do if things start going wrong.

Keeping track of the time

This chapter is supposed to be about the Arithmetic Reasoning subtest, so I think it's time for a practice question. Ready?

You have to take a math test consisting of 30 multiple-choice questions. You have 36 minutes to complete the test. How much time do you have for each question?

(A) 1 minute, 12 seconds

(B) 90 seconds

(C) 1 minute

(D) 1 minute, 20 seconds

First, convert the minutes to seconds so you don't have to deal with fractions or decimals: $36 \times 60 = 2,160$ seconds. Now, divide the total number of seconds by the number of test questions: $2,160 \div 30 = 72$ seconds. You have 72 seconds or Choice (A), 1 minute and 12 seconds, to complete each question.

That's not much time, considering that you have to read the question, determine what it's asking, translate the problem into mathematical equations, solve those equations, and then answer the question — and, if you have time, check your answer. But that's how Arithmetic Reasoning goes, at least on the paper test.

If you're taking the paper version of the ASVAB, you'll see a large clock clearly visible somewhere on the wall. The test proctor also posts the start time and end time of the subtest where you can easily see it. If you're taking the computerized version of the ASVAB, the time remaining for the subtest ticks down right there on your computer screen.

Don't spend too much time on any one question. If a question is stumping you, admit defeat, choose an answer (see the "Logical guessing" section later in this chapter), and move on. You don't want to find yourself in a position where you only have 15 minutes left and you're on question 3.

Choosing an answer and checking it twice

In Chapter 10, I mention that checking your answer to ensure it makes sense in relation to the question is always a good idea if you have time. You don't always have time on the Arithmetic Reasoning subtest, but if you find yourself running ahead of the clock, take a few seconds extra to check your answer.

Don't assume that just because the answer you got is one of the possible answer choices means it's the correct answer. Those crafty test makers often use common mistakes as possible answer choices.

If you're taking the paper version of the ASVAB, you should also leave enough time at the end of the subtest to check and make sure you've marked your answer sheet correctly. Make sure the answer blocks are completely filled in, and make sure you didn't make the rookie mistake of answering the wrong question with the right answer.

Using the answer choices: There's more than one way to skin an equation

If you're stumped and just can't seem to write equations to solve the problem, you can often answer the question by seeing which of the answer choices works. Look at the following example:

The product of two consecutive negative even integers is 24. Find the smallest number.

(A) –2

(B) –4

(C) –6

(D) –7

Correctly solving this problem involves factoring a quadratic equation (see the end of this section if that sentence scares you). Perhaps quadratic equations aren't your cup of tea, and you get stuck at $n^2 + 2n - 24 = 0$. (If so, Chapter 8 may be of some help.) But before giving up and making a wild guess, try seeing which of the answer choices works.

✔ **–2:** No negative even integer is larger than –2, so Choice (A) doesn't work.

✔ **–4:** $-4 \times -2 = 8$, so Choice (B) doesn't work.

✔ **–6:** $-6 \times -4 = 24$. Choice (C) works!

Don't use this method unless you're absolutely stuck. It uses up a lot of time. In essence, you're computing the problem (up to) four times.

Thought I forgot about the original problem? Here's the proper way to solve it. Let the first integer equal n. Then the next consecutive even integer is $n + 2$.

$$n(n+2) = 24$$
$$n^2 + 2n = 24$$
$$n^2 + 2n - 24 = 0$$
$$(n+6)(n-4) = 0$$
$$n = -6 \text{ and } n = 4$$

The answer can't be 4, because the problem asks for a negative number. The first number (the smallest, n) is –6, which means the second number ($n + 2$) is –4.

Logical guessing

Sometimes nothing else works, and you just have to guess. If you're taking the paper version of the ASVAB, you can always skip the hard questions and go back to them when you finish the other questions. If you choose to do so, remember to leave enough time to go back and answer, even if your method is "eeny-meeny-miny-mo." There is no penalty for wrong answers on the paper version of the ASVAB. If you get the question wrong, you get zero points. If you leave the answer blank, you also get zero points. If you make a wild guess, you have at least a one in four chance of getting the answer right and getting points. Be careful, however, of guessing a lot during the computer version. If you give a lot of wrong answers toward the end of the CAT-ASVAB, those pesky test creators will penalize you.

If you're taking the computerized version of the ASVAB, you can't leave the answer blank. The computer doesn't present you with the next question until you answer the current one. Unfortunately, that means you don't have the option of going back and giving the question another try when you finish the rest of the subtest. You have to decide whether to use more of your precious time to figure it out or guess and move on.

Guessing doesn't have to be wild, however. Sometimes you can improve your chances by eliminating obviously wrong answers. Consider the brain stumper from the preceding section:

The product of two consecutive negative even integers is 24. Find the smallest number.

(A) –2

(B) –4

(C) –6

(D) –7

Choice (A) is obviously incorrect because no number larger than –2 can be both negative and even. You can quickly see that Choice (D) is wrong because it's an odd number, and the question is asking for a negative even number. Now, if you have to guess, you've just changed the odds from a one in four chance to a 50/50 chance.

Taking Arithmetic Reasoning out for a Spin

I promised you a chance to practice, and here it is. In this section, I give you ten fairly simple math word problems, similar to what you see on the Arithmetic Reasoning subtest.

Don't worry about time here; use these questions to get used to the general test structure and to practice some of the concepts from this chapter and Chapter 10. When you're ready, you can move on to the full-blown AFQT practice tests later in the book.

1. If apples are on sale at 15 for $3, what is the cost of each apple?

   (A) 50¢

   (B) 25¢

   (C) 20¢

   (D) 30¢

2. A noncommissioned officer challenged her platoon of 11 enlisted women to beat her record of performing a 26-mile training run in four hours. If all the enlisted women match her record, how many miles will they have run?

   (A) 71.5 miles

   (B) 6.5 miles

   (C) 286 miles

   (D) 312 miles

3. Margaret gets her hair cut and colored at an expensive salon in town. She is expected to leave a 15 percent tip for services. If a haircut is $45 and a color treatment is $150, how much of a tip should Margaret leave?

   (A) $22.50

   (B) $29.25

   (C) $20.00

   (D) $195.00

4. A bag of sand holds 1 cubic foot of sand. How many bags of sand are needed to fill a square sandbox measuring 5 feet long and 1 foot high?

   (A) 5 bags

   (B) 10 bags

   (C) 15 bags

   (D) 25 bags

5. The day Samantha arrived at boot camp, the temperature reached a high of 90 degrees in the shade and a low of –20 degrees at night in the barracks. What is the average between the high and low temperatures for the day?

   (A) 35 degrees

   (B) 45 degrees

   (C) 70 degrees

   (D) 62 degrees

6. Farmer Beth has received an offer to sell her 320-acre farm for $3,000 per acre. She agrees to give the buyer $96,000 worth of land. What fraction of Farmer Beth's land is the buyer getting?

    (A) $\frac{1}{4}$

    (B) $\frac{1}{10}$

    (C) $\frac{1}{5}$

    (D) $\frac{2}{3}$

7. A map is drawn so that 1 inch equals 3 miles. On the map, the distance from Kansas City to Denver is 192.5 inches. How far is the round trip from Kansas City to Denver in miles?

    (A) 192.5 miles

    (B) 577.5 miles

    (C) 385 miles

    (D) 1,155 miles

8. Margaret and Julie can sell their store for $150,000. They plan to divide the proceeds according to the ratio of the money they each invested in the business. Margaret put in the most money, at a 3:2 ratio to Julie. How much money should Julie get from the sale?

    (A) $50,000

    (B) $30,000

    (C) $60,000

    (D) $90,000

9. In the military, $\frac{1}{4}$ of an enlisted person's time is spent sleeping and eating, $\frac{1}{12}$ is spent standing at attention, $\frac{1}{6}$ is spent staying fit, and $\frac{2}{5}$ is spent working. The rest of the time is spent at the enlisted person's own discretion. How many hours per day does this discretionary time amount to?

    (A) 6 hours

    (B) 1.6 hours

    (C) 2.4 hours

    (D) 3.2 hours

10. Train A is headed east at 55 mph. Train B is also heading east on an adjacent track at 70 mph. At the end of four hours, how much farther will train B have traveled than train A?

    (A) 40 miles

    (B) 50 miles

    (C) 60 miles

    (D) 70 miles

Answers and Explanations

Use this answer key to score the practice Arithmetic Reasoning questions.

1. **C.** Divide $3 by 15.

2. **C.** Multiply 26 × 11. The other information in the question is irrelevant; it's there to throw you off.

3. **B.** Add $45 and $150 and multiply the answer by 15 percent, or 0.15.

4. **D.** The volume formula for a square or rectangular box is $v = lwh$, so $v = 5 \times 5 \times 1 = 25$ cubic feet. Each bag holds 1 cubic foot of sand.

5. **A.** Add the two temperatures given and then divide by the number of terms, 2: $(90 + -20) \div 2 = 70 \div 2 = 35$.

6. **B.** $96,000 divided by $3,000 (the price per acre) equals 32 acres, and 32 acres divided by 320 acres (the total size of the farm) equals 10 percent, or $\frac{1}{10}$ of the land.

7. **D.** Multiply 192.5×3 to get the distance in miles and then double the answer to account for both legs of the trip.

8. **C.** According to the ratio, Margaret should get $\frac{3}{5}$ of the money and Julie should get $\frac{2}{5}$ of the money. The fractions are calculated by adding both sides of the ratio together $(3 + 2 = 5)$ to determine the denominator. Each side of the ratio then becomes a numerator, so Margaret's investment can be shown to be $\frac{3}{5}$ of the total investment, and Julie's is $\frac{2}{5}$ of the total investment. (You can check these fractions by adding $\frac{3}{5}$ and $\frac{2}{5}$ to get $\frac{5}{5}$ or 1, which is all the money.) Divide \$150,000 by 5, and then multiply the answer by 2 to determine Julie's share of the money.

9. **C.** Calculate this answer by first assigning a common denominator of 60 to all the fractions and adjusting the numerators accordingly: $\frac{15}{60}, \frac{5}{60}, \frac{10}{60}, \frac{24}{60}$. Add the fractions to find out how much time is allotted to all these tasks. The total is $\frac{54}{60}$, which leaves $\frac{6}{60}$ or $\frac{1}{10}$ of the day to the enlisted person's discretion. $\frac{1}{10}$ of 24 hours is 2.4 hours.

10. **C.** The distance formula is $d = rt$. Plug in the known values:

    - Train A: $d = 55 \times 4 = 220$ miles
    - Train B: $d = 70 \times 4 = 280$ miles

    Train B traveled $280 - 220 = 60$ miles farther than train A.

Part IV
AFQT Practice Exams

Checking Out the ASVAB AFQT Subtests

Subtest	Questions/Time (Paper Version)	Questions/Time (CAT-ASVAB)	Content
Arithmetic Reasoning	30 questions, 36 minutes	16 questions, 39 minutes	Math word problems
Word Knowledge	35 questions, 11 minutes	16 questions, 8 minutes	Correct meaning of a word and best synonym or antonym for a given word
Paragraph Comprehension	15 questions, 13 minutes	11 questions, 22 minutes	Questions based on paragraphs (usually a few hundred words) that you read
Mathematics Knowledge	25 questions, 24 minutes	16 questions, 20 minutes	High-school math

web extras

You can't take the four AFQT subtests alone; you have to take all nine ASVAB subtests. To find out more about the other five subtests, check out the free article that breaks them down at www.dummies.com/extras/asvabafqt.

In this part . . .

✔ Take four practice AFQT exams that simulate the paper version of the Arithmetic Reasoning, Word Knowledge, Paragraph Comprehension, and Mathematics Knowledge subtests.

✔ Score your tests and check your answers to see which topics you've mastered and which topics you need to spend more time on.

Chapter 12

Practice Exam 1

· ·

*T*he Armed Forces Qualification Test (AFQT) consists of four of the nine subtests given on the Armed Services Vocational Aptitude Battery (ASVAB). The four subtests used to determine your AFQT score are: Arithmetic Reasoning, Word Knowledge, Paragraph Comprehension, and Mathematics Knowledge.

The AFQT score is very important. Although all the ASVAB subtests are used to determine which military jobs you may qualify for, the AFQT score determines whether you're even qualified to join the military. All the military service branches have established minimum AFQT scores, according to their needs (see Chapter 2 for more information).

The AFQT is not a stand-alone test (it's part of the ASVAB), but, in this chapter, I present the subtests applicable to the AFQT in the same order in which you'll encounter them when you take the actual ASVAB.

After you complete the entire practice test, check your answers against the answer key in Chapter 13.

The test is scored by comparing your raw score to the scores of other people, which produces a scaled score. So just because you missed a total of 20 questions doesn't mean that your score is 80. (That would be too simple.) Turn to Chapter 2 to find out how the AFQT score is derived from these four subtests.

Your goal in taking this practice test is to determine which areas you may still need to study. If you miss only one question on the Word Knowledge subtest, but you miss 15 questions on Arithmetic Reasoning, you probably want to devote some extra study time to developing your math skills before you take the ASVAB.

Answer Sheet for Practice Exam 1
Part 1: Arithmetic Reasoning

1. Ⓐ Ⓑ Ⓒ Ⓓ   8. Ⓐ Ⓑ Ⓒ Ⓓ   15. Ⓐ Ⓑ Ⓒ Ⓓ   22. Ⓐ Ⓑ Ⓒ Ⓓ   29. Ⓐ Ⓑ Ⓒ Ⓓ
2. Ⓐ Ⓑ Ⓒ Ⓓ   9. Ⓐ Ⓑ Ⓒ Ⓓ   16. Ⓐ Ⓑ Ⓒ Ⓓ   23. Ⓐ Ⓑ Ⓒ Ⓓ   30. Ⓐ Ⓑ Ⓒ Ⓓ
3. Ⓐ Ⓑ Ⓒ Ⓓ   10. Ⓐ Ⓑ Ⓒ Ⓓ   17. Ⓐ Ⓑ Ⓒ Ⓓ   24. Ⓐ Ⓑ Ⓒ Ⓓ
4. Ⓐ Ⓑ Ⓒ Ⓓ   11. Ⓐ Ⓑ Ⓒ Ⓓ   18. Ⓐ Ⓑ Ⓒ Ⓓ   25. Ⓐ Ⓑ Ⓒ Ⓓ
5. Ⓐ Ⓑ Ⓒ Ⓓ   12. Ⓐ Ⓑ Ⓒ Ⓓ   19. Ⓐ Ⓑ Ⓒ Ⓓ   26. Ⓐ Ⓑ Ⓒ Ⓓ
6. Ⓐ Ⓑ Ⓒ Ⓓ   13. Ⓐ Ⓑ Ⓒ Ⓓ   20. Ⓐ Ⓑ Ⓒ Ⓓ   27. Ⓐ Ⓑ Ⓒ Ⓓ
7. Ⓐ Ⓑ Ⓒ Ⓓ   14. Ⓐ Ⓑ Ⓒ Ⓓ   21. Ⓐ Ⓑ Ⓒ Ⓓ   28. Ⓐ Ⓑ Ⓒ Ⓓ

Part 2: Word Knowledge

1. Ⓐ Ⓑ Ⓒ Ⓓ   8. Ⓐ Ⓑ Ⓒ Ⓓ   15. Ⓐ Ⓑ Ⓒ Ⓓ   22. Ⓐ Ⓑ Ⓒ Ⓓ   29. Ⓐ Ⓑ Ⓒ Ⓓ
2. Ⓐ Ⓑ Ⓒ Ⓓ   9. Ⓐ Ⓑ Ⓒ Ⓓ   16. Ⓐ Ⓑ Ⓒ Ⓓ   23. Ⓐ Ⓑ Ⓒ Ⓓ   30. Ⓐ Ⓑ Ⓒ Ⓓ
3. Ⓐ Ⓑ Ⓒ Ⓓ   10. Ⓐ Ⓑ Ⓒ Ⓓ   17. Ⓐ Ⓑ Ⓒ Ⓓ   24. Ⓐ Ⓑ Ⓒ Ⓓ   31. Ⓐ Ⓑ Ⓒ Ⓓ
4. Ⓐ Ⓑ Ⓒ Ⓓ   11. Ⓐ Ⓑ Ⓒ Ⓓ   18. Ⓐ Ⓑ Ⓒ Ⓓ   25. Ⓐ Ⓑ Ⓒ Ⓓ   32. Ⓐ Ⓑ Ⓒ Ⓓ
5. Ⓐ Ⓑ Ⓒ Ⓓ   12. Ⓐ Ⓑ Ⓒ Ⓓ   19. Ⓐ Ⓑ Ⓒ Ⓓ   26. Ⓐ Ⓑ Ⓒ Ⓓ   33. Ⓐ Ⓑ Ⓒ Ⓓ
6. Ⓐ Ⓑ Ⓒ Ⓓ   13. Ⓐ Ⓑ Ⓒ Ⓓ   20. Ⓐ Ⓑ Ⓒ Ⓓ   27. Ⓐ Ⓑ Ⓒ Ⓓ   34. Ⓐ Ⓑ Ⓒ Ⓓ
7. Ⓐ Ⓑ Ⓒ Ⓓ   14. Ⓐ Ⓑ Ⓒ Ⓓ   21. Ⓐ Ⓑ Ⓒ Ⓓ   28. Ⓐ Ⓑ Ⓒ Ⓓ   35. Ⓐ Ⓑ Ⓒ Ⓓ

Part 3: Paragraph Comprehension

1. Ⓐ Ⓑ Ⓒ Ⓓ   8. Ⓐ Ⓑ Ⓒ Ⓓ   15. Ⓐ Ⓑ Ⓒ Ⓓ
2. Ⓐ Ⓑ Ⓒ Ⓓ   9. Ⓐ Ⓑ Ⓒ Ⓓ
3. Ⓐ Ⓑ Ⓒ Ⓓ   10. Ⓐ Ⓑ Ⓒ Ⓓ
4. Ⓐ Ⓑ Ⓒ Ⓓ   11. Ⓐ Ⓑ Ⓒ Ⓓ
5. Ⓐ Ⓑ Ⓒ Ⓓ   12. Ⓐ Ⓑ Ⓒ Ⓓ
6. Ⓐ Ⓑ Ⓒ Ⓓ   13. Ⓐ Ⓑ Ⓒ Ⓓ
7. Ⓐ Ⓑ Ⓒ Ⓓ   14. Ⓐ Ⓑ Ⓒ Ⓓ

Part 4: Mathematics Knowledge

1. Ⓐ Ⓑ Ⓒ Ⓓ   8. Ⓐ Ⓑ Ⓒ Ⓓ   15. Ⓐ Ⓑ Ⓒ Ⓓ   22. Ⓐ Ⓑ Ⓒ Ⓓ
2. Ⓐ Ⓑ Ⓒ Ⓓ   9. Ⓐ Ⓑ Ⓒ Ⓓ   16. Ⓐ Ⓑ Ⓒ Ⓓ   23. Ⓐ Ⓑ Ⓒ Ⓓ
3. Ⓐ Ⓑ Ⓒ Ⓓ   10. Ⓐ Ⓑ Ⓒ Ⓓ   17. Ⓐ Ⓑ Ⓒ Ⓓ   24. Ⓐ Ⓑ Ⓒ Ⓓ
4. Ⓐ Ⓑ Ⓒ Ⓓ   11. Ⓐ Ⓑ Ⓒ Ⓓ   18. Ⓐ Ⓑ Ⓒ Ⓓ   25. Ⓐ Ⓑ Ⓒ Ⓓ
5. Ⓐ Ⓑ Ⓒ Ⓓ   12. Ⓐ Ⓑ Ⓒ Ⓓ   19. Ⓐ Ⓑ Ⓒ Ⓓ
6. Ⓐ Ⓑ Ⓒ Ⓓ   13. Ⓐ Ⓑ Ⓒ Ⓓ   20. Ⓐ Ⓑ Ⓒ Ⓓ
7. Ⓐ Ⓑ Ⓒ Ⓓ   14. Ⓐ Ⓑ Ⓒ Ⓓ   21. Ⓐ Ⓑ Ⓒ Ⓓ

Part 1

Arithmetic Reasoning

Time: 36 minutes for 30 questions

Directions: Arithmetic Reasoning is the second subtest of the ASVAB. These questions are designed to test your ability to use mathematics to solve various problems that may be found in real life — in other words, math word problems.

Each question is followed by four possible answers. Decide which answer is correct, and then mark the corresponding space on your answer sheet. Use your scratch paper for any figuring you want to do. You may not use a calculator.

1. Mike has $5.25 in quarters and dimes. He has exactly 15 dimes. How many quarters does he have?

   (A) 6

   (B) 12

   (C) 15

   (D) 21

2. Kelly used to pay $500 a month for rent. Now she pays $525 a month for rent. By what percent did her rent increase?

   (A) 0.5 percent

   (B) 5 percent

   (C) 10 percent

   (D) 12.5 percent

3. A bag has 8 pennies, 5 dimes, and 7 nickels. A coin is randomly chosen from the bag. What is the probability that the coin chosen is a dime?

   (A) $\frac{1}{20}$

   (B) $\frac{1}{4}$

   (C) $\frac{1}{3}$

   (D) $\frac{3}{10}$

4. There are 2 pints in 1 quart and 4 quarts in a gallon. How many pints are in 2 gallons?

   (A) 32 pints

   (B) 16 pints

   (C) 8 pints

   (D) 4 pints

5. Paul invests $2,000 in an account that pays 4 percent annual interest. How much will he earn in interest in one year?

   (A) $160

   (B) $80

   (C) $120

   (D) $800

6. One mile is equal to 5,280 feet. Sergeant Jeffries walked 1.2 miles. How many feet did he walk?

   (A) 7,392 ft

   (B) 1,056 ft

   (C) 5,780 ft

   (D) 6,336 ft

Go on to next page

7. A total of 200 people attended a conference. Use the chart to determine how many attendees were women.

Conference Attendance

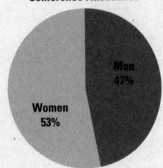

Illustration by Thomson Digital

(A) 94

(B) 212

(C) 53

(D) 106

8. Suppose you have $88 in your checking account. You pay $22 for a sweater and $8 for lunch, and then you deposit a $38 check. What is the balance in your account?

(A) $58

(B) $96

(C) $20

(D) $156

9. There are 24 right-handed students in a class of 30. A student is chosen from the class at random. What is the probability that the student is left-handed?

(A) $\frac{1}{2}$

(B) $\frac{1}{5}$

(C) $\frac{4}{5}$

(D) $\frac{1}{4}$

10. At a laundromat, it costs $1.75 to wash each load of laundry and $1.50 to dry each load of laundry. How much will you pay to wash and dry four loads of laundry?

(A) $2.25

(B) $20.00

(C) $20.25

(D) $13.00

11. Delia has been walking at a constant speed of 2.5 miles per hour for 12 minutes. How many miles has she walked?

(A) 0.2 miles

(B) 0.5 miles

(C) 2 miles

(D) 4.8 miles

12. A rectangular deck is 6 meters long and 8 meters wide. What is the distance from one corner of the deck to the opposite corner?

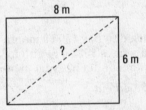

Illustration by Thomson Digital

(A) 10 m

(B) 12 m

(C) 14 m

(D) 15 m

13. Tom is going to hang three framed pictures side by side on a wall. How many different ways can he arrange the pictures?

(A) 9

(B) 5

(C) 6

(D) 27

Go on to next page

14. A cleaning company charges by the square foot. The company charged $600 to clean 4,800 square feet of space. How much would the company charge to clean 12,000 square feet of space?

(A) $950

(B) $1,200

(C) $1,400

(D) $1,500

15. Kendra earns $12 an hour. Her employer pays 1.5 times her normal pay rate for overtime. Last week, she worked 40 hours plus 4 hours overtime. How much did she earn last week?

(A) $552

(B) $528

(C) $1,400

(D) $480

16. A hot tub is 75 percent full with 600 gallons of water. How many gallons of water are in the hot tub when it's half full?

(A) 200 gallons

(B) 400 gallons

(C) 800 gallons

(D) 300 gallons

17. Angela has 15 quarters and dimes in the cash register. The total value of the quarters and dimes is $2.55. How many dimes are in the cash register?

(A) 8 dimes

(B) 7 dimes

(C) 3 dimes

(D) 10 dimes

18. A rectangular table top measures 48 inches long by 36 inches wide. A square game board that is 18 inches on each side is on the table top. Which amount of the table top's area is not covered by the game board?

(A) 1,710 in^2

(B) 1,404 in^2

(C) 1,656 in^2

(D) 96 in^2

19. A map of Texas has a scale of 1 cm = 11 km. The actual distance between Dallas and San Antonio is about 440 km. How far apart are the cities on the map?

(A) 11 cm

(B) 44 cm

(C) 40 cm

(D) 22 cm

20. Jake is four years older than Kenneth. Alicia is two years younger than Kenneth. The sum of Jake, Kenneth, and Alicia's ages is 38. What is Kenneth's age?

(A) 9

(B) 15

(C) 12

(D) 10

21. Mrs. Jacobs is making a large circular rug with a radius of 10 feet. Every square foot of material used to make the rug costs her $0.50. Approximately how much will the material for the entire rug cost?

(A) $157

(B) $167

(C) $628

(D) $314

22. John's quiz scores in science class are 8, 6, 10, 7, 9, and 5. What is John's average quiz score?

(A) 6

(B) 8

(C) 7.5

(D) 8.5

23. Robert charges a flat fee of $15 plus $20 per half hour to repair computers. He started one job at 8:45 a.m. and worked until he finished. The total charge for that job was $75. What time did he finish the job?

(A) 12:15 p.m.

(B) 11:45 a.m.

(C) 10:15 a.m.

(D) 9:30 a.m.

Go on to next page

24. The measure of angle P is 44°. Angle Q is 12° less than half the measure of the supplement of angle P. What is the measure of angle Q?

    (A) 136°

    (B) 80°

    (C) 68°

    (D) 56°

25. Rose and Carla play on the same basketball team. During the last game, Rose scored $\frac{3}{5}$ of the team's points. Carla scored 16 percent of the team's points. What percentage of the team's points were not scored by either Rose or Carla?

    (A) 76 percent

    (B) 66 percent

    (C) 24 percent

    (D) 34 percent

26. John and Garret are running in a marathon. John runs at a steady rate of 3.5 miles per hour, and Garret runs at a steady rate of 4.25 miles per hour. How far apart will they be 2 hours after the race starts?

    (A) 0.75 miles

    (B) 2.5 miles

    (C) 1.5 miles

    (D) 2.25 miles

27. Jim can repair a heating unit in 2 hours. Kyle can repair the same unit in 3 hours. How long will they take to repair the unit if they work together?

    (A) 1 hour and 10 minutes

    (B) 1 hour and 12 minutes

    (C) 48 minutes

    (D) 50 minutes

28. A square has an area of 121 cm². What is the perimeter?

    (A) 121 cm

    (B) 22 cm

    (C) 33 cm

    (D) 44 cm

29. How many gallons of water should you add to 4 gallons of a juice that is 20 percent water so the final mixture is 50 percent water?

    (A) 2.2 gallons

    (B) 2 gallons

    (C) 2.4 gallons

    (D) 1.4 gallons

30. David is at a car dealership trying to decide between buying a truck or a sedan. The truck is available in three colors, and the sedan is available in four colors. Each vehicle also has both a 2-wheel-drive and a 4-wheel-drive option in all available colors. How many different choices does he have?

    (A) 48

    (B) 14

    (C) 12

    (D) 6

STOP DO NOT TURN THE PAGE UNTIL TOLD TO DO SO. DO NOT RETURN TO A PREVIOUS TEST.

Part 2

Word Knowledge

Time: 11 minutes for 35 questions

Directions: The Word Knowledge subtest is the third subtest of the ASVAB. The questions are designed to measure your vocabulary knowledge. You'll see three types of questions on this subtest. The first type simply asks you to choose a word or words that most nearly mean the same as the underlined word in the question. The second type includes an underlined word used in a sentence, and you are to choose the word or words that most nearly mean the same as the underlined word, as used in the context of the sentence. The third type of question asks you to choose the word that has the opposite or nearly opposite meaning as the underlined word. Each question is followed by four possible answers. Decide which answer is correct, and then mark the corresponding space on your answer sheet.

1. Kindle most nearly means:
   - (A) devise
   - (B) ignite
   - (C) boil
   - (D) expire

2. The word most opposite in meaning to burnout is
   - (A) successful
   - (B) ruined
   - (C) enthusiasm
   - (D) fatigue

3. Blatant most nearly means:
   - (A) obvious
   - (B) overdrawn
   - (C) certain
   - (D) hidden

4. Hasten most nearly means:
   - (A) delay
   - (B) anxious
   - (C) rush
   - (D) stabilize

5. Objective most nearly means:
   - (A) massive
   - (B) favored
   - (C) neutral
   - (D) dependent

6. No one could convince the headstrong teen that he was wrong.
   - (A) cruel
   - (B) stubborn
   - (C) friendly
   - (D) unaffected

7. The thought of dissecting the frog made me cringe in disgust.
   - (A) recoil
   - (B) volunteer
   - (C) wail
   - (D) rally

8. Despite her wild past, Bobbi prefers to live a more domestic lifestyle these days.
   - (A) native
   - (B) homebound
   - (C) foreign
   - (D) elaborate

9. Grandma always taught us to be frugal and grateful for what we had.
   - (A) careless
   - (B) excessive
   - (C) cheap
   - (D) thrifty

Go on to next page ⟹

10. I wanted to <u>curtail</u> the date because of Bob's cat obsession.

    (A) develop

    (B) shorten

    (C) postpone

    (D) continue

11. The captain received many <u>accolades</u> for her bravery during the battle.

    (A) honors

    (B) criticisms

    (C) presents

    (D) promotions

12. <u>Covert</u> most nearly means:

    (A) tiresome

    (B) popular

    (C) secret

    (D) unruly

13. <u>Abhor</u> most nearly means:

    (A) commence

    (B) embrace

    (C) remove

    (D) dislike

14. The <u>mandate</u> to report at exactly 9 a.m. the next day was written on my boss's personal stationery.

    (A) invitation

    (B) greeting

    (C) command

    (D) permission

15. The word most opposite in meaning to <u>assortment</u> is

    (A) variety

    (B) difference

    (C) mixture

    (D) consistency

16. <u>Credible</u> most nearly means:

    (A) cynical

    (B) rehearsed

    (C) genuine

    (D) vague

17. <u>Reprieve</u> most nearly means:

    (A) on hold

    (B) complete

    (C) final

    (D) justice

18. <u>Tedious</u> most nearly means:

    (A) fresh

    (B) dreary

    (C) difficult

    (D) annoying

19. Jackson's music was so loud he was <u>oblivious</u> to the honking car behind him.

    (A) cognizant

    (B) superfluous

    (C) ignorant

    (D) perceptive

20. The coach knew how to <u>bolster</u> the team's morale in the final moments.

    (A) recruit

    (B) demean

    (C) allude

    (D) encourage

21. The word most opposite in meaning to <u>abstract</u> is

    (A) exclusive

    (B) realistic

    (C) imaginative

    (D) far-fetched

22. The rain <u>hampered</u> the runner's ability to break the record.

    (A) facilitated

    (B) eased

    (C) forced

    (D) hindered

23. <u>Cower</u> most nearly means:

    (A) attack

    (B) celebrate

    (C) cringe

    (D) sublime

Go on to next page →

24. <u>Tangent</u> most nearly means:
    (A) detour
    (B) angular
    (C) focus
    (D) perfect

25. <u>Nullify</u> most nearly means:
    (A) suggest
    (B) cancel
    (C) perform
    (D) promote

26. <u>Tangible</u> most nearly means:
    (A) theoretical
    (B) fragile
    (C) possessive
    (D) physical

27. <u>Absolution</u> most nearly means:
    (A) condemnation
    (B) owing a debt
    (C) assurance
    (D) forgiveness

28. <u>Abrogate</u> most nearly means:
    (A) materialize
    (B) terminate
    (C) embark
    (D) constitute

29. I wanted to <u>temper</u> the dinner conversation so Grandpa wouldn't walk out.
    (A) ignore
    (B) irritate
    (C) soothe
    (D) anger

30. <u>Plethora</u> most nearly means:
    (A) scarcity
    (B) infection
    (C) unique
    (D) abundance

31. Mary was <u>tentative</u> about buying the more expensive car.
    (A) unhappy
    (B) optimistic
    (C) hesitant
    (D) certain

32. The word most opposite in meaning to <u>retaliation</u> is
    (A) vengeance
    (B) forgiveness
    (C) recognition
    (D) payback

33. Jennifer tried to <u>admonish</u> me about asking Mr. Michelson questions because of his long-winded nature.
    (A) encourage
    (B) punish
    (C) spurn
    (D) warn

34. The memo was more like a <u>diatribe</u> of all the things Kathy hated about work.
    (A) novel
    (B) tirade
    (C) compliment
    (D) dispute

35. The word most opposite in meaning to <u>memento</u> is
    (A) rubbish
    (B) souvenir
    (C) jewel
    (D) prize

STOP DO NOT TURN THE PAGE UNTIL TOLD TO DO SO.
DO NOT RETURN TO A PREVIOUS TEST.

Part 3
Paragraph Comprehension

Time: 13 minutes for 15 questions

Directions: Paragraph Comprehension is the fourth subtest on the ASVAB. The questions are designed to measure your ability to understand what you read. This section includes one or more paragraphs of reading material, followed by incomplete statements or questions. Read the paragraph and select the choice that best completes the statement or answers the question. Then mark the corresponding space on your answer sheet.

Question 1 refers to the following passage.

Terry always wanted to move back to Chicago, the city of her birth, because of fond childhood memories. After convincing her husband, Jim, to leave sunny California, her dream was coming true. They moved in the fall, just in time to catch the leaves changing. However, the worst winter in the city's history was too much for their beach bum mentality, and Terry soon regretted her decision. Her dream wasn't the same as reality, and she realized you can't always go back.

1. Why does Terry feel like "you can't always go back?"

    (A) Chicago is too far.

    (B) She is no longer a child.

    (C) California had changed her.

    (D) Winter was her favorite season.

Questions 2 and 3 refer to the following passage.

A new study shows that since the 1970s, the number of households with pets has almost tripled. Yet despite this increased pet ownership, the number of animals euthanized at shelters each year is still between 2.5 and 3 million. In fact, according to the Humane Society of the United States, in 2012, only 30 percent of the 62 percent of households with pets got the animals from shelters or rescue organizations. Furthermore, many of the euthanized animals are healthy, and 25 percent of the dogs euthanized are purebred. There is still a lot of work to do to spread the word about rescue pets to ensure healthy animals don't meet this fate.

2. What is the main point of the passage?

    (A) Americans have more pets than ever before.

    (B) More households should adopt rescue animals.

    (C) More cats are adopted than dogs.

    (D) Shelters house only sick or hurt dogs.

3. Of the households that had pets in 2012, how many of them got their pets from a shelter or rescue organization?

    (A) 62 percent

    (B) 25 percent

    (C) 3 percent

    (D) 30 percent

Question 4 refers to the following passage.

Christo and Jeanne-Claude were an artistic couple known for their elaborate and grandiose projects. Their projects involved giant sheets of nylon wrapped or hanging in an unlikely environment. They achieved notoriety for their artistic installations, such as Valley Curtain, which displayed a 200,200-square-foot curtain hanging between two Colorado mountains. Although their unconventional penchant for wrapping monuments and buildings wasn't understood by everyone, no one can dispute that their work was respected nonetheless.

4. In this passage, <u>penchant</u> means

    (A) inclination

    (B) disinterest

    (C) incompetence

    (D) experience

Go on to next page

Question 5 refers to the following passage.

Despite having used her new shoes for only three months during her frequent marathon training, Tara was having pains in her feet while running. All the articles she read said that running shoes should last at least six months if used an average of two to three times a week. Tara decided she had bought the wrong shoes.

5. Based on the passage, what other reason could Tara's shoes be worn out sooner than six months?

(A) She runs with bad form.

(B) The shoes are cheap.

(C) She runs more than average.

(D) She damaged her shoes on rough terrain.

Question 6 refers to the following passage.

Robert De Niro may never have won his first Academy Award if he had gotten the role he wanted as Michael Corleone in *The Godfather*. In 1975, he received his first nomination and win for his role as young Vito Corleone in *The Godfather: Part II*. By 2013, he'd scored six more nominations (including another win in 1981).

6. According to the passage, how many Academy Awards has Robert De Niro been nominated for?

(A) 3

(B) 6

(C) 7

(D) 0

Questions 7 and 8 refer to the following passage.

Tiffany often wished her family lived closer to another airport. It seemed like her flights were always either canceled or delayed due to weather. In fact, she missed Christmas one year because of a blizzard, and her flight home from her grandma's birthday celebration was postponed for five hours because of a thunderstorm. But she couldn't do anything about it. The region just had terrible weather sometimes.

7. What is the main point of the passage?

(A) Tiffany doesn't like visiting her family.

(B) The region's weather is unpredictable.

(C) Tiffany's local airport is terrible.

(D) Tiffany has bad luck.

8. In this passage, <u>postponed</u> means

(A) ruined

(B) over

(C) expedited

(D) delayed

Question 9 refers to the following passage.

Historical battle reenactments date back to the Middle Ages, when actors would perform scenes from Ancient Rome to entertain a public audience. The most famous reenactments, of course, are those pertaining to the American Civil War, which became popular during the war's centennial celebration in 1961. Almost 50,000 people gathered to commemorate the beginning of the Civil War, which started on April 12, 1861. These days, anywhere from 500 to 20,000 people will congregate to reenact a famous battle from the war. Both the Confederate and Union armies are equally represented.

9. How many years does a centennial celebration recognize?

(A) 20,000

(B) 100

(C) 500

(D) 1,861

Questions 10 and 11 refer to the following passage.

When you're driving in snow, a few bits of knowledge can be the difference between a safe trip and an accident. Never slam on the brakes in the snow. Tapping the brakes helps you slow down without skidding. If you are skidding, turn into the direction of the skid, not away from it. This approach will help you gain control of the vehicle.

Go on to next page

10. The author wrote this passage to

    (A) convince the reader to drive in the snow

    (B) provide driving tips for snowy conditions

    (C) make sure your brakes are tuned

    (D) scare the reader about driving in the snow

11. Driving safely in snowy conditions means

    (A) understanding the results of your actions

    (B) avoiding braking

    (C) avoiding busy roads

    (D) relinquishing control

Question 12 refers to the following passage.

The crowd at the store was growing quickly. Children reached for their favorite-colored backpack. Notebooks flew off the shelves, and pencils of different shapes and sizes were running low in stock. Back-to-school shopping had definitely begun.

12. What is the author telling the reader in the passage?

    (A) that school supplies are scarce

    (B) that the store isn't prepared

    (C) that parents spend too much money on supplies

    (D) that the beginning of school is approaching

Questions 13 and 14 refer to the following passage.

The 70-year career of Frank Lloyd Wright is one of the most remarkable and renowned in the architecture world. He designed 1,141 buildings, and 532 of those designs were actually developed. The 409 that remain are considered individual works of art. His name is as famous as Bruce Springsteen's in modern-day society.

13. How many buildings were constructed from Frank Lloyd Wright's designs?

    (A) 532

    (B) 1,141

    (C) 70

    (D) 409

14. In this passage, <u>renowned</u> means

    (A) common

    (B) popular

    (C) misunderstood

    (D) famous

Question 15 refers to the following passage.

Sailors don't like to share the water with motorboaters because of the massive wake left by the high-speed boats. The waves disrupt the easy flow of the sailboats, causing them to twist and turn in the wind. The sentiment between sailors and speedboaters is similar to that between skiers and snowboarders.

15. How do skiers feel about snowboarders?

    (A) They think snowboarders are a great addition to the slopes.

    (B) They hate snowboarders.

    (C) They don't like to share the mountain with snowboarders.

    (D) They think snowboarders lack a high level of skill.

STOP DO NOT TURN THE PAGE UNTIL TOLD TO DO SO.
DO NOT RETURN TO A PREVIOUS TEST.

Part 4

Mathematics Knowledge

Time: 24 minutes for 25 questions

Directions: Mathematics Knowledge is the fifth subtest on the ASVAB. The questions are designed to test your ability to solve general mathematical problems. Each question is followed by four possible answers. Decide which answer is correct, and then mark the corresponding space on your answer sheet. Use your scratch paper for any figuring you want to do. You may not use a calculator.

1. $(-5)^3 =$

    (A) −125

    (B) −15

    (C) 15

    (D) 125

2. If $42 < 2x$, which is true about the value of x?

    (A) x is less than 21.

    (B) x is greater than 21.

    (C) x is less than or equal to 21.

    (D) x is greater than or equal to 21.

3. $473 + 220 + 27 =$

    (A) 710

    (B) 620

    (C) 720

    (D) 711

4. In the decimal 45.21, which digit is in the tenths place?

    (A) 4

    (B) 5

    (C) 2

    (D) 1

5. What are the coordinates of point P?

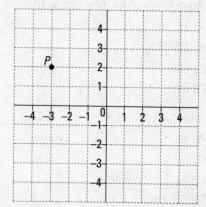

Illustration by Thomson Digital

    (A) (−3, −2)

    (B) (3, −2)

    (C) (−3, 2)

    (D) (2, −3)

6. Express $\frac{11}{4}$ as a decimal.

    (A) 2.25

    (B) 2.5

    (C) 2.75

    (D) 3.25

7. If $-2 + y = 8$, then $y =$

    (A) −10

    (B) −6

    (C) 6

    (D) 10

Go on to next page

8. A circle has a circumference of 9.42 centimeters. What is the diameter of the circle?

   (A) 1.5 cm

   (B) 3 cm

   (C) 3.14 cm

   (D) 6 cm

9. What is 28 percent of 40?

   (A) 9.4

   (B) 10.2

   (C) 11.2

   (D) 12.5

10. Which is equal to $10^3 \times 10^{-6} \times 10^2$?

    (A) 10

    (B) 100

    (C) 0.1

    (D) 0.01

11. Simplify: $2 + 2y + 4 + y$

    (A) $3y + 6$

    (B) $3y + 8$

    (C) $8y$

    (D) $2y^2 + 6$

12. What is the value of x?

    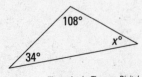

    Illustration by Thomson Digital

    (A) 54°

    (B) 34°

    (C) 58°

    (D) 38°

13. $(5 - 2)! =$

    (A) 118

    (B) 12

    (C) 6

    (D) 3

14. $\frac{1}{2} + \frac{1}{16} + \frac{1}{4} =$

    (A) $\frac{3}{22}$

    (B) $\frac{13}{22}$

    (C) $\frac{13}{16}$

    (D) $\frac{7}{16}$

15. How many factors does the number 51 have?

    (A) Four

    (B) Three

    (C) Two

    (D) One

16. The number 0.405 is what percent of 0.9?

    (A) 4.5 percent

    (B) 45 percent

    (C) 25 percent

    (D) 50 percent

17. The measure of angle P is $m°$. What is the measure of the complement of angle P?

    (A) $(180 - m)°$

    (B) $(90 - m)°$

    (C) $(m - 90)°$

    (D) $(m - 180)°$

18. What is the length b in the right triangle?

    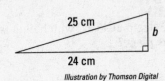

    Illustration by Thomson Digital

    (A) 4 cm

    (B) 5 cm

    (C) 6 cm

    (D) 7 cm

Go on to next page

19. Translate the following sentence into an equation: "x decreased by 11 is twice x."

    (A) $11 - x = 2x$

    (B) $x - 11 = 2$

    (C) $11 - x = 2$

    (D) $x - 11 = 2x$

20. The mean of 5, 7, 8, 10, 4, and x is 7.5. What is the value of x?

    (A) 7

    (B) 8

    (C) 10

    (D) 11

21. $(9 - 3 \cdot 2)^2 - 0.5(-2) =$

    (A) 10

    (B) 145

    (C) 8

    (D) 143

22. Simplify: $9 - 4(5x - 2)$

    (A) $17 - 20x$

    (B) $25x - 2$

    (C) $7 - 20x$

    (D) $25x - 10$

23. The height, h, of a cylinder is twice the radius r. What is the volume of the cylinder?

    (A) πr^3

    (B) $4\pi r^3$

    (C) $2\pi r^3$

    (D) $8\pi r^2$

24. Find the area of the entire region shown.

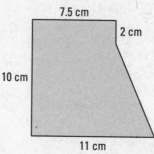

Illustration by Thomson Digital

    (A) 85 cm^2

    (B) 89 cm^2

    (C) 125 cm^2

    (D) 719 cm^2

25. Of 260 students at a local elementary school, 140 are boys. Express the ratio of girls to boys as a simplified fraction.

    (A) $\frac{6}{7}$

    (B) $\frac{7}{6}$

    (C) $\frac{13}{7}$

    (D) $\frac{7}{13}$

STOP DO NOT TURN THE PAGE UNTIL TOLD TO DO SO.
DO NOT RETURN TO A PREVIOUS TEST.

Chapter 13

Practice Exam 1: Answers and Explanations

• •

Did you do well on the first practice exam? I sure hope so! Use this answer key to score the practice exam in Chapter 12. If you don't do well, don't worry — there are three more full-length practice tests in this book to help you hone your English and math skills.

The AFQT isn't scored based on number correct, number wrong, or even percent of questions correct. Instead, the score is derived by comparing your raw score with the raw score of others who have taken the test before you. In determining the raw score, harder questions are worth more points than easier questions. (For more on scoring, turn to Chapter 2.)

Don't waste time trying to equate your score on this practice test with your potential score on the actual AFQT. It can't be done. Instead, use the results of this practice test to determine which areas you should devote more study time to.

Part 1: Arithmetic Reasoning

Mathematical word problems can be tough. You have to develop a skill for determining which factors are relevant to the problem and then be able to convert those factors into a mathematical formula to arrive at a correct solution. Yikes! No wonder so many math books are on the market! A few good ones that may help are *Math Word Problems For Dummies, Algebra I For Dummies,* and *Algebra II For Dummies,* all by Mary Jane Sterling; *Geometry For Dummies,* 2nd Edition, and *Calculus For Dummies,* both by Mark Ryan; and *SAT II Math For Dummies,* by Scott Hatch, JD, and Lisa Zimmer Hatch, MA — all published by Wiley.

Reviewing Chapters 8 and 10 and the additional practice questions in Chapter 11 may also help. Finally, Chapters 20 and 21 may help you improve your scores.

1. **C. 15**

   If Mike has 15 dimes, he has (15)($0.10) = $1.50 in dimes. Subtract that from the total to find out how much he has in quarters: $5.25 – $1.50 = $3.75. Then, divide that result by $0.25 to determine how many quarters he has: $3.75/$0.25 = 15.

2. **B. 5 percent**

   The percent increase is the amount of increase, $25, divided by the original amount, $500: 25/500 = 0.05. Convert 0.05 to a percent by multiplying 0.05 by 100 to get 5 percent.

3. **B. $\frac{1}{4}$**

   The probability of randomly selecting a dime is equal to the number of dimes in the bag, 5, divided by the total number of coins in the bag, 20: 5 ÷ 20 = 1/4.

4. **B. 16 pints**

If 1 gallon contains 4 quarts, 2 gallons contain 8 quarts. Multiply that number by the number of pints per quart, 2, to get 16 pints in 8 quarts.

5. **B. $80**

Use the interest formula $I = Prt$, where I is the interest, P is the principal, r is the interest rate (as a decimal), and t is the time in years.

$I = \$2,000(0.04)(1) = \$80$.

6. **D. 6,336 ft**

Convert miles to feet by multiplying 1.2 miles by the conversion factor, 5,280 feet: $1.2(5,280) = 6,336$ ft.

7. **D. 106**

According to the chart, 53 percent of the attendees were women. Multiply the percent of women (0.53) by the number of attendees (200): $0.53(200) = 106$.

8. **B. $96**

Subtract the purchase amounts ($22 and $8) from the amount in your checking account: $\$88 - \$22 - \$8 = \$58$. Then add the amount of deposit: $\$58 + \$38 = \$96$.

9. **B. $\dfrac{1}{5}$**

The probability of choosing one of the six left-handed students in the class (remember, it's a class of 30, and 24 students are right-handed) is easy to find. Because $\dfrac{6}{30}$ students are left-handed, reduce the fraction to come up with the probability. $\dfrac{6}{30} = \dfrac{1}{5}$. You have a one-in-five chance of randomly choosing a leftie.

10. **D. $13.00**

Each total load costs $3.25 ($1.75 + $1.50). Multiply that by 4 to get the total cost of all your laundry: $3.25 \times 4 = \$13$. You might be better off taking it to your parents' house, where it's free (and your mom feeds you)!

11. **B. 0.5 miles**

Convert the minutes to hours by dividing 12 by 60: $12 \div 60 = 0.2$ hours. Use the distance formula, $d = rt$, to find the distance in miles that she walked: $d = 2.5(0.2) = 0.5$ miles.

12. **A. 10 m**

Use the Pythagorean theorem, $a^2 + b^2 = c^2$, to find the length of the diagonal, c:

$$6^2 + 8^2 = c^2$$
$$36 + 64 = c^2$$
$$100 = c^2$$
$$\pm\sqrt{100} = c^2$$
$$\pm 10 = c^2$$

Use the positive answer because length is always positive.

13. C. 6

For the first picture to be hung on the wall, there are three choices. After he hangs the first picture, there are two choices left for the second picture, and then one choice left for the last picture. Multiply to find the number of different ways he can arrange the three pictures: $(3)(2)(1) = 6$ ways.

14. D. $1,500

The easiest way to figure out how much the cleaning company would charge is to first determine how much it charges per square foot. Divide $600 by 4,800 to find that out: $600 \div 4,800 = \$0.125$ per square foot. You want the company to clean 12,000 square feet, so multiply that number by the per-square-foot rate: $12,000 \times \$0.125 = \$1,500$.

15. A. $552

Kendra earned $12(40) = \$480$ for the 40 hours she worked. Her overtime pay rate is $1.5(\$12) = \$18$ per hour. She earned an additional $18(4) = \$72$ in overtime pay. Her total pay last week was $\$480 + \$72 = \$552$.

16. B. 400 gallons

Seventy-five percent of the total amount of water the tub will hold, x, is equal to 600 gallons. You can represent this fact with the equation $0.75x = 600$. Solve the equation to determine how many gallons the tub holds when full:

$$0.75x = 600$$
$$x = \frac{600}{0.75}$$
$$x = 800$$

The full hot tub holds 800 gallons of water. Half of 800 gallons is 400 gallons.

17. A. 8 dimes

Let q equal the number of quarters and d equal the number of dimes. The value of the quarters is $25q$, and the value of the dimes is $10d$. So the value of dimes and quarters is $25q + 10d = 255$.

You also know that the total number of coins is 15, so $q + d = 15$. You can rearrange this equation to isolate q: $q = 15 - d$. Now you can substitute that for the q in the first equation and solve for d:

$$25(15 - d) + 10d = 255$$
$$375 - 25d + 10d = 255$$
$$375 - 15d = 255$$
$$-15d = -120$$
$$d = 8$$

18. B. 1,404 in²

Use the formula for a rectangle, $a = lw$, to find the area of the table top: $a = 48(36) = 1,728$ in². The formula for the area of a square is $a = s^2$, where s is the length of one side. Use it to find the area of the game board: $a = 18^2 = 324$ in². Then you can find the amount of area not covered by the game board by subtracting the area of the game board from the area of the table top: $1,728$ in² $- 324$ in² $= 1,404$ in².

19. **C. 40 cm**

    Let x represent the distance between the cities on the map. Write and solve an equation to find x:

    $$\frac{x}{440} = \frac{1}{11}$$
    $$11x = 440$$
    $$x = 440 \div 11$$
    $$x = 40$$

20. **C. 12**

    Let x represent Kenneth's age. You can then write Jake's age as $x + 4$ and Alicia's age as $x - 2$. The sum of their ages is 38. Write and solve an equation to find x:

    $$x + x + 4 + x - 2 = 38$$
    $$3x + 2 = 38$$
    $$3x = 36$$
    $$x = 12$$

21. **A. $157**

    The area of a circle is $a = \pi r^2$. If the radius is 10 feet, then the area is $a = \pi r^2 = 3.14(10)^2 = 3.14(100) = 314$ ft^2. Multiply the area by the cost per square foot: $314(\$0.50) = \$157$.

22. **C. 7.5**

    John took six quizzes in science class. To find his average, first add all of his scores together: $8 + 6 + 10 + 7 + 9 + 5 = 45$. Then, divide that number by 6 (the number of quizzes John took):

    $$\frac{45}{6} = 7.5$$

    His average score was 7.5.

23. **C. 10:15 a.m.**

    Subtract the $15 base fee from $75 to find Robert's total hourly earnings: $75 − $15 = $60. Divide $60 by $20 to find the number of half hours that he worked: $60 ÷ $20 = 3 half hours. Three half hours equal 1.5 hours, so add this amount of time to 8:45 a.m. to discover that he finished the job at 10:15 a.m.

24. **D. 56°**

    If two angles are supplementary, the sum of their measures is equal to 180°. To find the supplement of angle P, subtract its measure from 180°: $180° − 44° = 136°$. Angle Q is 12° less than half the supplement of angle P, so divide 136° by 2 and then subtract 12°:
    $$\frac{136°}{2} − 12° = 68° − 12° = 56°.$$

25. **C. 24 percent**

    Write the fraction of points scored by Rose as a percent: $\frac{3}{5} = 0.6 = 60\%$.

    Together, Rose and Carla scored 60 percent + 16 percent = 76 percent of the points scored by the team. So the percentage of points not scored by either player is 100 percent − 76 percent = 24 percent.

26. **C. 1.5 miles**

This problem uses the distance formula: $d = rt$. John's distance is the product of his rate (3.5 mph) and the time (2 hours): $d = 3.5(2) = 7$ miles. Garret's distance is the product of his rate (4.25 mph) and the time (2 hours): $d = 4.25(2) = 8.5$ miles. After 2 hours, they're 8.5 miles – 7 miles = 1.5 miles apart.

27. **B. 1 hour and 12 minutes**

Use the formula $\frac{a \times b}{a+b}$, where a is the amount of time Jim takes to repair the unit and b is the amount of time Kyle takes to repair the unit:

$$\frac{2 \times 3}{2+3} = \frac{6}{5} = 1\frac{1}{5}$$

To figure out how many minutes are in $\frac{1}{5}$ of an hour, multiply that fraction by 60 minutes:

$$\frac{1}{5}\left(\frac{60}{1}\right) = \frac{60}{5} = 12$$

An alternate way to solve this problem is by finding out how much Jim and Kyle can do in the same unit of time, such as 1 hour. Jim can do half of a heating unit in 1 hour, while Kyle can do one-third of a heating unit in 1 hour. Adding their times in a formula like this can be very useful:

$$\frac{\frac{1}{2}}{1} + \frac{\frac{1}{3}}{1} = \frac{\frac{5}{6}}{1}$$

Together, they can do $\frac{5}{6}$ of a unit in 1 hour, leaving $\frac{1}{6}$ of the unit to go. It takes 12 minutes longer for them to finish the unit (1 hour = 60 minutes; $60 \div 5 = 12$, which tells you that they need 12 more minutes).

28. **D. 44 cm**

To find the length of one side of the square, find the square root of the area: $\sqrt{121} = 11$. Multiply the side length by 4 to find the perimeter: $4 \times 11 = 44$.

29. **C. 2.4 gallons**

Let x represent the amount of water to be added to the 20 percent mixture, and then make a chart to help solve the problem.

	# gallons	% water	Amount water
Water	x	100	$100x$
Juice	4	20	4(20)
Mixture	$x + 4$	50	$50(x + 4)$

Illustration by Thomson Digital

From the table, you know that the amount of added water is $100x$, and the amount of juice is 4(20). The sum of these two amounts is equal to the amount of mixture, $50(x + 4)$. Write and solve an equation to find x:

$$100x + 4(20) = 50(x+4)$$
$$100x + 80 = 50x + 200$$
$$50x = 120$$
$$x = 2.4$$

30. **B. 14**

   The number of different trucks David can choose from is the product of the number of colors (3) and the number of drive options (2). So he has 3(2) = 6 choices of truck.

   Similarly, the number of sedans he can choose from is the product of the number of colors (4) and drive options (2). So he has 4(2) = 8 choices of sedan.

   The total number of options is the sum of the number of choices of truck and sedan: 6 + 8 = 14.

Part 2: Word Knowledge

I hope you did well on this subtest. (I was crossing my fingers the whole time!) If not, you may want to take another gander at Chapter 4 and the practice questions in Chapter 5. Chapters 20 and 21 may also help.

If you need additional study references to improve your vocabulary ability, you may want to consider *Vocabulary For Dummies,* by Laurie E. Rozakis, PhD, and *SAT Vocabulary For Dummies,* by Suzee Vlk (both published by Wiley).

1. **B. ignite**

   Kindle is a verb that means to arouse or ignite something.

2. **C. enthusiasm**

   Burnout is a noun that means to be strained or tired of something.

3. **A. obvious**

   Blatant is an adjective that describes something evident or noticeable.

4. **C. rush**

   Hasten is a verb that means to speed up or move quickly.

5. **C. neutral**

   Objective is an adjective that means free from bias or personal preference.

6. **B. stubborn**

   Headstrong is an adjective that means determined not to follow orders or advice.

7. **A. recoil**

   Cringe is a verb that means to react to something with discomfort through a physical motion.

8. **B. homebound**

   As used in this sentence, *domestic* is an adjective describing a person or thing related to the home.

9. **D. thrifty**

   Thrifty is an adjective that means being careful with resources.

10. **B. shorten**

   Curtail is a verb that means to decrease the length of something.

11. **A. honors**

Accolade is a noun that means praise or high recognition.

12. **C. secret**

Covert is an adjective that describes something not intended for public knowledge.

13. **D. dislike**

Abhor is a verb that means to reject something or disapprove.

14. **C. command**

Mandate is a noun that means an official order or decree.

15. **D. consistency**

Assortment is a noun that means a collection of things that differ.

16. **C. genuine**

Credible is an adjective meaning something believable or convincing.

17. **A. on hold**

Reprieve is a noun that means a temporary relief or break from something.

18. **B. dreary**

Tedious is an adjective meaning something boring or repetitive.

19. **C. ignorant**

Oblivious is an adjective that means unaware.

20. **D. encourage**

Bolster is a verb that means to make more confident through support.

21. **B. realistic**

Used as an adjective, abstract means conceptual or irregular.

22. **D. hindered**

As used in this sentence, hamper is a verb that means to make more difficult.

23. **C. cringe**

Cower is a verb that means to cringe or move away from something in fear.

24. **A. detour**

Tangent is a noun that means a change or digression from the current topic.

25. **B. cancel**

Nullify is a verb that means to make something invalid.

26. **D. physical**

Tangible is an adjective describing something material or able to be touched.

27. **D. forgiveness**

Absolution is a noun that means a pardon for wrongful deeds.

28. B. terminate

Abrogate is a verb that means to formally end an agreement or contract.

29. C. soothe

When used as a verb, *temper* means to alleviate or soften.

30. D. abundance

Plethora is a noun meaning a large or excessive amount.

31. C. hesitant

Tentative is an adjective that means apprehensive or cautious.

32. B. forgiveness

Retaliation is a noun that means to harm someone for harming you.

33. D. warn

Admonish is a verb that means to caution or advise against.

34. B. tirade

Diatribe is a noun that means an abusive criticism.

35. A. rubbish

Memento is a noun that describes something special that is kept.

Part 3: Paragraph Comprehension

So, how did you do? If you didn't do very well on this subtest, you may want to engage in some more reading practice. Improving your vocabulary can also help improve your reading comprehension skills; see Chapter 6 for some tips. You may also want to try a few of the practice questions in Chapter 7.

1. C. California had changed her.

The author doesn't explicitly state that California changed Terry, but you can infer the correct answer from the phrase "too much for their beach bum mentality." Based on that phrase and the distinction between sunny California and the worst winter, you can determine that the weather in California had ruined her ability to handle cold weather. The other answer choices can't be inferred from the limited information given in the paragraph.

2. B. More households should adopt rescue animals.

You may think that the paragraph is about the increased number of pets in American households, but that's only a small piece of information. The other information about pets in shelters and rescue facilities dominates the rest of the paragraph, with the main idea presented in the last sentence. All the information supports the idea that Americans need to adopt more rescue pets.

3. D. 30 percent

You'll notice that all the percentage numbers fall within the middle two sentences. You may be tempted by Choice (A), but read carefully and you'll see that it's the total number of households with pets, not the number with rescue pets.

4. **A. inclination**

The paragraph describes how the artists were known for their preference, or inclination, for undertaking these large and unconventional projects.

5. **C. She runs more than average.**

The passage states that shoes last six months for average use, so that's the only information that could lead to a logical assumption about Tara or her shoes. The other answers aren't related to the presented information.

6. **C. 7**

The passage says that De Niro was nominated for six other awards in addition to the Oscar he won in 1975. That makes seven nominations in all.

7. **B. The region's weather is unpredictable.**

Although Tiffany certainly seems to have bad luck with flights, the passage describes the different inclement weather conditions for her region. The use of "sometimes" at the end signifies its unpredictability.

8. **D. delayed**

The passage states that the thunderstorm caused her flight to be delayed for five hours, which is the meaning of *postponed*.

9. **B. 100**

The term centennial means 100 years, but even if you didn't know this fact, you read that the people gathered in 1961 to celebrate a war that started a hundred years earlier, in 1861.

10. **B. provide driving tips for snowy conditions**

The passage provides safe driving tips for snowy conditions in order to prevent safety hazards. The first part of the first sentence states the focus.

11. **A. understanding the results of your actions**

The passage describes what to do and what not to do when driving in snow. The author explains the results of each action. Therefore, you can infer that knowing what actions are dangerous in the snow will help you drive more safely.

12. **D. that the beginning of school is approaching**

If back-to-school shopping has begun, the beginning of school must be around the corner. Nothing in the passage suggests any of the other answers are correct.

13. **A. 532**

The passage states that 532 of his designs were developed.

14. **D. famous**

The last sentence of the passage says that Frank Lloyd Wright is as famous as Bruce Springsteen. You can infer that his career is famous as well.

15. **C. They don't like to share the mountain with snowboarders.**

The passage states that sailors and skiers share similar feelings toward their respective fellow athletes. Sailors don't like to share the water with motorboaters, so the inference you can draw is that skiers don't like to share the mountain with snowboarders.

Part 4: Mathematics Knowledge

This subtest would have been much easier if the ASVAB folks allowed you to use a calculator, wouldn't it? I mean, what are these folks, electronically challenged or something? Even so, the problems on this subtest are designed so they can be solved using only scratch paper, the ol' No. 2 pencil, and a little brain sweat.

If you're still having difficulty, give Chapter 8 another gander. *Algebra I For Dummies* and *Algebra II For Dummies,* both by Mary Jane Sterling; *Geometry For Dummies,* 2nd Edition, and *Calculus For Dummies,* both by Mark Ryan; and *SAT II Math For Dummies,* by Scott Hatch, JD, and Lisa Zimmer Hatch, MA (all published by Wiley) can also help you improve your math knowledge score. You can find additional practice questions in Chapter 9.

1. **A. –125**

   The value of $(-5)^3$ is equal to –5 multiplied by itself three times:

   $$(-5)^3 = (-5)(-5)(-5) = 25(-5) = -125$$

2. **B. *x* is greater than 21.**

   To get *x* alone on one side of the inequality, divide both sides of the inequality $42 < 2x$ by 2:

   $$42 < 2x$$
   $$\frac{42}{2} < x$$
   $$21 < x$$
   $$x > 21$$

3. **C. 720**

   This one is simple addition.

4. **C. 2**

   The digit 4 is in the tens place, the digit 5 is in the ones place, the digit 2 is in the tenths place, and the digit 1 is in the hundredths place.

5. **C. (–3, 2)**

   Locate point *P* by starting at the origin and moving along the *x*-axis until you're even with point *P*. That's the –3 mark, so –3 is your *x* coordinate. Now move along the *y*-axis until you reach point *P*. It's at the 2 mark, so 2 is the *y* coordinate.

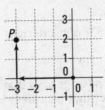

Illustration by Thomson Digital

6. **C. 2.75**

Divide 11 by 4 using long division.

$$
\begin{array}{r}
2.75 \\
4\overline{)11.00} \\
\underline{-8} \\
30 \\
\underline{-28} \\
20 \\
\underline{-20} \\
0
\end{array}
$$

7. **D. 10**

To get y by itself on one side of the equal sign, add 2 to both sides of the equation: $-2 + y + 2 = 8 + 2$. The -2 and 2 on the left side cancel each other, so $y = 10$.

8. **B. 3 cm**

The formula for the circumference of a circle is $C = \pi d$. Substitute 9.42 for C and 3.14 for π and then solve for d by dividing both sides by 3.14.

$$9.42 = 3.14d$$
$$\frac{9.42}{3.14} = d$$
$$3 = d$$

9. **C. 11.2**

Write 28 percent as a decimal: 28 percent $= 28/100 = 0.28$. Multiply: $0.28(40) = 11.2$.

10. **C. 0.1**

To multiply terms with the same base, add the exponents:

$$10^{3 + (-6) + 2} = 10^{-1}$$

Simplify: $10^{-1} = \frac{1}{10} = 0.1$

11. **A. 3y + 6**

This expression has two pairs of like terms. First, 2 and 4 are like terms and have a sum of 6. The terms $2y$ and y are also like terms and have a sum of $3y$ (remember that y is the same as $1y$).

12. **D. 38°**

The sum of the angles of a triangle is always equal to 180°. To find the value of x, subtract 34° and 108° from 180°: $180° - 34° - 108° = 38°$.

13. **C. 6**

Using the order of operations, simplify inside the parentheses first: $(5 - 2)! = 3!$. The expression $3!$ is the product of all whole numbers from 3 down to 1: $3! = 3(2)(1) = 6$.

14. **C.** $\frac{13}{16}$

To add these fractions, you have to find their common denominator, which is the least common multiple (LCM) of all three denominators. In this case, the common denominator is 16. Multiply the numerator and denominator of each fraction by the number that makes each denominator 16. (You don't have to do anything to the middle fraction because it already has the common denominator.)

$$\frac{1 \times 8}{2 \times 8} + \frac{1}{16} + \frac{1 \times 4}{4 \times 4} = \frac{8}{16} + \frac{1}{16} + \frac{4}{16}$$
$$= \frac{8 + 1 + 4}{16}$$
$$= \frac{13}{16}$$

15. **A. Four**

The factors of a number are all the numbers, including the number and 1, that divide into the number without a remainder. The number 51 has four factors: 1, 3, 17, and 51.

16. **B. 45 percent**

Write this sentence as an equation, using x to represent the percent you're trying to find: $0.405 = 0.9x$. Divide both sides by 0.9 to get x alone on one side of the equal sign.

$$0.405 = 0.9x$$
$$\frac{0.405}{0.9} = x$$
$$x = 0.45$$

You convert the decimal 0.45 to a percent by multiplying 0.45 by 100: $0.45(100) = 45$ percent.

17. **B. $(90 - m)°$**

If two angles are complementary, the sum of their measures is 90°. Because the measure of angle P is $m°$, you find the complement of angle P by subtracting its measure from 90°.

18. **D. 7 cm**

Because the triangle is a right triangle, you need the Pythagorean theorem: $a^2 + b^2 = c^2$. You know the lengths of side a and the hypotenuse (c), so plug those values into the theorem and solve for b:

$$24^2 + b^2 = 25^2$$
$$576 + b^2 = 625$$
$$b^2 = 49$$
$$b = \pm 7$$

Use the positive answer because a length is never negative.

19. **D. $x - 11 = 2x$**

When you decrease something, you're subtracting from it. In this instance, you're taking 11 away from x; that means you have $x - 11$. "Is" means "equals" in mathematical terms (and you know that every equation must have an equal sign). "Twice x" means $2x$. Your equation will look like this: $x - 11 = 2x$.

20. **D. 11**

The mean is the sum of all values divided by the number of values, or the average. First, find the sum of the values: $5 + 7 + 8 + 10 + 4 + x = 34 + x$. Because there are six values, you'll set this side of the equation up as a fraction:

$$\frac{34+x}{6}$$

You already know the answer to the equation is 7.5, so your equation will look like this:

$$\frac{34+x}{6} = 7.5$$
$$34+x = 45$$
$$x = 11$$

21. **A. 10**

Use the order of operations: simplify inside the parentheses first, compute all exponents next, multiply and divide from left to right after that, and then add and subtract from left to right:

$$(9-3\cdot2)^2 -0.5(-2) = (9-6)^2 - 0.5(-2)$$
$$= (3)^2 - 0.5(-2)$$
$$= 9 - 0.5(-2)$$
$$= 9 - (-1)$$
$$= 9 + 1$$
$$= 10$$

22. **A. 17 – 20x**

First, use the distributive property to remove the parentheses: $9 - 20x + 8$. Then, simplify by adding 9 and 8 to get $17 - 20x$.

23. **C. $2\pi r^3$**

The formula for the volume of a right cylinder is $V = \pi r^2 h$. Substitute $h = 2r$ in to the formula:

$$V = \pi r^2(2r)$$

Reorder the terms:

$$V = \pi \cdot r^2 \cdot 2r$$
$$V = 2\pi \cdot r^2 \cdot r$$
$$V = 2\pi r^3$$

24. **B. 89 cm²**

    You can break the figure down into a rectangle on the left with dimensions 7.5 cm by 10 cm and a right triangle on the right whose base is 11 − 7.5 = 3.5 cm and whose height is 10 − 2 = 8 cm.

    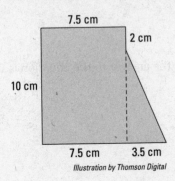

    7.5 cm

    2 cm

    10 cm

    7.5 cm   3.5 cm

    Illustration by Thomson Digital

    The area of the rectangle is $a = lw = (10)(7.5) = 75$ cm², and the area of the triangle is $A = \frac{bh}{2} = \frac{(3.5)(8)}{2} = 14$ cm². Add the two areas to find the total area: 75 + 14 = 89 cm².

25. **A. $\frac{6}{7}$**

    The problem only gives you the number of boys, so first you have to find the number of girls by subtracting 140 from 260: 260 − 140 = 120. When you need to express the number of girls to boys as a fraction, there are 120 girls for every 140 boys; that means 120:140 or 120/140, which simplifies to 6/7.

    On the ASVAB, you have to pay close attention to wording; if they'd asked for the ratio of boys to girls, Choice (B) would've been correct.

Answer Key

Part 1: Arithmetic Reasoning

1. C	7. D	13. C	19. C	25. C
2. B	8. B	14. D	20. C	26. C
3. B	9. B	15. A	21. A	27. B
4. B	10. D	16. B	22. C	28. D
5. B	11. B	17. A	23. C	29. C
6. D	12. A	18. B	24. D	30. B

Part 2: Word Knowledge

1. B	8. B	15. D	22. D	29. C
2. C	9. D	16. C	23. C	30. D
3. A	10. B	17. A	24. A	31. C
4. C	11. A	18. B	25. B	32. B
5. C	12. C	19. C	26. D	33. D
6. B	13. D	20. D	27. D	34. B
7. A	14. C	21. B	28. B	35. A

Part 3: Paragraph Comprehension

1. C	4. A	7. B	10. B	13. A
2. B	5. C	8. D	11. A	14. D
3. D	6. C	9. B	12. D	15. C

Part 4: Mathematics Knowledge

1. A	6. C	11. A	16. B	21. A
2. B	7. D	12. D	17. B	22. A
3. C	8. B	13. C	18. D	23. C
4. C	9. C	14. C	19. D	24. B
5. C	10. C	15. A	20. D	25. A

Chapter 14

Practice Exam 2

The Armed Services Vocational Aptitude Battery (ASVAB) includes four subtests that make up the Armed Forces Qualification Test (AFQT) score: Arithmetic Reasoning, Word Knowledge, Paragraph Comprehension, and Mathematics Knowledge.

The military services use the AFQT score as an initial qualifier to determine whether the military considers you to be "trainable." Each service has established its own minimum score. You can find much more information about how the AFQT is scored, and how the services use those scores, in Chapter 2.

You can't take the AFQT by itself. You have to take the entire ASVAB exam, which includes nine total subtests. All the subtests of the ASVAB are used to determine military job qualifications, while the four subtests that make up the AFQT score are used to determine military qualification.

After you complete the entire sample test, check your answers against the answer key in Chapter 15. On the actual AFQT, hard questions are worth more points than easy questions, so you can't score your test by a simple number correct or number wrong. (Chapter 2 explains how the AFQT is scored.)

Use this test as a progress check after a week or two of study. Adjust your study plan accordingly.

Answer Sheet for Practice Exam 2

Part 1: Arithmetic Reasoning

1. Ⓐ Ⓑ Ⓒ Ⓓ   8. Ⓐ Ⓑ Ⓒ Ⓓ   15. Ⓐ Ⓑ Ⓒ Ⓓ   22. Ⓐ Ⓑ Ⓒ Ⓓ   29. Ⓐ Ⓑ Ⓒ Ⓓ
2. Ⓐ Ⓑ Ⓒ Ⓓ   9. Ⓐ Ⓑ Ⓒ Ⓓ   16. Ⓐ Ⓑ Ⓒ Ⓓ   23. Ⓐ Ⓑ Ⓒ Ⓓ   30. Ⓐ Ⓑ Ⓒ Ⓓ
3. Ⓐ Ⓑ Ⓒ Ⓓ   10. Ⓐ Ⓑ Ⓒ Ⓓ   17. Ⓐ Ⓑ Ⓒ Ⓓ   24. Ⓐ Ⓑ Ⓒ Ⓓ
4. Ⓐ Ⓑ Ⓒ Ⓓ   11. Ⓐ Ⓑ Ⓒ Ⓓ   18. Ⓐ Ⓑ Ⓒ Ⓓ   25. Ⓐ Ⓑ Ⓒ Ⓓ
5. Ⓐ Ⓑ Ⓒ Ⓓ   12. Ⓐ Ⓑ Ⓒ Ⓓ   19. Ⓐ Ⓑ Ⓒ Ⓓ   26. Ⓐ Ⓑ Ⓒ Ⓓ
6. Ⓐ Ⓑ Ⓒ Ⓓ   13. Ⓐ Ⓑ Ⓒ Ⓓ   20. Ⓐ Ⓑ Ⓒ Ⓓ   27. Ⓐ Ⓑ Ⓒ Ⓓ
7. Ⓐ Ⓑ Ⓒ Ⓓ   14. Ⓐ Ⓑ Ⓒ Ⓓ   21. Ⓐ Ⓑ Ⓒ Ⓓ   28. Ⓐ Ⓑ Ⓒ Ⓓ

Part 2: Word Knowledge

1. Ⓐ Ⓑ Ⓒ Ⓓ   8. Ⓐ Ⓑ Ⓒ Ⓓ   15. Ⓐ Ⓑ Ⓒ Ⓓ   22. Ⓐ Ⓑ Ⓒ Ⓓ   29. Ⓐ Ⓑ Ⓒ Ⓓ
2. Ⓐ Ⓑ Ⓒ Ⓓ   9. Ⓐ Ⓑ Ⓒ Ⓓ   16. Ⓐ Ⓑ Ⓒ Ⓓ   23. Ⓐ Ⓑ Ⓒ Ⓓ   30. Ⓐ Ⓑ Ⓒ Ⓓ
3. Ⓐ Ⓑ Ⓒ Ⓓ   10. Ⓐ Ⓑ Ⓒ Ⓓ   17. Ⓐ Ⓑ Ⓒ Ⓓ   24. Ⓐ Ⓑ Ⓒ Ⓓ   31. Ⓐ Ⓑ Ⓒ Ⓓ
4. Ⓐ Ⓑ Ⓒ Ⓓ   11. Ⓐ Ⓑ Ⓒ Ⓓ   18. Ⓐ Ⓑ Ⓒ Ⓓ   25. Ⓐ Ⓑ Ⓒ Ⓓ   32. Ⓐ Ⓑ Ⓒ Ⓓ
5. Ⓐ Ⓑ Ⓒ Ⓓ   12. Ⓐ Ⓑ Ⓒ Ⓓ   19. Ⓐ Ⓑ Ⓒ Ⓓ   26. Ⓐ Ⓑ Ⓒ Ⓓ   33. Ⓐ Ⓑ Ⓒ Ⓓ
6. Ⓐ Ⓑ Ⓒ Ⓓ   13. Ⓐ Ⓑ Ⓒ Ⓓ   20. Ⓐ Ⓑ Ⓒ Ⓓ   27. Ⓐ Ⓑ Ⓒ Ⓓ   34. Ⓐ Ⓑ Ⓒ Ⓓ
7. Ⓐ Ⓑ Ⓒ Ⓓ   14. Ⓐ Ⓑ Ⓒ Ⓓ   21. Ⓐ Ⓑ Ⓒ Ⓓ   28. Ⓐ Ⓑ Ⓒ Ⓓ   35. Ⓐ Ⓑ Ⓒ Ⓓ

Part 3: Paragraph Comprehension

1. Ⓐ Ⓑ Ⓒ Ⓓ   8. Ⓐ Ⓑ Ⓒ Ⓓ   15. Ⓐ Ⓑ Ⓒ Ⓓ
2. Ⓐ Ⓑ Ⓒ Ⓓ   9. Ⓐ Ⓑ Ⓒ Ⓓ
3. Ⓐ Ⓑ Ⓒ Ⓓ   10. Ⓐ Ⓑ Ⓒ Ⓓ
4. Ⓐ Ⓑ Ⓒ Ⓓ   11. Ⓐ Ⓑ Ⓒ Ⓓ
5. Ⓐ Ⓑ Ⓒ Ⓓ   12. Ⓐ Ⓑ Ⓒ Ⓓ
6. Ⓐ Ⓑ Ⓒ Ⓓ   13. Ⓐ Ⓑ Ⓒ Ⓓ
7. Ⓐ Ⓑ Ⓒ Ⓓ   14. Ⓐ Ⓑ Ⓒ Ⓓ

Part 4: Mathematics Knowledge

1. Ⓐ Ⓑ Ⓒ Ⓓ   8. Ⓐ Ⓑ Ⓒ Ⓓ   15. Ⓐ Ⓑ Ⓒ Ⓓ   22. Ⓐ Ⓑ Ⓒ Ⓓ
2. Ⓐ Ⓑ Ⓒ Ⓓ   9. Ⓐ Ⓑ Ⓒ Ⓓ   16. Ⓐ Ⓑ Ⓒ Ⓓ   23. Ⓐ Ⓑ Ⓒ Ⓓ
3. Ⓐ Ⓑ Ⓒ Ⓓ   10. Ⓐ Ⓑ Ⓒ Ⓓ   17. Ⓐ Ⓑ Ⓒ Ⓓ   24. Ⓐ Ⓑ Ⓒ Ⓓ
4. Ⓐ Ⓑ Ⓒ Ⓓ   11. Ⓐ Ⓑ Ⓒ Ⓓ   18. Ⓐ Ⓑ Ⓒ Ⓓ   25. Ⓐ Ⓑ Ⓒ Ⓓ
5. Ⓐ Ⓑ Ⓒ Ⓓ   12. Ⓐ Ⓑ Ⓒ Ⓓ   19. Ⓐ Ⓑ Ⓒ Ⓓ
6. Ⓐ Ⓑ Ⓒ Ⓓ   13. Ⓐ Ⓑ Ⓒ Ⓓ   20. Ⓐ Ⓑ Ⓒ Ⓓ
7. Ⓐ Ⓑ Ⓒ Ⓓ   14. Ⓐ Ⓑ Ⓒ Ⓓ   21. Ⓐ Ⓑ Ⓒ Ⓓ

Part 1

Arithmetic Reasoning

Time: 36 minutes for 30 questions

Directions: Arithmetic Reasoning is the second subtest of the ASVAB. These questions are designed to test your ability to use mathematics to solve various problems that may be found in real life — in other words, math word problems.

Each question is followed by four possible answers. Decide which answer is correct, and then mark the corresponding space on your answer sheet. Use your scratch paper for any figuring you want to do. You may not use a calculator.

1. Marty is building a rectangular fence in his back yard and has 200 feet of fencing he can use. If the yard is to be 15 feet wide, how long will it be?

   (A) 27 ft

   (B) 72 ft

   (C) 85 ft

   (D) 87 ft

2. Henry is 48 inches tall. His older brother is 25 percent taller. How tall is Henry's brother?

   (A) 60 in

   (B) 64 in

   (C) 63 in

   (D) 73 in

3. Janet, Alice, and Gabriel are collecting cans for recycling. Altogether, they collected 473 cans. Janet collected 124 cans, and Alice collected 205 cans. How many cans did Gabriel collect?

   (A) 329

   (B) 142

   (C) 144

   (D) 167

4. The floor of Mr. Gilbert's office is in the shape of a rectangle with an area of 168 square feet. The length of the floor is 12 feet. What is the width?

   (A) 12 ft

   (B) 14 ft

   (C) 9 ft

   (D) 16 ft

5. There are 10 decimeters in a meter and 10 meters in a decameter. How many decimeters are there in 3 decameters?

   (A) 3,000

   (B) 0.03

   (C) 300

   (D) 30

6. At 9:00 a.m., the outside temperature was –14° Fahrenheit. By noon, the temperature increased by 21° Fahrenheit. What was the outside temperature at noon?

   (A) 7°F

   (B) 6°F

   (C) –7°F

   (D) –35°F

7. An airplane flew a distance of 180 miles in an hour and a half. What was the speed of the plane?

   (A) 120 mph

   (B) 110 mph

   (C) 180 mph

   (D) 270 mph

Go on to next page

8. The ratio of cars to trucks is 3:4. There are 15 cars. How many trucks are there?

   (A) 24

   (B) 10

   (C) 12

   (D) 20

9. A grocery store sells raisins for $3.50 per pound, and almonds for $4 per pound. Keith bought just enough raisins and almonds to make a 2-pound mixture that is 40 percent raisins. How much did he pay for the raisins?

   (A) $2.85

   (B) $3.50

   (C) $3.20

   (D) $2.80

10. Patricia's age is one-third Ms. Chang's age. The sum of their ages is 56 years. What is Ms. Chang's age?

    (A) 38

    (B) 44

    (C) 42

    (D) 14

11. Ed worked 10 hours and earned $125. John also worked 10 hours, but his hourly rate is $0.50 less than Ed's hourly rate. How much did John earn for 10 hours of work?

    (A) $118.75

    (B) $60.00

    (C) $119.50

    (D) $120.00

12. A game board is in the shape of a square with a perimeter of 60 inches. What is the length of one side of the game board?

    (A) 1 ft

    (B) 1.25 ft

    (C) 1.5 ft

    (D) 1.75 ft

13. A recipe calls for $2\frac{3}{4}$ cups of milk, but you have only $1\frac{1}{2}$ cups of milk available. How much more milk do you need for the recipe?

    (A) $1\frac{3}{4}$ cups

    (B) $1\frac{1}{4}$ cups

    (C) $1\frac{1}{5}$ cups

    (D) $\frac{3}{4}$ cup

14. Maria invests $2,500 into a savings account. After 1 year, she earns $100 in interest. What is the annual interest rate for the account?

    (A) 4.5 percent

    (B) 0.4 percent

    (C) 4 percent

    (D) 2.5 percent

15. What is the area of the region in this figure?

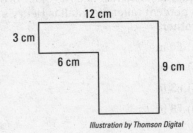

Illustration by Thomson Digital

    (A) 72 cm²

    (B) 36 cm²

    (C) 90 cm²

    (D) 30 cm²

16. Martha is teaching her first cooking class. 60 percent of the class — or 21 students — burned their quiche. How many total students are in the class?

    (A) 27

    (B) 31

    (C) 35

    (D) 39

Go on to next page

17. Keisha walked a distance of 4.5 miles at a rate of 3 miles per hour. She started her walk at 3:40 p.m. What time did she finish her walk?

    (A) 4:10 p.m.

    (B) 3:55 p.m.

    (C) 4:20 p.m.

    (D) 5:10 p.m.

18. You earn $9.75 an hour and need to earn at least $150. Which inequality shows the number of hours, h, you must work?

    (A) $9.75 < 150h$

    (B) $9.75h \geq 150$

    (C) $9.75h \leq 150$

    (D) $\dfrac{9.75}{h} \geq 150$

19. Carlos has a model of his father's new truck. The model truck is 32 centimeters long. If the scale of the model is 2 centimeters = 0.25 meters, what is the approximate length of his father's truck?

    (A) 4 m

    (B) 8 m

    (C) 10 m

    (D) 12 m

20. Joan is selling 3 paintings. She places them in a row so the cost increases by $15 from left to right. The painting on the far left costs $29. What is the cost of the painting on the far right?

    (A) $59

    (B) $15

    (C) $75

    (D) $75

21. Megan is in a hurry to get to her grandmother's Thanksgiving dinner in Wyoming. If she is traveling a constant 50 miles per hour, how many hours will it take her to travel the 600-mile trip?

    (A) 30 hours

    (B) 12 hours

    (C) 60 hours

    (D) 15 hours

22. In a certain city, the formula for calculating a speeding fine, F, is $F = 10(x - 60) + 80$, where x is the speed of the car in miles per hour. If Steve was fined $230 for speeding, how fast was he driving?

    (A) 70 mph

    (B) 75 mph

    (C) 85 mph

    (D) 80 mph

23. Nick recorded the odometer reading of 65,034 before filling his car with gas. The next time he filled his car with gas, the odometer reading was 65,322. He needed 12 gallons of gas to fill his tank. What is the best estimate of the car's gas mileage in miles per gallon (mpg)?

    (A) 12 mpg

    (B) 24 mpg

    (C) 18 mpg

    (D) 32 mpg

24. A can of beans is in the shape of a cylinder. The can has a diameter of 8 centimeters and a height of 10 centimeters. What is the volume of the can?

    (A) 160π cm^3

    (B) 640π cm^3

    (C) 80π cm^3

    (D) $1{,}600\pi$ cm^3

25. Matt must pay a $15 co-pay for each of his visits to a chiropractor. Then the insurance company pays 60 percent of the remaining cost of the visit. He made 10 visits to the chiropractor, each costing $305. How much did Matt pay for his chiropractor visits in total?

    (A) $2,900

    (B) $1,310

    (C) $1,160

    (D) $1,180

Go on to next page

26. Marco can replace a truck tire in 20 minutes. His brother takes 10 minutes longer to do the same job. How long will replacing a truck tire take them if they work together?

    (A) 18 minutes

    (B) 16 minutes

    (C) 12 minutes

    (D) 25 minutes

27. Each squeeze of a spray bottle's trigger emits 0.024 ounces of water. Ten squeezes of the trigger emit 2 percent of the total amount of water the bottle holds. How many ounces of water can the bottle hold?

    (A) 16 oz

    (B) 20 oz

    (C) 24 oz

    (D) 12 oz

28. A shoe box has a length of 30 centimeters, a width of 15 centimeters, and a height of 10 centimeters. What is the surface area of the shoe box?

    (A) 3,600 cm²

    (B) 4,500 cm²

    (C) 1,800 cm²

    (D) 900 cm²

29. Two runners start in the same place and run in opposite directions. The first runner averages 5 miles per hour, and the second runner averages 6 miles per hour. After how many hours will they be 11 miles apart?

    (A) 1 hour

    (B) 2 hours

    (C) 1.5 hours

    (D) 1.1 hours

30. The coach bought pepperoni pizzas for the entire soccer team, including himself. Each pizza cost $12. When they were all finished eating, $2\frac{3}{4}$ pizzas were left over. Each of the 15 players on the team ate a quarter of a pizza, and the coach ate half of a pizza. How much did the coach pay for the pizzas, before tax?

    (A) $72

    (B) $180

    (C) $84

    (D) $88

STOP DO NOT TURN THE PAGE UNTIL TOLD TO DO SO.
DO NOT RETURN TO A PREVIOUS TEST.

Part 2
Word Knowledge

Time: 11 minutes for 35 questions

Directions: The Word Knowledge subtest is the third subtest of the ASVAB. The questions are designed to measure your vocabulary knowledge. You'll see three types of questions on this subtest. The first type simply asks you to choose a word or words that most nearly mean the same as the underlined word in the question. The second type includes an underlined word used in a sentence, and you are to choose the word or words that most nearly mean the same as the underlined word, as used in the context of the sentence. The third type of question asks you to choose the word that has the opposite or nearly opposite meaning as the underlined word. Each question is followed by four possible answers. Decide which answer is correct, and then mark the corresponding space on your answer sheet.

1. The word most opposite in meaning to savor is
   (A) deny
   (B) enjoy
   (C) detest
   (D) keep

2. Lackluster most nearly means:
   (A) exuberant
   (B) benign
   (C) mediocre
   (D) sharp

3. The word most opposite in meaning to participate is
   (A) abstain
   (B) join
   (C) contribute
   (D) shove

4. The word most opposite in meaning to organize is
   (A) arrange
   (B) mess up
   (C) juggle
   (D) disturb

5. Unkempt most nearly means:
   (A) clean
   (B) orderly
   (C) disastrous
   (D) messy

6. I knew the preliminary interview was merely to get my foot in the door.
   (A) falling
   (B) first
   (C) closing
   (D) binding

7. The clash between Mary and her mother-in-law was inevitable because of their different values.
   (A) unlikely
   (B) unavoidable
   (C) unrelenting
   (D) unusual

8. Toby took the sunset as a good omen for his new life in Florida.
   (A) fact
   (B) letter
   (C) decree
   (D) sign

Go on to next page

9. The <u>frigid</u> wind on the chairlift was enough to give someone frostbite.

   (A) stale

   (B) warm

   (C) cold

   (D) boring

10. No one voted for Michael because he was such a <u>tyrant</u> last semester.

    (A) leader

    (B) oppressor

    (C) guide

    (D) teacher

11. <u>Counterfeit</u> most nearly means:

    (A) authentic

    (B) soiled

    (C) phony

    (D) credible

12. The word most opposite in meaning to <u>burden</u> is

    (A) relieve

    (B) bother

    (C) trouble

    (D) support

13. The word most opposite in meaning to <u>animate</u> is

    (A) deflect

    (B) stir

    (C) enliven

    (D) subdue

14. <u>Plausible</u> most nearly means:

    (A) impossible

    (B) factual

    (C) reasonable

    (D) perishable

15. <u>Pliable</u> most nearly means:

    (A) dormant

    (B) flexible

    (C) stiff

    (D) spontaneous

16. <u>Resignation</u> most nearly means:

    (A) approval

    (B) acceptance

    (C) denial

    (D) disbelief

17. <u>Obliterate</u> most nearly means:

    (A) pamper

    (B) wound

    (C) destroy

    (D) control

18. <u>Heed</u> most nearly means:

    (A) betray

    (B) abide

    (C) ignore

    (D) escape

19. Sean felt <u>immense</u> pride as he accepted the gold medal.

    (A) massive

    (B) contained

    (C) minute

    (D) similar

20. Jenny made a choice to <u>pursue</u> her dream of dancing despite her parents' disapproval.

    (A) follow

    (B) ignore

    (C) mediate

    (D) bring forth

21. I was impressed by how <u>tactful</u> my father was regarding my recent breakup.

    (A) cruel

    (B) oblivious

    (C) sensitive

    (D) doting

22. I loved watching my jock brother <u>endure</u> my sister's ballet recitals.

    (A) tolerate

    (B) approve

    (C) deny

    (D) abstain

Go on to next page

23. Charli's <u>longevity</u> during the marathon training was better than she expected.

    (A) brevity

    (B) distance

    (C) number

    (D) endurance

24. The girl had to <u>console</u> her friend, who couldn't stop crying.

    (A) compartment

    (B) comfort

    (C) hide

    (D) push away

25. When the coach claps his hands, we're supposed to <u>disperse</u> to our positions in the field.

    (A) run

    (B) gather

    (C) scatter

    (D) formulate

26. <u>Enshrouded</u> most nearly means:

    (A) illuminated

    (B) enclosed

    (C) revealed

    (D) covered

27. <u>Repudiate</u> most nearly means:

    (A) disown

    (B) waver

    (C) reclaim

    (D) adjust

28. <u>Oblique</u> most nearly means:

    (A) forward

    (B) cordial

    (C) indirect

    (D) candid

29. <u>Acquiesce</u> most nearly means:

    (A) agree with

    (B) argue with

    (C) hide from

    (D) move into

30. <u>Tenuous</u> most nearly means:

    (A) stable

    (B) flimsy

    (C) firm

    (D) buoyant

31. The children were <u>unbridled</u> during playtime, looking more like wild animals than 5-year-olds.

    (A) organized

    (B) relieving

    (C) rampant

    (D) joyous

32. I won't <u>ostracize</u> the new girl just because the other kids are jealous.

    (A) ridicule

    (B) befriend

    (C) exclude

    (D) restrict

33. <u>Replete</u> most nearly means:

    (A) full

    (B) barren

    (C) meager

    (D) coarse

34. <u>Enigma</u> most nearly means:

    (A) accessible

    (B) mystery

    (C) transparent

    (D) profound

35. Carlton stepped in to <u>assuage</u> the patron's fury after a waiter spilled soup on the man.

    (A) pacify

    (B) replace

    (C) order

    (D) determine

Part 3

Paragraph Comprehension

Time: 13 minutes for 15 questions

Directions: Paragraph Comprehension is the fourth subtest on the ASVAB. The questions are designed to measure your ability to understand what you read. This section includes one or more paragraphs of reading material, followed by incomplete statements or questions. Read the paragraph and select the choice that best completes the statement or answers the question. Then mark the corresponding space on your answer sheet.

Questions 1 and 2 refer to the following passage.

Dog training isn't for the faint of heart. You have to be tough and let the dog know who's boss, or it'll never listen to anything you say. Sometimes, you have to punish it, and it'll cry or look at you in anger or surprise. If your dog is a puppy, you may have to put it in a crate when you leave the house, which will cause it to whine and become anxious. All these actions can be difficult when you're looking into the face of an adorable dog, so you have to be firm in your resolve even when you feel bad.

1. What is the main point of the passage?

    (A) Crate training is the best way to train a dog.

    (B) Dogs are easy to train.

    (C) All dogs require training.

    (D) Trainers should avoid becoming emotional.

2. In this passage, <u>resolve</u> means

    (A) determination

    (B) indecision

    (C) prowess

    (D) fear

Question 3 refers to the following passage.

The sudden death of Dale Earnhardt was a shock to not only the NASCAR community but also the world. His aggressiveness on the track and success behind the wheel made him a well-known figure and a household name. He started his career in 1975, racing as part of the Winston Cup Series in Charlotte, North Carolina. Before his fatal crash in 2001 during the Daytona 500, he won more than 76 races, including one Daytona 500 race in 1998. He shares the record for the most NASCAR Winston Cup Championships with Richard Petty at seven apiece.

3. How many Daytona 500 races did Dale Earnhardt win?

    (A) 7

    (B) 76

    (C) 1

    (D) none of the above

Question 4 refers to the following passage.

Bipolar disorder is a mental illness that involves acute swings in mood, ranging from a heightened state of mania and an extreme state of depression. More than 4 percent of the population lives with bipolar disorder, which can be a debilitating factor in day-to-day functioning. The cause is still a topic of research for scientists, although they suspect that genetics and environment are responsible, at least in part, for the onset of the illness.

Go on to next page

4. As used in this passage, <u>acute</u> most nearly means

   (A) pointed

   (B) severe

   (C) sensitive

   (D) mild

Questions 5 and 6 refer to the following passage.

For a sport to get into the Olympic Games, the International Olympic Committee must first recognize the activity as an official sport, and the sport must have a governing agency that isn't politically affiliated. In 2014, 12 sports were added to the Winter Olympics in Sochi, Russia, but many more have come and gone over the years. For instance, rugby was added and dropped from the games three times between 1900 and 1928. However, the sport has been added again to the 2016 Summer Olympics in Rio de Janeiro, Brazil, due to a gap in the roster created by the elimination of softball and baseball from the 2012 Summer Games in London, England.

5. How many times has rugby been added to the roster of Olympic sports?

   (A) 3

   (B) 12

   (C) 4

   (D) 1

6. According to the passage, what country hosts the 2016 Summer Olympics?

   (A) Holland

   (B) England

   (C) Russia

   (D) Brazil

Question 7 refers to the following passage.

Making bread and cooking are different beasts. You can easily substitute ingredients and improvise the recipe as you go in cooking, but you must use exact ingredients and measurements for breadmaking. For example, if you want to use whole-grain flour instead of bread flour, you have to change the ratio of wet ingredients to get the same texture. Cooking is much more flexible than breadmaking.

7. What is the author trying to convey in this paragraph?

   (A) Making bread is easier than cooking.

   (B) Anyone can measure ingredients.

   (C) Breadmaking is more exact than cooking.

   (D) Whole grains are better for cooking.

Questions 8 and 9 refer to the following passage.

The history of the bald eagle in the United States is an interesting tale; the national bird came very close to extinction in the mid-20th century. An act of Congress in 1940 barred the trapping and killing of the eagles in the United States, but their numbers continued to decline. It was discovered that the pesticide DDT caused a calcium breakdown in bald eagles, resulting in sterilization or fragile egg shells and therefore low reproduction rates. With the ban of DDT use in 1972, the slow regrowth of the species began. In 1995, the eagles were removed from the endangered species list; in 1998, they were removed from the threatened species list. The bald eagles now live in abundance in North America.

8. In the passage, <u>barred</u> means

   (A) promoted

   (B) outlawed

   (C) approved

   (D) disowned

Go on to next page

9. In what year did the action that eventually led to the growth of the bald eagle population begin?

   (A) 1972

   (B) 1998

   (C) 1995

   (D) 1940

Question 10 refers to the following passage.

Jill has danced her best many times in front of audiences, but this performance is the most important one of her life. Her audition for the famed Joffrey Ballet company is the end of a long journey of schooling and competitions, all of which were in preparation for this moment. She has spent the last 15 years improving her skills, and she is confident in her ability to achieve her goal. Dancing with the Joffrey Ballet would be a dream come true for Jill.

10. What is the main point of this passage about Jill?

   (A) Jill is a skilled ballet dancer.

   (B) Ballet is Jill's preferred form of exercise.

   (C) Joining the Joffrey Ballet is Jill's life's goal.

   (D) Jill is overly determined.

Question 11 refers to the following passage.

A good quilt was once simply fluffy, decorative, and cozy, creating the image of a grandmother lovingly sewing patches of material together by hand. Today, however, the art of quilting is more lucrative than just a hobby. National and international quilting contests are regular annual events with hundreds of entrants. The quilts depict a variety of scenes, from landscapes to skylines, and the prizes for best in show can reach up to $10,000. Quilting has become a serious activity for many, and the results are impressive.

11. According to the passage, quilt makers

   (A) have plenty of time on their hands

   (B) have opportunities to make a lot of money

   (C) are in short supply

   (D) only make quilts with squares

Question 12 refers to the following passage.

For sale: Inflatable lifeboat for use in calm, shallow water. Has some puncture holes on the surface. Water typically fills the bottom, and air must be pumped periodically to avoid sinking. This boat isn't good for water deeper than four feet or for people who don't swim. Asking market price of $200.

12. According to this advertisement, the lifeboat would be safe to use in

   (A) a lake

   (B) the ocean

   (C) a river

   (D) none of the above

Questions 13 and 14 refer to the following passage.

A new study indicates that childhood obesity begins in the early years of life. Researchers followed more than 7,500 obese students between kindergarten (age 5) and eighth grade. The findings indicated that two-thirds of the children who were obese in kindergarten remained obese in eighth grade. The study also showed that children who were obese in eighth grade were likely to remain that way into adulthood. The researchers measured the children seven times for height and weight over the period of the study, and determinations of "obese" or "overweight" were made using body mass index levels.

Go on to next page

13. Based on the information in the passage, which step could likely reduce adolescent obesity?

    (A) promoting extracurricular activities

    (B) removing a child from school

    (C) forming a support group for obese children

    (D) preventing a child from becoming overweight before the age of 5

14. According to the passage, approximately how many children who participated in the study fell out of the obese range?

    (A) one-third

    (B) 7,500

    (C) two-thirds

    (D) 25 percent

Question 15 refers to the following passage.

Crispin Glover is a cult actor famous for his dark and brooding characters. Finding success first in the thriller *The River's Edge*, he became the most famous nerd in the world with his portrayal of outcast bookworm George McFly in the box office hit *Back to the Future*. He is often referred to as a shape shifter for his ability to fully become his characters. His role as the slick samurai in the movie adaptation of the TV series *Charlie's Angels* was no exception.

15. In this passage, <u>adaptation</u> can best be defined as

    (A) version

    (B) copy

    (C) continuation

    (D) screenplay

STOP DO NOT TURN THE PAGE UNTIL TOLD TO DO SO.
DO NOT RETURN TO A PREVIOUS TEST.

Part 4

Mathematics Knowledge

Time: 24 minutes for 25 questions

Directions: Mathematics Knowledge is the fifth subtest on the ASVAB. The questions are designed to test your ability to solve general mathematical problems. Each question is followed by four possible answers. Decide which answer is correct, and then mark the corresponding space on your answer sheet. Use your scratch paper for any figuring you want to do. You may not use a calculator.

1. Which number is prime?
   - (A) 1
   - (B) 2
   - (C) 10
   - (D) 51

2. Which decimal is equal to eleven thousandths?
   - (A) 1.1
   - (B) 0.11
   - (C) 0.011
   - (D) 0.101

3. $1.091 + 0.19 =$
   - (A) 1.181
   - (B) 1.182
   - (C) 1.281
   - (D) 1.11

4. An equilateral triangle has a perimeter of 54 feet. What is the length of one side of the triangle?
   - (A) 18 ft
   - (B) 16 ft
   - (C) 27 ft
   - (D) 162 ft

5. What is 40 percent of 220?
   - (A) 8.8
   - (B) 55
   - (C) 44
   - (D) 88

6. What is $\frac{26}{8}$ as a decimal?
   - (A) 4.25
   - (B) 3.5
   - (C) 2.75
   - (D) 3.25

7. Which is equal to $p^3 \times p^{-1}$?
   - (A) p^2
   - (B) $2p^2$
   - (C) p^{-3}
   - (D) p

8. $\frac{8}{25} - \frac{3}{25} =$
   - (A) $\frac{5}{50}$
   - (B) $\frac{1}{5}$
   - (C) $\frac{1}{4}$
   - (D) $\frac{5}{0}$

9. For which value of y is the inequality $y + 2 < -6$ true?
   - (A) –9
   - (B) –8
   - (C) 7
   - (D) 9

10. Simplify: $3(x - 5) + 4x$.
    - (A) $7x - 5$
    - (B) $7x - 15$
    - (C) $7x + 35$
    - (D) $12x - 15$

Go on to next page

11. The longest side of a right triangle has a length of 17 feet, and the shortest side has a length of 8 feet. What is the length of the remaining side?

    (A) 10 ft

    (B) 12 ft

    (C) 15 ft

    (D) 16 ft

12. What is the result when the quotient of 40 and 20 is decreased by the sum of 1 and 5?

    (A) –5.5

    (B) 2

    (C) 14

    (D) –4

13. $15 - 3 \times 2^2 =$

    (A) –21

    (B) 576

    (C) 3

    (D) 48

14. What is the least common multiple of 12 and 20?

    (A) 2

    (B) 60

    (C) 120

    (D) 240

15. What is the product of $\frac{3}{4}$ and $\frac{8}{7}$?

    (A) $\frac{6}{7}$

    (B) $\frac{11}{28}$

    (C) 1

    (D) $\frac{24}{11}$

16. $3(-4)(1)(-2) =$

    (A) –24

    (B) 12

    (C) 18

    (D) 24

17. $\sqrt[3]{64} =$

    (A) 8 and –8

    (B) 4 and –4

    (C) 8 only

    (D) 4 only

18. $\frac{2}{5} + \frac{1}{3} =$

    (A) $\frac{5}{50}$

    (B) $\frac{1}{5}$

    (C) $\frac{11}{15}$

    (D) $\frac{5}{0}$

19. The length of one side of the square is 20 meters. Find the area of the region that is inside the square but outside the circle.

    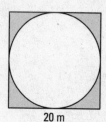

    20 m

    Illustration by Thomson Digital

    (A) 314 m²

    (B) 86 m²

    (C) 856 m²

    (D) 234 m²

20. The sum of three consecutive odd integers is 63. What is the middle number?

    (A) 21

    (B) 23

    (C) 25

    (D) 27

21. Solve the equation $x^2 + 4 = 20$.

    (A) 16 only

    (B) 8 and –8

    (C) 4 only

    (D) 4 and –4

Go on to next page

22. The measure of the supplement of an angle is equal to twice the measure of the angle. What is the measure of the angle?

    (A) 60°

    (B) 30°

    (C) 45°

    (D) 90°

23. Solve for x: $\dfrac{9}{x} = \dfrac{81}{10}$

    (A) 90

    (B) $1\dfrac{1}{9}$

    (C) $\dfrac{1}{9}$

    (D) $2\dfrac{1}{9}$

24. Simplify: $\dfrac{x^2 - 16}{x - 4}$

    (A) $\dfrac{1}{x - 4}$

    (B) $\dfrac{x - 16}{x + 4}$

    (C) $x + 4$

    (D) $x - 4$

25. The measures of the angles of a given quadrilateral are 55, 90, 111, and $2n$. What is the value of n?

    (A) 45°

    (B) 90°

    (C) 110°

    (D) 52°

STOP DO NOT TURN THE PAGE UNTIL TOLD TO DO SO.
DO NOT RETURN TO A PREVIOUS TEST.

Chapter 15

Practice Exam 2: Answers and Explanations

• •

T he answers and explanations in the following sections help you determine how well you performed on the practice test in Chapter 14 — and give you some hints about where you may have dropped a decimal point or two. Don't worry, it happens to the best of us.

Don't focus too much on scores. On the actual AFQT, harder questions are worth more points than easier questions. The AFQT is one of those rare tests on which you can miss some questions and still max out your test score. As always, use the results to decide where you want to concentrate your study time. Do you need more work on math or reading/verbal skills? This chapter helps you find out.

Part 1: Arithmetic Reasoning

The Arithmetic Reasoning subtest is not only one of the important subtests that make up the AFQT, but it's also used as a qualification factor for many of the military jobs you can choose from. You may want to glance at *ASVAB For Dummies* by yours truly (published by Wiley) to see which military jobs require you to do well on this subtest. If you missed more than five or six questions, it's time to dig out that old high-school math textbook and wrap your brain around some math problems. Chapters 8 and 10 may also help you out. Some other great books that may help you score better on this subtest include *Math Word Problems For Dummies, Algebra I For Dummies,* and *Algebra II For Dummies,* all by Mary Jane Sterling; *Geometry For Dummies,* 2nd Edition, and *Calculus For Dummies,* both by Mark Ryan; and *SAT II Math For Dummies,* by Scott Hatch, JD, and Lisa Zimmer Hatch, MA — all published by Wiley.

1. **C. 85 ft**

   Marty has 200 feet of fencing and wants to fence in a rectangular yard. If the yard is to be 15 feet wide, then use the formula for perimeter to find the length:

   $$P = 2(l + w)$$
   $$200 = 2(l + 15)$$
   $$\frac{200}{2} = \frac{2(l + 15)}{2}$$
   $$100 - 15 = l + 15 - 15$$
   $$85 = l$$

   You can check your work by plugging the numbers for length and width back into the equation to make sure the answer comes out to 200 or less (the total amount of fencing Marty has).

2. A. 60 in

First, find 25 percent of 48: 0.25(48) = 12 inches. Henry's brother's height is 48 + 12 = 60 inches.

3. C. 144

Together, Janet and Alice collected 329 cans: 124 + 205 = 329. Because the group collected 473 cans, subtract Janet and Alice's number to find out how much Gabriel pitched in: 473 − 329 = 144 cans.

4. B. 14 ft

The area formula for a rectangle is $a = lw$, where a = area, l = length, and w = width. Substitute the known values into this formula and then isolate w by dividing both sides by 12:

$$168 = 12w$$
$$\frac{168}{12} = w$$
$$14 = w$$

5. C. 300

A decameter equals 10 meters, so 3 decameters equals 30 meters. Because there are 10 decimeters in a meter, you multiply that number by the total number of meters: 10(30) = 300 decimeters in a decameter.

6. A. 7°F

Because the temperature increased, add to find the outside temperature at noon: −14 + 21 = 21 + (−14) = 21 − 14 = 7° Fahrenheit.

7. A. 120 mph

The distance formula is $d = rt$, where d is the distance, r is the rate, and t is the time. Substitute the known values into this formula and then isolate r by dividing both sides by 1.5:

$$180 = r(1.5)$$
$$\frac{180}{1.5} = r$$
$$120 = r$$

8. D. 20

Let x = the number of trucks, and express the number of cars to trucks as a fraction. So $\frac{3}{4} = \frac{15}{x}$ because you know there are 15 cars. Use the cross-products rule to solve for x.

$$\frac{3}{4} = \frac{15}{x}$$
$$3x = 4(15)$$
$$3x = 60$$
$$x = \frac{60}{3} = 20$$

9. D. $2.80

Forty percent of 2 pounds is 0.4(2) = 0.8 pounds. The amount he paid for the raisins is 0.8($3.50) = $2.80.

10. **C. 42**

If x is Patricia's age, then Ms. Chang's age is $3x$. Set up the equation and solve for x:

$$x + 3x = 56$$
$$4x = 56$$
$$x = \frac{56}{4}$$
$$x = 14$$

Patricia's age is 14, so Ms. Chang's age is $3(14) = 42$. As a double-check, add the two ages together to make sure they equal 56 as the problem indicates: $14 + 42 = 56$.

11. **D. $120.00**

Ed's hourly rate is $125 \div 10 = \$12.50$ per hour. John's hourly rate is $\$12.50 - \$0.50 = \$12$ per hour. For 10 hours of work, John earns $10(\$12) = \$120$.

12. **B. 1.25 ft**

The length of one side of the square game board is $\frac{60}{4} = 15$ inches. There are 12 inches in 1 foot, so 15 inches is 1 foot and 3 inches, or $1\frac{3}{12} = 1\frac{1}{4} = 1.25$ feet.

13. **B. $1\frac{1}{4}$ cups**

Write each mixed number as an improper fraction. Multiply the denominator by the whole number and then add the result to the numerator:

$$2\frac{3}{4} = \frac{4 \times 2 + 3}{4} = \frac{8+3}{4} = \frac{11}{4}$$
$$1\frac{1}{2} = \frac{2 \times 1 + 1}{2} = \frac{2+1}{2} = \frac{3}{2}$$

Subtract to find the amount of milk you need. The common denominator is 4 because 4 is the least common multiple (LCM) of 4 and 2:

$$\frac{11}{4} - \frac{3}{2} = \frac{11}{4} - \frac{6}{4}$$
$$= \frac{11-6}{4}$$
$$= \frac{5}{4}$$
$$= 1\frac{1}{4}$$

14. **C. 4 percent**

Use the interest formula $I = Prt$, where I is the interest, P is the principal, r is the interest rate (as a decimal), and t is the time in years. Substitute known values into the formula and solve for r.

$$100 = 2,500\,(r)\,(1)$$
$$100 = 2,500r$$
$$\frac{100}{2,500} = r$$
$$r = \frac{1}{25} = 0.04$$

Write 0.04 as a percent by moving the decimal point two places to the right: $0.04 = 4$ percent.

15. **A. 72 cm²**

Divide the region into two rectangles and find the length of the missing sides.

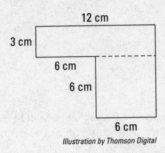

12 cm
3 cm
6 cm
6 cm
6 cm

Illustration by Thomson Digital

The formula for the area of a rectangle is $a = lw$. Find the area of the upper rectangle and add it to the area of the lower rectangle.

Upper rectangle: $a = 3(12) = 36$ cm²

Lower rectangle: $a = 6(6) = 36$ cm²

The area of the total region is $36 + 36 = 72$ cm².

16. **C. 35**

If 60 percent of Martha's cooking class is equal to 21, you must find the total number of students by using x for the total number of people in the class.

Write the equation like this:

$$0.60x = 21$$

Divide both sides by 0.60:

$$\frac{0.60x}{0.60} = \frac{21}{0.60}$$
$$x = 35$$

So there are 35 total students in the class.

17. **D. 5:10 p.m.**

The distance formula is $d = rt$, where d is the distance, r is the rate, and t is the time. Substitute the known values and solve for t to find out how long Keisha walked.

$$4.5 = 3t$$
$$\frac{4.5}{3} = t$$
$$1.5 = t$$

One hour and 30 minutes after 3:40 p.m. is 4:10 p.m.

18. **B. 9.75h ≥ 150**

The amount you earn is the product of your hourly rate and the number of hours worked, which can be expressed as $9.75h$. Your earnings must be greater than or equal to $150, which is represented by the symbol $\geq$.

amount earned $\geq$ $150

$9.75h \geq$ $150

19. **B. 8 m**

Let x = the length of Carlos's father's truck. The ratio of the model length to the length of the actual truck should equal the ratio of 2 centimeters to 0.25 m.

Set the two ratios equal to each other to make an equation. Use the cross-products rule to solve for x.

$$\frac{32}{x} = \frac{2}{0.25}$$
$$32\,(0.25) = 2x$$
$$8 = x$$

20. **A. $59**

Use a sequence of numbers to represent the cost of the paintings in order from left to right. The first number on the left is 29. Add 15 to find the cost of the next painting: 29, 44, 59. The painting on the far right costs $59.

21. **B. 12 hours**

Find how many hours it will take Megan to travel by using the distance formula ($d = rt$) where $d = 600$ and $r = 50$:

$$d = rt$$
$$600 = (50)t$$
$$\frac{600}{50} = \frac{(50)t}{50}$$
$$12 = t$$

It will take Megan 12 hours to get to her grandmother's house.

22. **B. 75 mph**

Substitute $F = 230$ into the formula and solve for x.

$$230 = 10\,(x - 60) + 80$$
$$230 = 10x - 600 + 80$$
$$230 = 10x - 520$$
$$750 = 10x$$
$$75 = x$$

23. **B. 24 mpg**

Subtract to find the number of miles traveled: 65,322 – 65,034 = 288 miles. The car's gas mileage is the distance traveled divided by the number of gallons of gas used: $\frac{288}{12} = 24$.

24. **A. 160π cm³**

The formula for the volume of a cylinder is $V = \pi r^2 h$, where r is the radius and h is the height. The radius of the can is equal to half the diameter: $r = d/2 = 8/2 = 4$. Substitute known values into the formula to find the volume: $V = \pi(4^2)(10) = \pi(16)(10) = 160\pi$.

25. **B. $1,310**

Subtract the co-pay for one visit from the cost of one visit: $305 – $15 = $290. The insurance company pays 60 percent of the cost after the co-pay, so Matt pays 40 percent of the cost. Find 40 percent of $290: 0.4($290) = $116. Add Matt's portion after the co-pay to the co-pay: $15 + $116 = $131 total for each visit. Multiply Matt's total cost for one visit to the chiropractor by 10: 10($131) = $1,310.

26. C. 12 minutes

You can figure out how long it will take Marco and his brother to change a tire together by determining how much work each person does in a set amount of time. Use one hour (60 minutes) to keep it simple: Marco can repair one tire in 20 minutes, so he can finish three tires in an hour. His brother can repair two tires in one hour.

Let a = the amount of time Marco needs and b = the amount of time his brother needs. In one hour together, they repair

$$\frac{3}{1} + \frac{2}{1} = \frac{5}{1}$$

The number of tires is expressed in the numerator, and the unit of time is expressed in the denominator. Because they can repair five tires in one hour together, divide the 60 minutes of an hour by 5 to get the time it takes them to repair just one.

$$60 \div 5 = 12$$

27. D. 12 oz

First, find out how many ounces of water ten squeezes of the trigger emit: $10(0.024) = 0.24$ ounces. So 0.24 ounces of water is 2 percent of the total amount of water that the bottle can hold.

Let x = the total number of ounces of water that the bottle will hold. You know that 2 percent of x is equal to 0.24, so write an equation and then solve for x.

$$0.02x = 0.24$$
$$x = \frac{0.24}{0.02}$$
$$x = \frac{24}{2}$$
$$x = 12$$

28. C. 1,800 cm²

A shoe box is a rectangular box. The formula for the surface area of a rectangular box is $SA = 2lw + 2wh + 2lh$, where l = length, w = width, and h = height. Substitute the known values into the formula and simplify.

$$SA = 2(30)(15) + 2(15)(10) + 2(30)(10)$$
$$= 60(15) + 30(10) + 60(10)$$
$$= 900 + 300 + 600$$
$$= 1,800$$

29. A. 1 hour

Let x represent the amount of time the runners take to run 11 miles in opposite directions, and then make a chart to help solve the problem.

	Rate ×	Time =	Distance
Runner 1	5	x	$5x$
Runner 2	6	x	$6x$

Illustration by Thomson Digital

You need to figure out how far each runner ran using a variation of the distance formula, $d = rt$, where d = distance, r = rate, and t = time. The table shows you that Runner 1 will run a distance of $5x$ and Runner 2 will run a distance of $6x$. Because they are running in opposite directions and you want to know when they are 11 miles apart, you add the two distances together and set the sum equal to 11. The equation looks like this:

$$5x + 6x = 11$$
$$11x = 11$$
$$x = 1$$

It will take the runners 1 hour to get 11 miles apart.

30. **C. $84**

Use the amount of pizza eaten to determine how many pizzas the coach bought. Excluding the coach, the team ate $15\left(\frac{1}{4}\right) = \frac{15}{4} = 3\frac{3}{4}$ pizzas. Add the amount of pizza the coach ate and the amount of pizza left over: $3\frac{3}{4} + \frac{1}{2} + 2\frac{3}{4}$. Write each as an improper fraction with a common denominator and add to find the total number of pizzas:

$$\frac{15}{4} + \frac{2}{4} + \frac{11}{4} = \frac{15 + 2 + 11}{4}$$
$$= \frac{28}{4}$$
$$= 7$$

For 7 pizzas, the total cost before tax is $7(\$12) = \$84$.

Part 2: Word Knowledge

The Word Knowledge subtest is nothing more than a vocabulary test. However, it can be hard for some people. The good news is that vocabulary isn't an innate talent. It's something that everyone can improve. If you find you need to improve your vocabulary, see Chapter 4. A couple of other great study references are *Vocabulary For Dummies* by Laurie E. Rozakis (Wiley) and *SAT Vocabulary For Dummies* by Suzee Vlk (Wiley). Additionally, see Chapter 5 for more practice questions.

1. **C. detest**

   Savor is a verb that means to appreciate something.

2. **C. mediocre**

   Lackluster is an adjective meaning a lack of life or energy.

3. **A. abstain**

   Participate is a verb that means to take part in.

4. **B. mess up**

   Organize is a verb that means to coordinate or make orderly.

5. **D. messy**

   Unkempt is an adjective describing something disorderly.

6. **B. first**

   Preliminary is an adjective describing something introductory.

7. **B. unavoidable**

   Inevitable is an adjective that means bound to happen.

8. **D. sign**

   Omen is a noun describing something prophetic.

9. **C. cold**

   As used in this sentence, *frigid* is an adjective meaning extremely cold.

10. **B. oppressor**

    Tyrant is a noun describing someone who rules over others unjustly.

11. **C. phony**

    As used in this sentence, *counterfeit* is an adjective meaning fake or forged.

12. **A. relieve**

    Used as a verb, *burden* means to provide a load or a difficult task to someone.

13. **D. subdue**

    Used as a verb, *animate* means to rouse or make lively.

14. **C. reasonable**

    Plausible is an adjective that means something looks to be true or believable, though it may or may not actually be so.

15. **B. flexible**

    Pliable is an adjective that means easily bent or changeable.

16. **B. acceptance**

    Resignation is a noun that means a reluctant agreement.

17. **C. destroy**

    Obliterate is a verb that means to demolish or annihilate.

18. **B. abide**

    Heed is a verb meaning to take warning or advice in earnest.

19. **A. massive**

    Immense is an adjective meaning very large or colossal.

20. **A. follow**

    Pursue is a verb meaning to go after something or someone.

21. **C. sensitive**

    Tactful is an adjective that means being thoughtful or delicate.

22. **A. tolerate**

    Endure is a verb that means to exercise toleration in a difficult moment.

23. **D. endurance**

    In this sentence, *longevity* is a noun meaning a prolonged ability.

24. **B. comfort**

    As used in this sentence, *console* is a verb meaning to provide relief.

25. **C. scatter**

    Disperse is a verb that means to move in different directions.

26. **D. covered**

    Enshrouded is a verb meaning to encompass or obscure something.

27. **A. disown**

    Repudiate is a verb that means to renounce or strongly deny something or someone.

28. **C. indirect**

    Oblique is an adjective meaning not straight or not straightforward.

29. **A. agree with**

    Acquiesce is a verb meaning to consent by way of giving in.

30. **B. flimsy**

    Tenuous is an adjective describing something weak or lacking substance.

31. **C. rampant**

    Unbridled is an adjective meaning uncontrolled.

32. **C. exclude**

    Ostracize is a verb meaning to leave out intentionally.

33. **A. full**

    Replete is an adjective that means ample or fully supplied.

34. **B. mystery**

    Enigma is a noun that means something not clear or not understandable.

35. **A. pacify**

    Assuage is a verb meaning to appease or calm.

Part 3: Paragraph Comprehension

The Paragraph Comprehension subtest can be a bit tricky, but you need to get a good score on this subtest if you want to ace the AFQT. So pay special attention if you've missed more than a couple of these answers — you need some study time (see Chapter 6). Remember that rereading the paragraph several times to make sure that you have the right answer is perfectly fine. The best method of improving your reading comprehension skills is simply to read more. You can find additional practice questions in Chapter 7.

1. **D. Trainers should avoid becoming emotional.**

    The first sentence states the point: "Dog training isn't for the faint of heart." In other words, sometimes you have to discipline the dog without becoming an emotional wreck.

2. **A. determination**

The last sentence of the passage lets you know that your *resolve* will be tested because you may feel guilty for training your dog. You have to be very determined to train your pet because pity could make you want to drop everything and play.

3. **C. 1**

A quick scan of the passage shows you that it clearly says "including one Daytona 500 race." You can answer questions like these quickly on the ASVAB, so read the question thoroughly, find your answer, and move on.

4. **B. severe**

The description of the mood swings states that they range from a heightened place to an extreme state of depression. *Severe* is the only word that describes the large range experienced.

5. **C. 4**

The passage states that rugby has been added and dropped three times but is coming back in 2016. The first three times plus the most recent equals four times rugby has been added to the Olympic Games.

6. **D. Brazil**

The passage lists many locations, but careful scanning shows you that the 2016 Olympics are in Rio de Janeiro, Brazil.

7. **C. Breadmaking is more exact than cooking.**

The paragraph gives examples of how, unlike cooking, making bread uses exact measurements and ratios to get the desired result. The last sentence also states the answer in different terms.

8. **B. outlawed**

The paragraph states that the number of bald eagles continued to decline despite trapping and killing having been barred. The term *despite* tells you that barred signifies an action against trapping and killing. In fact, the act banned, or outlawed, those practices against the eagle.

9. **A. 1972**

The passage indicates that DDT was responsible for the decline of the species. Thus, the banning of DDT in 1972 would be the beginning of the repopulation of the bald eagle. You may have been tempted by 1940, but the congressional act didn't contribute to the population regrowth. When an ASVAB question asks you for a specific date, scan the paragraph quickly for numbers; you'll be able to find the answer easily.

10. **C. Joining the Joffrey Ballet is Jill's life's goal.**

Although many of these things could be true about Jill, the question asks for the main point of the passage. The passage stresses the importance of her audition and how being accepted by the Joffre Ballet would be "a dream come true," so the main point is that she has been eagerly anticipating this moment for some time.

11. **B. have opportunities to make a lot of money**

The paragraph describes the popularity of quilting and mentions contests with best in show prizes reaching $10,000. Therefore, you can assume quilters today can make a good amount of money.

12. D. none of the above

Although areas of the other answers may have depths of less than four feet, they can all have deeper areas. Because the seller clearly says the lifeboat should not be used by people who cannot swim, it shouldn't be used in open water.

13. D. preventing a child from becoming overweight before the age of 5

The information states that children obese at age 5 were more likely to be obese in adolescence. Although the passage doesn't explicitly state that weight management before the age of 5 is desirable, you can reason that from the information provided. The other three answers aren't stated in the passage, so you can quickly rule them out as possible answers.

14. A. one-third

The passage states that approximately two-thirds of the children involved in the study remained obese in their later years, so you can reason that one-third became thinner.

15. A. version

The movie is based on the TV show, so an *adaptation* is another version of the show.

Part 4: Mathematics Knowledge

Some folks find math to be a breeze and can't understand why the rest of us approach math problems with all the enthusiasm of a trip to the dentist. However, the military considers math skills to be important, and it's right. If you miss more than four or five questions, you should consider brushing up on your basic math skills — Chapter 8 can help with this. As with the Arithmetic Reasoning subtest, the following *For Dummies* books may also be of some help: *Algebra I For Dummies* and *Algebra II For Dummies,* both by Mary Jane Sterling; *Geometry For Dummies,* 2nd Edition, and *Calculus For Dummies,* both by Mark Ryan; and *SAT II Math For Dummies,* by Scott Hatch, JD, and Lisa Zimmer Hatch, MA (all published by Wiley). Chapter 9 also has some additional practice questions.

1. B. 2

A prime number is a number that is bigger than 1 and has only itself and 1 as factors. The number 2 is the only choice that fits the definition of a prime number.

2. C. 0.011

Eleven thousandths is the same as $\frac{11}{1,000}$. When dividing a number by 1,000, move the decimal point 3 places to the left: $\frac{11}{1,000} = 0.011$.

3. C. 1.281

When adding decimals, arrange the numbers in an addition column with the decimal points lined up.

$$\begin{array}{r} \overset{1}{1.091} \\ +0.19 \\ \hline 1.281 \end{array}$$

When adding the 9s in the hundredths column, remember to carry the 1 to the tenths column.

4. A. 18 ft

An equilateral triangle has three equal sides. The perimeter is the sum of all three sides. To find the length of one side, divide the perimeter by 3: $54 \div 3 = 18$ ft.

5. **D. 88**

   Write 40 percent as a decimal: 40 percent = 0.4. Multiply 0.4 by 220: 0.4(220) = 88.

6. **D. 3.25**

   Divide 26 by 8 using long division.

$$
\begin{array}{r}
3.25 \\
8\overline{)\,26.00} \\
-24 \\
\hline
20 \\
-16 \\
\hline
40 \\
-40 \\
\hline
0
\end{array}
$$

7. **A. p^2**

   To multiply terms with the same base, add the exponents: $p^{3 + (-1)} = p^{3-1} = p^2$.

8. **B. $\frac{1}{5}$**

   To subtract fractions with the same denominator, subtract the numerators but keep the denominators the same. You can then simplify the difference $\frac{5}{25}$ to $\frac{1}{5}$.

   $$\frac{8}{25} - \frac{3}{25} = \frac{8-3}{25} = \frac{5}{25} = \frac{1}{5}$$

9. **A. –9**

   Get y alone on one side of the inequality symbol by subtracting 2 from both sides:

   $$
   \begin{aligned}
   y+2 &< -6 \\
   y+2-2 &< -6-2 \\
   y &< -8
   \end{aligned}
   $$

   So y can be any number less than –8. The only answer choice that is less than –8 is –9.

10. **B. $7x - 15$**

    Use the distributive property to remove the parentheses. Then add like terms $3x$ and $4x$.

    $$
    \begin{aligned}
    3(x-5)+4x &= 3x-15+4x \\
    &= 7x-15
    \end{aligned}
    $$

11. **C. 15 ft**

    Use the Pythagorean theorem $a^2 + b^2 = c^2$ to find the length of the remaining side. Remember that the hypotenuse, c, is always the longest side of a right triangle. Let a represent the length of the remaining side.

    $$
    \begin{aligned}
    a^2 + 8^2 &= 17^2 \\
    a^2 + 64 &= 289 \\
    a^2 &= 289 - 64 \\
    a^2 &= 225 \\
    a &= \pm\sqrt{225} = \pm 15
    \end{aligned}
    $$

    Use the positive answer because length is always positive.

12. **D. –4**

The quotient of 40 and 20 is $40 \div 20 = 2$. The sum of 1 and 5 is 6. Decrease 2 by 6 using subtraction: $2 - 6 = -4$.

13. **C. 3**

Use the order of operations, which says to simplify inside the parentheses first, compute all exponents, multiply and divide from left to right, and then add and subtract from left to right. (You might know this order of operations as PEMDAS.) This equation has no parentheses, so start with the exponents:

$$15 - 3 \times 2^2 = 15 - 3 \times 4$$
$$= 15 - 12$$
$$= 3$$

14. **B. 60**

To find the least common multiple (LCM) of two numbers, write out the multiples of each number and find the smallest number that they have in common.

Multiples of 12: 12, 24, 36, 48, 60

Multiples of 20: 20, 40, 60

The LCM is 60.

15. **A. $\frac{6}{7}$**

Product means multiplication. When multiplying two fractions, multiply the numerators by each other and multiply the denominators by each other.

$$\frac{3}{4} \cdot \frac{8}{7} = \frac{3 \cdot 8}{4 \cdot 7} = \frac{24}{28}$$

Remember to simplify all fractions. Simplify this fraction by dividing the numerator and denominator by the greatest common divisor, 4:

$$\frac{24 \div 4}{28 \div 4} = \frac{6}{7}$$

16. **D. 24**

This question asks for the product of four numbers. You can multiply two numbers at a time, moving from left to right. Remember that the product of two numbers with the same sign is positive, and the product of two numbers with different signs is negative.

$$3(-4)(1)(-2) = -12(1)(-2)$$
$$= -12(-2)$$
$$= 24$$

17. **D. 4 only**

A cube root is a number that when multiplied by itself three times equals the number under the radical sign. Because $4(4)(4) = 64$, 4 is the cube root of 64.

18. **C. $\frac{11}{15}$**

You need to find the common denominator for these two fractions. The common denominator is the least common multiple of 5 and 3.

Multiples of 5: 5, 10, 15

Multiples of 3: 3, 6, 9, 12, 15

The common denominator for these two fractions is 15. Multiply the numerator and denominator of each fraction by the number that makes each denominator 15.

$$\frac{2}{5}+\frac{1}{3}=\frac{2\cdot3}{5\cdot3}+\frac{1\cdot5}{3\cdot5}$$
$$=\frac{6}{15}+\frac{5}{15}$$
$$=\frac{6+5}{15}$$
$$=\frac{11}{15}$$

19. **B. 86 m^2**

First, find the area of the square by using the formula $a = s^2$, where s is the length of one side of the square. Because $s = 20$ meters, the area of the square is $20^2 = 400$ m^2.

Next, find the area of the circle by using the formula $a = \pi r^2$, where r is the radius of the circle. Because the diameter of the circle runs the length of one side of the square, the radius is half the length of one side of the square, so $r = 10$ meters. The area of the circle is $a = \pi(10^2) = 3.14(100) = 314$ m^2.

To find the area of the region inside the square and outside the circle, subtract the area of the circle from the area of the square: $400 - 314 = 86$ m^2.

20. **A. 21**

Let x represent the middle number. Next add and subtract 2 (to represent the other odd numbers), written as $(x + 2)$ and $(x - 2)$.

$$(x+2)+x+(x-2)=63$$
$$3x=63$$
$$\frac{3x}{3}=\frac{63}{3}$$
$$x=21$$

21. **D. 4 and –4**

This equation is a quadratic equation because the unknown quantity (x) has an exponent of 2. To solve it, first isolate the variable by subtracting 4 from both sides:

$$x^2+4=20$$
$$x^2+4-4=20-4$$
$$x^2=16$$

Next, use the square root rule, which says that if $x^2 = k$, then $x=\pm\sqrt{k}$:

$$x=\pm\sqrt{16}$$
$$x=\pm4$$

22. **A. 60°**

If two angles are supplementary, the sum of their measures is 180°. Label the angle you're trying to find as x and the supplement as $2x$. You can then set up an equation:

$$x+2x=180$$
$$3x=180$$
$$x=\frac{180}{3}$$
$$x=60$$

23. **B.** $1\frac{1}{9}$

To solve for x, cross-multiply and isolate the variable:

$$\frac{9}{x} = \frac{81}{10}$$
$$9(10) = 81x$$
$$90 = 81x$$
$$\frac{90}{81} = x$$

Use long division to write the answer as a mixed number.

$$\begin{array}{r} 1 \\ 81\overline{)90} \\ \underline{-81} \\ 9 \end{array}$$

The quotient forms the whole number; the reminder, 9, is the numerator of the fraction, and the divisor, 81, is the denominator: $1\frac{9}{81}$. You can simplify this number to $1\frac{1}{9}$.

24. **C. 24.** $x + 4$

The numerator is a difference of two squares. Use the formula $x^2 - a^2 = (x - a)(x + a)$ to factor the numerator. The factor $x - 4$ cancels out in the numerator and in the denominator.

$$\frac{x^2 - 16}{x - 4} = \frac{(x-4)(x+4)}{x-4}$$
$$= \frac{\cancel{(x-4)}(x+4)}{\cancel{x-4}}$$
$$= x + 4$$

25. **D. 52°**

The sum of the angles in a quadrilateral always measure 360°. Write an equation to find the value of n: $55 + 90 + 111 + 2n = 360$

To solve this equation, isolate the variable:

$$256 + 2n = 360$$
$$256 + 2n - 256 = 360 - 256$$
$$2n = 104$$
$$n = 52$$

Answer Key

Part 1: Arithmetic Reasoning

1. C	7. A	13. B	19. B	25. B
2. A	8. D	14. C	20. A	26. C
3. C	9. D	15. A	21. B	27. D
4. B	10. C	16. C	22. B	28. C
5. C	11. D	17. D	23. B	29. A
6. A	12. B	18. B	24. A	30. C

Part 2: Word Knowledge

1. C	8. D	15. B	22. A	29. A
2. C	9. C	16. B	23. D	30. B
3. A	10. B	17. C	24. B	31. C
4. B	11. C	18. B	25. C	32. C
5. D	12. A	19. A	26. D	33. A
6. B	13. D	20. A	27. A	34. B
7. B	14. C	21. C	28. C	35. A

Part 3: Paragraph Comprehension

1. D	4. B	7. C	10. C	13. D
2. A	5. C	8. B	11. B	14. A
3. C	6. D	9. A	12. D	15. A

Part 4: Mathematics Knowledge

1. B	6. D	11. C	16. D	21. D
2. C	7. A	12. D	17. D	22. A
3. C	8. B	13. C	18. C	23. B
4. A	9. A	14. B	19. B	24. C
5. D	10. B	15. A	20. A	25. D

Chapter 16

Practice Exam 3

· ·

*I*n the sections that follow, you find the four subtests of the Armed Services Vocational Aptitude Battery (ASVAB), which make up the Armed Forces Qualification Test (AFQT) score: Arithmetic Reasoning, Word Knowledge, Paragraph Comprehension, and Mathematics Knowledge.

I note in Chapter 2 that the military services use the scores derived from these four subtests to determine your overall AFQT score, and that the AFQT score is the primary factor that decides whether or not you are qualified to enlist in the military branch of your choice. Remember to use the results of the following practice exam to decide which areas you should dedicate more study to.

Use the answer key and explanations in Chapter 17 to score your practice exam. Remember not to be too concerned with how many you get right and how many you get wrong. Some of the questions on the practice exam are hard, and others are very easy. When you take the actual subtests as part of the ASVAB, harder questions are awarded more points than easier questions. See Chapter 2 to see exactly how this works, and how it affects your overall AFQT score.

Take this practice exam about a week before you're scheduled to take the actual ASVAB. Use the results to determine which AFQT subjects need a little extra attention.

Answer Sheet for Practice Exam 3

Part 1: Arithmetic Reasoning

1. (A) (B) (C) (D)   8. (A) (B) (C) (D)   15. (A) (B) (C) (D)   22. (A) (B) (C) (D)   29. (A) (B) (C) (D)
2. (A) (B) (C) (D)   9. (A) (B) (C) (D)   16. (A) (B) (C) (D)   23. (A) (B) (C) (D)   30. (A) (B) (C) (D)
3. (A) (B) (C) (D)   10. (A) (B) (C) (D)   17. (A) (B) (C) (D)   24. (A) (B) (C) (D)
4. (A) (B) (C) (D)   11. (A) (B) (C) (D)   18. (A) (B) (C) (D)   25. (A) (B) (C) (D)
5. (A) (B) (C) (D)   12. (A) (B) (C) (D)   19. (A) (B) (C) (D)   26. (A) (B) (C) (D)
6. (A) (B) (C) (D)   13. (A) (B) (C) (D)   20. (A) (B) (C) (D)   27. (A) (B) (C) (D)
7. (A) (B) (C) (D)   14. (A) (B) (C) (D)   21. (A) (B) (C) (D)   28. (A) (B) (C) (D)

Part 2: Word Knowledge

1. (A) (B) (C) (D)   8. (A) (B) (C) (D)   15. (A) (B) (C) (D)   22. (A) (B) (C) (D)   29. (A) (B) (C) (D)
2. (A) (B) (C) (D)   9. (A) (B) (C) (D)   16. (A) (B) (C) (D)   23. (A) (B) (C) (D)   30. (A) (B) (C) (D)
3. (A) (B) (C) (D)   10. (A) (B) (C) (D)   17. (A) (B) (C) (D)   24. (A) (B) (C) (D)   31. (A) (B) (C) (D)
4. (A) (B) (C) (D)   11. (A) (B) (C) (D)   18. (A) (B) (C) (D)   25. (A) (B) (C) (D)   32. (A) (B) (C) (D)
5. (A) (B) (C) (D)   12. (A) (B) (C) (D)   19. (A) (B) (C) (D)   26. (A) (B) (C) (D)   33. (A) (B) (C) (D)
6. (A) (B) (C) (D)   13. (A) (B) (C) (D)   20. (A) (B) (C) (D)   27. (A) (B) (C) (D)   34. (A) (B) (C) (D)
7. (A) (B) (C) (D)   14. (A) (B) (C) (D)   21. (A) (B) (C) (D)   28. (A) (B) (C) (D)   35. (A) (B) (C) (D)

Part 3: Paragraph Comprehension

1. Ⓐ Ⓑ Ⓒ Ⓓ   8. Ⓐ Ⓑ Ⓒ Ⓓ   15. Ⓐ Ⓑ Ⓒ Ⓓ
2. Ⓐ Ⓑ Ⓒ Ⓓ   9. Ⓐ Ⓑ Ⓒ Ⓓ
3. Ⓐ Ⓑ Ⓒ Ⓓ   10. Ⓐ Ⓑ Ⓒ Ⓓ
4. Ⓐ Ⓑ Ⓒ Ⓓ   11. Ⓐ Ⓑ Ⓒ Ⓓ
5. Ⓐ Ⓑ Ⓒ Ⓓ   12. Ⓐ Ⓑ Ⓒ Ⓓ
6. Ⓐ Ⓑ Ⓒ Ⓓ   13. Ⓐ Ⓑ Ⓒ Ⓓ
7. Ⓐ Ⓑ Ⓒ Ⓓ   14. Ⓐ Ⓑ Ⓒ Ⓓ

Part 4: Mathematics Knowledge

1. Ⓐ Ⓑ Ⓒ Ⓓ   8. Ⓐ Ⓑ Ⓒ Ⓓ   15. Ⓐ Ⓑ Ⓒ Ⓓ   22. Ⓐ Ⓑ Ⓒ Ⓓ
2. Ⓐ Ⓑ Ⓒ Ⓓ   9. Ⓐ Ⓑ Ⓒ Ⓓ   16. Ⓐ Ⓑ Ⓒ Ⓓ   23. Ⓐ Ⓑ Ⓒ Ⓓ
3. Ⓐ Ⓑ Ⓒ Ⓓ   10. Ⓐ Ⓑ Ⓒ Ⓓ   17. Ⓐ Ⓑ Ⓒ Ⓓ   24. Ⓐ Ⓑ Ⓒ Ⓓ
4. Ⓐ Ⓑ Ⓒ Ⓓ   11. Ⓐ Ⓑ Ⓒ Ⓓ   18. Ⓐ Ⓑ Ⓒ Ⓓ   25. Ⓐ Ⓑ Ⓒ Ⓓ
5. Ⓐ Ⓑ Ⓒ Ⓓ   12. Ⓐ Ⓑ Ⓒ Ⓓ   19. Ⓐ Ⓑ Ⓒ Ⓓ
6. Ⓐ Ⓑ Ⓒ Ⓓ   13. Ⓐ Ⓑ Ⓒ Ⓓ   20. Ⓐ Ⓑ Ⓒ Ⓓ
7. Ⓐ Ⓑ Ⓒ Ⓓ   14. Ⓐ Ⓑ Ⓒ Ⓓ   21. Ⓐ Ⓑ Ⓒ Ⓓ

Part 1

Arithmetic Reasoning

Time: 36 minutes for 30 questions

Directions: Arithmetic Reasoning is the second subtest of the ASVAB. These questions are designed to test your ability to use mathematics to solve various problems that may be found in real life — in other words, math word problems.

Each question is followed by four possible answers. Decide which answer is correct, and then mark the corresponding space on your answer sheet. Use your scratch paper for any figuring you want to do. You may not use a calculator.

1. Luis has 15 quarters and 22 dimes. What is the dollar value of these coins?

   (A) $4.95
   (B) $5.95
   (C) $5.85
   (D) $6.05

2. A pool has 4,856 gallons of water. How many gallons of water remain after 919 gallons are drained from the pool?

   (A) 3,917 gallons
   (B) 5,775 gallons
   (C) 3,937 gallons
   (D) 4,937 gallons

3. One mile is equal to 5,280 ft. Use this conversion to estimate the number of feet in 50 miles.

   (A) about 250,000 ft
   (B) about 350,000 ft
   (C) about 25,000 ft
   (D) about 300,000 ft

4. Cooking one package of noodles requires 3 cups of water. How many cups of water do you need to cook one and a half dozen packages of noodles?

   (A) 18 cups
   (B) 21 cups
   (C) 54 cups
   (D) 64 cups

5. A boat is carrying 40 passengers, 18 of whom are male. What is the ratio of male to female passengers?

   (A) $\frac{11}{9}$
   (B) $\frac{9}{11}$
   (C) $\frac{9}{20}$
   (D) $\frac{1}{2}$

6. Minnie earned $175 for 14 hours of work. What is her hourly pay rate?

   (A) $12.00
   (B) $9.50
   (C) $12.50
   (D) $13.25

7. Candace made 42 phone calls during the fundraiser. Fred made 6 fewer calls than Candace. How many calls did Fred make?

   (A) 36
   (B) 48
   (C) 7
   (D) 38

Go on to next page

8. A bicycle wheel has a diameter of 32 inches. When the bicycle is upright, how far is the center of the wheel from the ground?

(A) 8 in

(B) 24 in

(C) 64 in

(D) 16 in

9. A builder needs 420 nails to build a garage. The nails he wants come in boxes of 50. How many boxes of nails must he buy to build the garage?

(A) 8 boxes

(B) 42 boxes

(C) 9 boxes

(D) 5 boxes

10. Ricardo bought a bottle of flavored water for $2.25. He gave the cashier a $5 bill and got $3.25 in change. Which describes this transaction?

(A) Ricardo got $0.50 more change than he should have.

(B) Ricardo got $0.75 more change than he should have.

(C) Ricardo got the right amount of change.

(D) Ricardo got $0.50 less change than he should have.

11. Carl has a day job and a night job. He earns $9.50 an hour at the day job and $12 an hour at the night job. Last week he worked 8 hours at each job. How much more did he earn from his night job than his day job?

(A) $40

(B) $20

(C) $22

(D) $36

12. One hour into the potluck, there were $9\frac{1}{3}$ pies on the dessert table. Throughout the rest of the lunch, the guests ate $2\frac{1}{6}$ pies. How many pies were left on the table at the end of the potluck?

(A) $7\frac{1}{6}$

(B) $6\frac{1}{6}$

(C) $7\frac{1}{3}$

(D) $6\frac{1}{7}$

13. A sheet of construction paper is three-eighteths of an inch thick. A ream of this paper has 240 sheets. How thick is a ream of paper?

(A) 6 in

(B) 4.5 in

(C) 9 in

(D) 18 in

14. Mr. Franklin invests $4,000 into a savings account. After one year, he earns $200 in interest. What is the annual interest rate for the account?

(A) 5.5 percent

(B) 4.5 percent

(C) 5 percent

(D) 20 percent

15. How far will a car travel in 90 minutes if it is traveling at a constant speed of 70 miles per hour?

(A) 115 miles

(B) 95 miles

(C) 100 miles

(D) 105 miles

16. The weight in pounds of five different rocks is 8.1, 7.2, 6.5, 4.4, and 10.3. What is the average of the weights of these rocks?

(A) 7.6 pounds

(B) 6.5 pounds

(C) 7 pounds

(D) 7.3 pounds

17. At 3:30 p.m., the outside temperature was –12° Fahrenheit. By 4:45 p.m., the temperature dropped another 8° Fahrenheit. What was the temperature at 4:45 p.m.?

(A) –20° Fahrenheit

(B) –4° Fahrenheit

(C) –10° Fahrenheit

(D) 4° Fahrenheit

Go on to next page

18. One ounce is equal to about 28 grams. Roughly how many grams are in $1\frac{1}{5}$ ounces?

    (A) $29\frac{3}{5}$ grams

    (B) $33\frac{1}{5}$ grams

    (C) $33\frac{3}{5}$ grams

    (D) $35\frac{4}{5}$ grams

19. To ride the roller coaster, a person's height (x) in inches must satisfy the inequality $2x - 84 > 0$. A person with which height cannot ride the roller coaster?

    (A) 43 in

    (B) 42 in

    (C) 46 in

    (D) 62 in

20. The bed of a flatbed truck is in the shape of a rectangle and has an area of 72 square feet. What is the perimeter of the flatbed if the width is 6 feet?

    (A) 42 ft

    (B) 36 ft

    (C) 18 ft

    (D) 60 ft

21. Patrick charges $1.25 for every square foot of wall that he paints. A rectangular wall has a length of 25 feet and a height of 10 feet. How much will Patrick charge to paint this wall?

    (A) $325.50

    (B) $315.00

    (C) $312.50

    (D) $316.75

22. A coat that originally sold for $80 is on sale at a 20 percent discount. What is the discount price of the coat?

    (A) $60.00

    (B) $64.00

    (C) $72.00

    (D) $56.00

23. James is twice as old as Kiki. In 5 years, the sum of their ages will be 28. How old is James now?

    (A) 14

    (B) 6

    (C) 16

    (D) 12

24. A rectangular playground is 5 yards longer than it is wide. Its area is 300 square yards. What is the length of the playground?

    (A) 15 yd

    (B) 20 yd

    (C) 14 yd

    (D) 25 yd

25. A car lot has 140 new vehicles for sale. The graph shows the percent of the cars that are available in blue, yellow, green, and red. How many more blue cars are available than red cars?

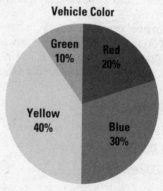

Vehicle Color

Illustration by Thomson Digital

    (A) 42

    (B) 28

    (C) 14

    (D) 40

Go on to next page

26. Convert $-15°C$ to degrees Fahrenheit. Use the formula $\frac{9}{5}C + 32°$.

   (A) $5°$ Fahrenheit

   (B) $10°$ Fahrenheit

   (C) $-10°$ Fahrenheit

   (D) $59°$ Fahrenheit

27. At a grocery store, hot dogs come in packages of 8; hot dog buns come in packages of 6; and small bags of chips come in packages of 16. How many packages of each do you need to buy so you have an equal number of hot dogs, hot dog buns, and bags of chips?

   (A) 8 packages of hot dogs, 6 packages of buns, and 3 packages of chips

   (B) 6 packages of hot dogs, 8 packages of buns, and 4 packages of chips

   (C) 6 packages of hot dogs, 8 packages of buns, and 3 packages of chips

   (D) 8 packages of hot dogs, 8 packages of buns, and 12 packages of chips

28. Each wheel on Adam's bicycle has a diameter of 20 inches. When riding down his driveway, Adam moved exactly 6,280 inches. How many full revolutions did each wheel make during his trip?

   (A) 50 revolutions

   (B) 100 revolutions

   (C) 1,000 revolutions

   (D) 500 revolutions

29. Alexa is selling carnival tickets. Each adult ticket costs 40 percent more than a child's ticket. She's sold 10 child tickets and 12 adult tickets for $134. How much does a single adult ticket cost?

   (A) $12

   (B) $8

   (C) $5

   (D) $7

30. A parking meter contains $3.40 in quarters, dimes, and nickels. There are 8 nickels and twice as many quarters as dimes. How many quarters are in the parking meter?

   (A) 10 quarters

   (B) 5 quarters

   (C) 15 quarters

   (D) 8 quarters

STOP DO NOT TURN THE PAGE UNTIL TOLD TO DO SO.
DO NOT RETURN TO A PREVIOUS TEST.

Part 2

Word Knowledge

Time: 11 minutes for 35 questions

Directions: The Word Knowledge subtest is the third subtest of the ASVAB. The questions are designed to measure your vocabulary knowledge. You'll see three types of questions on this subtest. The first type simply asks you to choose a word or words that most nearly mean the same as the underlined word in the question. The second type includes an underlined word used in a sentence, and you are to choose the word or words that most nearly mean the same as the underlined word, as used in the context of the sentence. The third type of question asks you to choose the word that has the opposite or nearly opposite meaning as the underlined word. Each question is followed by four possible answers. Decide which answer is correct, and then mark the corresponding space on your answer sheet.

1. Perjury most nearly means:

    (A) order

    (B) remark

    (C) oath

    (D) lie

2. Dynamic most nearly means:

    (A) special

    (B) vibrant

    (C) ordinary

    (D) dull

3. The word most opposite in meaning to abandon is

    (A) discard

    (B) maintain

    (C) remove

    (D) become

4. Momentous most nearly means:

    (A) major

    (B) minute

    (C) heavy

    (D) brief

5. Vital most nearly means:

    (A) perfect

    (B) intentional

    (C) critical

    (D) deep

6. Drone most nearly means:

    (A) shout

    (B) hum

    (C) cackle

    (D) engage

7. Stifle most nearly means:

    (A) regurgitate

    (B) reward

    (C) release

    (D) restrain

8. Caroline's new apartment was small but very quaint.

    (A) grand

    (B) charming

    (C) boring

    (D) outlandish

9. Trying to teach the old dog new tricks is futile.

    (A) worthy

    (B) robust

    (C) pointless

    (D) doomed

Go on to next page

10. The student's essay about Martians at Thanksgiving was pure <u>drivel</u>.

    (A) poetry

    (B) nonsense

    (C) logic

    (D) fantasy

11. The chef tried to change the negative <u>stereotype</u> against vegetarian cooks.

    (A) label

    (B) identity

    (C) lie

    (D) characteristic

12. The word most opposite in meaning to <u>betray</u> is

    (A) protect

    (B) deceive

    (C) annoy

    (D) rely

13. <u>Amble</u> most nearly means:

    (A) stroll

    (B) navigate

    (C) accelerate

    (D) rush

14. The skier wanted to <u>garner</u> a few more medals at this year's event.

    (A) cherish

    (B) generate

    (C) gain

    (D) display

15. The flat, <u>monotonous</u> section of the cross-country course challenged even the most enthusiastic runners.

    (A) varied

    (B) manic

    (C) exciting

    (D) dull

16. The politician's promises were <u>dubious</u> because of his checkered past.

    (A) honest

    (B) questionable

    (C) forthright

    (D) manipulative

17. <u>Quarantine</u> most nearly means:

    (A) gather

    (B) reunite

    (C) isolate

    (D) dispel

18. The word most opposite in meaning to <u>endorse</u> is

    (A) condemn

    (B) approve

    (C) promote

    (D) quibble

19. <u>Mitigate</u> most nearly means:

    (A) concede

    (B) enhance

    (C) reduce

    (D) support

20. Faith was so <u>complacent</u> with her life that she frequently passed up new opportunities.

    (A) content

    (B) unsatisfied

    (C) daring

    (D) concerned

21. The word most opposite in meaning to <u>dominate</u> is

    (A) control

    (B) govern

    (C) surrender

    (D) ignore

22. The police officer had to <u>commandeer</u> Julie's bike during a foot chase.

    (A) portray

    (B) seize

    (C) divide

    (D) return

23. <u>Vindicate</u> most nearly means:

    (A) succeed

    (B) blame

    (C) win

    (D) justify

Go on to next page

24. Mrs. Magan was a <u>staunch</u> advocate for animal rights.

    (A) smelly

    (B) grotesque

    (C) devoted

    (D) bloated

25. The professor took off points for the <u>colloquial</u> content in the student's midterm paper.

    (A) unique

    (B) commonplace

    (C) avant garde

    (D) intellectual

26. <u>Atrophy</u> most nearly means:

    (A) shrivel

    (B) explode

    (C) tire

    (D) awaken

27. The authorities were on the hunt for the <u>insurgent</u> behind the uprising.

    (A) scout

    (B) partner

    (C) scapegoat

    (D) rebel

28. The choreographer requested they <u>augment</u> the music with a longer section to fit the routine.

    (A) replace

    (B) enlarge

    (C) trade

    (D) diminish

29. <u>Intermittent</u> most nearly means:

    (A) regular

    (B) variable

    (C) uniform

    (D) abnormal

30. The residents were in a <u>quandary</u> after the only bridge accessing their town was destroyed.

    (A) solution

    (B) puzzle

    (C) resolution

    (D) predicament

31. The doctor gave the diagnosis with a <u>stoic</u> demeanor.

    (A) intelligent

    (B) anxious

    (C) unemotional

    (D) overwrought

32. <u>Aversion</u> most nearly means:

    (A) distracter

    (B) dislike

    (C) goal

    (D) element

33. <u>Garish</u> most nearly means:

    (A) gaudy

    (B) frightening

    (C) boisterous

    (D) inappropriate

34. <u>Intrepid</u> most nearly means:

    (A) random

    (B) nervous

    (C) brave

    (D) fearful

35. The word most opposite in meaning to <u>vanquish</u> is

    (A) bemoan

    (B) conquer

    (C) crush

    (D) yield

STOP DO NOT TURN THE PAGE UNTIL TOLD TO DO SO.
DO NOT RETURN TO A PREVIOUS TEST.

Part 3

Paragraph Comprehension

Time: 13 minutes for 15 questions

Directions: Paragraph Comprehension is the fourth subtest on the ASVAB. The questions are designed to measure your ability to understand what you read. This section includes one or more paragraphs of reading material, followed by incomplete statements or questions. Read the paragraph and select the choice that best completes the statement or answers the question. Then mark the corresponding space on your answer sheet.

Questions 1 and 2 refer to the following passage.

People are often confused about the difference between the fiddle and the violin. The truth is that there's no difference except for the way they're played. Violins are often part of orchestras, and the music tends more toward classical and composed pieces. The sounds are played fluidly and in long notes. On the other hand, the fiddle is often played in country or bluegrass bands. The notes are more melodic and tend to be shorter and repetitive. Although they sound like separate instruments, the fiddle and violin are the same and can be played in both styles.

1. What is the main point of the passage?

   (A) The violin is not as popular as the fiddle.

   (B) Country music is more entertaining than classical music.

   (C) Violins are only used in orchestras.

   (D) Fiddles and violins are the same instrument.

2. In the passage, the term <u>fluidly</u> most nearly means

   (A) smoothly

   (B) roughly

   (C) staccato

   (D) broken

Question 3 refers to the following passage.

Acupuncture is becoming more accepted in modern society as a form of healing; however, the practice of acupuncture has been used for healing in the Eastern world for centuries. The Chinese first began the art of moving *qi* by applying pressure or creating a release in a *chakra,* or energy zone in the body, more than 2,000 years ago. Although acupuncture treatments have taken on a boutique quality, becoming popular features at full-service spas, the ideas behind this ancient form of healing have remained: Moving the stagnant or blocked *qi* in the body allows the life force to move freely and heal the body of physical ailments and medical conditions.

3. What is the author trying to convey with the phrase "boutique quality"?

   (A) Acupuncture is not done properly.

   (B) Acupuncture is done in hair salons.

   (C) Acupuncture has become trendy in spa settings.

   (D) Acupuncture is different in America.

Go on to next page

Questions 4 and 5 refer to the following passage.

Researchers from two leading universities in the United States have discovered what may be the answer to the prayers of many parents. Findings reveal that ingesting negligible amounts of peanuts or peanut proteins may help reduce the sensitivity of allergic reactions through contact. The number of children who suffer from peanut allergies in America is in the hundreds of thousands, and many parents live in fear of their children being exposed to peanut oil or other byproducts that could cause severe and sometimes deadly reactions. Researchers say that in order for this treatment to work, daily to weekly doses of peanut products may be required for up to four to five years.

4. How many children in America have peanut allergies?

    (A) less than 1,000

    (B) about 10,000

    (C) hundreds of thousands

    (D) just under a million

5. How could this research help parents of children with peanut allergies?

    (A) It means their children could eat peanuts again.

    (B) It could reduce their anxiety about exposure.

    (C) It could help pay for the medical treatment.

    (D) None of the above.

Question 6 refers to the following passage.

Residents of suburban communities throughout the western United States are becoming increasingly concerned about coming face-to-face with a mountain lion in their backyards. In the last year, mountain lions have been found prowling neighborhoods in Colorado, Utah, California, and other areas where urban and rural communities rest at the base or within mountainous regions. The main concern for these owners, according to a recent poll, is that their small pets will become prey for the wild animals. Although officials from the Department of Wildlife and Fisheries have provided strategies to protect households, such as clearing the ground of bushes and vegetation to remove possible hiding spots, they say the main cause of the problem is urban sprawl, which continues to displace mountain lions from their natural habitat.

6. According to the passage, why are mountain lions appearing in residential neighborhoods?

    (A) to hide in low bushes

    (B) to eat small pets

    (C) because of urban sprawl

    (D) to access better vegetation

Question 7 refers to the following passage.

Despite hailing from Chicago, Illinois, in 1927, the Harlem Globetrotters took the name of the Manhattan neighborhood to represent the African American community that was large and prevalent in Harlem, New York. However, the team known for its outlandish antics and moves on the basketball court didn't play in its namesake city until the late 1960s.

7. As used in this paragraph, <u>outlandish</u> most nearly means

    (A) run of the mill

    (B) perfect

    (C) bizarre

    (D) illegal

Go on to next page

Question 8 refers to the following passage.

Lou Gehrig was known in major league base-ball as "The Iron Horse" for his strength and prowess in the batter's box. Gehrig played first base for the New York Yankees from 1923 to 1938. He set many major-league baseball records, including most consecutive games played (2,130), that stood the test of time until the second half of the 20th century. His nickname turned out to be quite ironic after the famed Yankee was diagnosed with a debilitating and fatal disease (now referred to as Lou Gehrig's disease) that attacks the central nervous system. The disease all but shuts down motor function, though the sufferer's mind remains coherent. The greatest first baseman in the history of base-ball died in 1941, two years after his diagnosis.

8. How many years did Lou Gehrig play major league baseball?

(A) 2,130

(B) 15

(C) 38

(D) 20

Questions 9 and 10 refer to the following passage.

Learning to ski is much different for children than for adults. First, adults have farther to fall, so the fear factor is greater. Second, children are still learning about their coordination and can adjust their body positions more quickly than adults can. Third, children follow directions better than adults do. Fourth, adults have a life-time of injuries that make them afraid of getting hurt, and they heal more slowly than children do. Fifth, children don't worry about health insurance and hefty medical bills if they get hurt.

9. What is the author saying about children in this passage?

(A) They are more talented.

(B) They are better skiers.

(C) They learn to ski more easily.

(D) They are better at sports.

10. According to the passage, what would make learning to ski easier for adults?

(A) being less fearful

(B) better directions

(C) lessons

(D) better equipment

Question 11 refers to the following passage.

The drive-in movie theater industry was once a booming pastime, but since its heyday in the late 1950s, the number of drive-ins has been reduced by almost 90 percent. Once a fun week-end activity with the family or a hangout for teens, the drive-in has been reduced to only 500 viable theaters around the country. Experts say that one of the main causes of drive-in decline is growing real estate prices. Perhaps if landowners appreci-ated the piece of history they had on their prop-erty, they would help keep these relics alive for families and teens to enjoy forever.

11. The author is using the word <u>heyday</u> to mean

(A) end

(B) prime

(C) country

(D) farm

Question 12 refers to the following passage.

Fidgety children lined in front of the build-ing, eager parents pacing by their sides. Some of the kids were talking to themselves, and some were counting on their fingers or being quizzed by their parents. But on everyone's face was the anticipation of greatness. The national spelling bee was only moments away.

12. According to the passage, some of the children waiting to compete in the spelling bee seemed

(A) bored

(B) calm

(C) nervous

(D) spoiled

Go on to next page

Questions 13 and 14 refer to the following passage.

Perhaps the most famous gymnast of all time is Romanian Nadia Comaneci, who was the first female gymnast to receive a perfect ten score in an Olympic gymnastics competition. She did so at the 1976 Olympic Games in Montreal, Quebec, where she achieved the feat seven times. Her strong suits were the uneven bars and the balance beam, but she often won the top place in the vault and, less often, the floor routine. After her coaches defected during a tour in the United States in 1981, Comaneci, seen as a Romanian national treasure, was heavily guarded and forbidden to travel. She finally found her freedom in 1989 when she defected to the United States. She eventually found a new home in Canada, but she will always be remembered as the 14-year-old phenomenon at the Summer Olympics.

13. Why was Nadia Comaneci considered a phenomenon at the Summer Olympic Games?

    (A) She was from Romania.

    (B) She excelled at the vault.

    (C) She was the youngest gymnast to compete.

    (D) She achieved the highest score given in Olympic gymnastics.

14. In what year did Nadia Comaneci defect from Romania?

    (A) 1989

    (B) 1976

    (C) 1980

    (D) 1981

Question 15 refers to the following passage.

Natural gas vehicles (NGVs) are good not only for the environment but also for drivers' wallets. They offer cleaner emissions and better gas mileage than gasoline-burning vehicles, and the price of a gallon of compressed natural gas is more than $1 cheaper than a gallon of gasoline. However, only slightly more than 100,000 NGVs are on the roads in the United States. If Americans knew about these savings, they would likely purchase more NGVs.

15. According to the passage, why do most Americans drive gasoline-burning vehicles?

    (A) lack of knowledge about prices

    (B) preference for fossil fuel emissions

    (C) inability to drive them

    (D) high cost of natural gas

STOP DO NOT TURN THE PAGE UNTIL TOLD TO DO SO. DO NOT RETURN TO A PREVIOUS TEST.

Part 4
Mathematics Knowledge

Time: 24 minutes for 25 questions

Directions: Mathematics Knowledge is the fifth subtest on the ASVAB. The questions are designed to test your ability to solve general mathematical problems. Each question is followed by four possible answers. Decide which answer is correct, and then mark the corresponding space on your answer sheet. Use your scratch paper for any figuring you want to do. You may not use a calculator.

1. $45 - 6 + 15 =$

   (A) 24

   (B) 54

   (C) 35

   (D) 0

2. What is 30 percent of 720?

   (A) 216

   (B) 21.6

   (C) 44

   (D) 12.6

3. In the logarithm 7.13824, what is the 7 called?

   (A) conversion

   (B) mantissa

   (C) decimal

   (D) characteristic

4. Express the decimal 0.026 as a percent.

   (A) 2.6 percent

   (B) 0.26 percent

   (C) 26 percent

   (D) 260 percent

5. What is 234,678 rounded to the nearest thousand?

   (A) 234,700

   (B) 230,000

   (C) 235,000

   (D) 200,000

6. In the decimal 845.721, which digit is in the hundredths place?

   (A) 8

   (B) 4

   (C) 7

   (D) 2

7. $4! =$

   (A) 12

   (B) 24

   (C) 120

   (D) 9

8. Evaluate $\frac{m}{-7}$ if $m = 28$.

   (A) -4

   (B) 4

   (C) 21

   (D) -21

9. Solve: $-55 = m - 17$

   (A) -38

   (B) 38

   (C) -72

   (D) 935

10. What is the percent increase when 20 is increased to 23?

   (A) 3 percent

   (B) 17 percent

   (C) 15 percent

   (D) 7.5 percent

Go on to next page

11. Write 0.00000436 using scientific notation.

    (A) 4.36×10^6

    (B) 4.36×10^{-5}

    (C) 436×10^{-6}

    (D) 4.36×10^{-6}

12. Which point has coordinates (–3, 2)?

    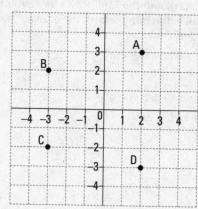

    Illustration by Thomson Digital

    (A) Point A

    (B) Point B

    (C) Point C

    (D) Point D

13. $5\frac{1}{3} - 4\frac{1}{2} = ?$

    (A) $\frac{1}{6}$

    (B) $1\frac{1}{6}$

    (C) $\frac{5}{6}$

    (D) $1\frac{1}{5}$

14. Simplify: $7(-3m)$

    (A) $4m$

    (B) $-3 + 7m$

    (C) $21m$

    (D) $-21m$

15. The lengths of the three sides of a triangle are 14, y, and 6. Which could be a value of y?

    (A) 19

    (B) 21

    (C) 25

    (D) 31

16. $10 + 2(5 - 3)^2 =$

    (A) 48

    (B) 18

    (C) 26

    (D) 36

17. What is 12 divided by $\frac{3}{4}$?

    (A) $12\frac{3}{4}$

    (B) 9

    (C) 16

    (D) $\frac{1}{16}$

18. $p^4 = \sqrt{x}$

    (A) p^{16}

    (B) p^2

    (C) p^8

    (D) p^4

19. A number is equal to 12 less than the product of 4 and –2.5. What is the number?

    (A) –2

    (B) –22

    (C) 2

    (D) 22

20. What are the measures of the three angles of the triangle?

    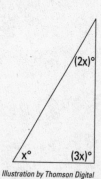

    Illustration by Thomson Digital

    (A) 30°, 75°, 75°

    (B) 36°, 72°, 108°

    (C) 36°, 54°, 90°

    (D) 30°, 60°, 90°

Go on to next page

21. $(3x^2 - 4x + y) - (2y - 6x^2) =$

    (A) $9x^2 - 4x - y$

    (B) $-3x^2 - 4x - y$

    (C) $9x^2 - 4x + y$

    (D) $-3x^2 - 4x + y$

22. What is the quotient of 4.8×10^{-4} and 1.2×10^{-9}?

    (A) 2.5×10^{-3}

    (B) 4×10^5

    (C) 4×10^{-5}

    (D) 4×10^{-13}

23. $\sqrt{66 - 2 \cdot 5^2} = ?$

    (A) $\sqrt{44}$

    (B) 10

    (C) 4

    (D) 40

24. Evaluate $\dfrac{45}{x} - \dfrac{39}{y}$ if $x = -5$ and $y = 3$.

    (A) 4

    (B) –4

    (C) 22

    (D) –22

25. The radius of a circle is m centimeters. The radius of another circle is $3 + m$ centimeters. What is the difference of the areas of the two circles?

    (A) $(9m\pi + 6\pi)$ cm^2

    (B) 9π cm^2

    (C) $(9\pi + 6m\pi)$ cm^2

    (D) $54m^2\pi$ cm^2

STOP DO NOT TURN THE PAGE UNTIL TOLD TO DO SO.
DO NOT RETURN TO A PREVIOUS TEST.

Chapter 17

Practice Exam 3: Answers and Explanations

● ●

A re you getting tired of math and English yet? I certainly hope not. If you still want more practice after finishing the exams in this book, I recommend you head to your favorite book seller and pick up a copy of *ASVAB For Dummies,* written by yours truly (published by Wiley).

Use the answer keys in the following sections to find out how you did on the AFQT practice exam in Chapter 16. The accompanying explanations tell you how to get to the correct answer if you got somewhat lost along the way.

Part 1: Arithmetic Reasoning

If you already took three practice AFQT exams, and the temperature is a steady 87 degrees, what is the probability that you got most of the questions right on all four subtests? Okay, that's not a real arithmetic reasoning question (insufficient data, as my computer friends say), but I'm betting you've done pretty well. Now it's time to see how you did on this Arithmetic Reasoning practice subtest.

If you need more practice doing arithmetic reasoning–type problems, Chapters 8 and 10 are a good place to start. You can also check out *Math Word Problems For Dummies, Algebra I For Dummies,* and *Algebra II For Dummies,* all by Mary Jane Sterling; *Geometry For Dummies,* 2nd Edition, and *Calculus For Dummies,* both by Mark Ryan; and *SAT II Math For Dummies,* by Scott Hatch, JD, and Lisa Zimmer Hatch, MA — all published by Wiley.

1. **B. $5.95**

    Because you want dollar values, write the value of a quarter as $0.25 and the value of a dime as $0.10. The value of the quarters is 15($0.25) = $3.75, and the value of the dimes is 22($0.10) = $2.20. Add to find the answer: $3.75 + $2.20 = $5.95.

2. **C. 3,937 gallons**

    This problem just uses simple subtraction. However, remember that this subtraction involves borrowing.

$$\begin{array}{r} {\scriptstyle 3\ \ 18\ \ 4\ \ 16} \\ 4,8\,5\,6 \\ -\ \ 9\,1\,9 \\ \hline 3,9\,3\,7 \end{array}$$

3. **A. 250,000 ft**

    Because you're estimating, you don't actually need to multiply 5,280 by 50. Instead, round 5,280 down to 5,000 and then multiply: 50(5,000) = 250,000.

4. **C. 54 cups**

One dozen is equal to 12 packages, and half of a dozen is 6 packages. So you want to find out how much water you need for 12 + 6 = 18 packages of noodles. Multiply to find the answer: 3(18) = 54.

5. **B. $\frac{9}{11}$**

To find this ratio, you need to find the number of female passengers by subtracting the number of males from the total number of passengers: 40 − 18 = 22 female passengers. Write the ratio of male to female passengers by using a fraction. Simplify by dividing the numerator and denominator by their greatest common factor (GCF, the largest number that will go into both), which is 2:

$$\frac{male}{female} = \frac{18}{22} = \frac{18 \div 2}{22 \div 2} = \frac{9}{11}$$

6. **C. $12.50**

To find her hourly pay rate, you need to divide 175 by 14:

$$
\begin{array}{r}
12.5 \\
14\overline{)175.0} \\
-14 \\
\hline
35 \\
-28 \\
\hline
70 \\
-70 \\
\hline
0
\end{array}
$$

Her pay rate is $12.50 an hour.

7. **A. 36**

If Fred made 6 fewer calls than Candace, you subtract 6 from 42 to find out how many calls Fred made: 42 − 6 = 36.

8. **D. 16 in**

The distance between the center of the wheel and the outside of the wheel (where the wheel touches the ground) is the radius. A circle's radius equals half its diameter, so the center is 16 inches from the ground.

9. **C. 9 boxes**

Divide 420 by 50 to find out how many whole boxes of nails the builder needs: $420 \div 50 = 8$ with a remainder of 20. So eight boxes aren't enough for the project because the builder still needs 20 more nails. The builder needs 9 boxes.

10. **A. Ricardo got $0.50 more change than he should have.**

Subtract $2.25 from $5 to find the correct amount of change Ricardo should have received: $5 − $2.25 = $2.75. Compare this amount to the change Ricardo actually received ($3.25) to see that he received too much in change. Subtract $2.75 from $3.25 to find the amount of the discrepancy: $3.25 − $2.75 = $0.50.

11. **B. $20**

Multiply to find out how much Carl earned at his day job: 8($9.50) = $76. Multiply again to find out how much he earned at his night job: 8($12) = $96. So he earned $96 − $76 = $20 more at his night job last week.

12. **A. $7\dfrac{1}{6}$**

Write each mixed number as an improper fraction:

$$9\frac{1}{3} = \frac{3 \times 9 + 1}{3} = \frac{27 + 1}{3} = \frac{28}{3}$$

$$2\frac{1}{6} = \frac{6 \times 2 + 1}{6} = \frac{12 + 1}{6} = \frac{13}{6}$$

Subtract to find how many pies remain. The common denominator is 6, so don't forget to multiply the numerator and denominator of that first fraction by 2:

$$\frac{28}{3} - \frac{13}{6} = \frac{56}{6} - \frac{13}{6}$$
$$= \frac{56 - 13}{6}$$
$$= \frac{43}{6}$$
$$= 7\frac{1}{6}$$

13. **C. 9 in.**

A fraction written in words isn't much help, so make it into a fraction: three-eightieths $= \dfrac{3}{80}$. Now multiply this fraction by 240 to find the answer:

$$\frac{3}{80} \cdot 240 = \frac{3}{_{1}\cancel{80}} \cdot \frac{\cancel{240}^{3}}{1} = \frac{9}{1} = 9$$

14. **C. 5 percent**

Use the interest formula, $I = Prt$, where I is the interest, P is the principal, r is the interest rate (as a decimal), and t is the time in years. Substitute the known values into the formula and solve for r.

$$200 = 4,000(r)(1)$$
$$200 = 4,000r$$
$$\frac{200}{4,000} = r$$
$$r = \frac{1}{20} = 0.05$$

Write 0.05 as a percent by moving the decimal point two places to the right: $0.05 = 5$ percent.

15. **D. 105 miles**

The first thing you should notice about this problem is that the speed is in miles per hour but the time traveled is in minutes. You can't solve the problem until you convert the minutes to hours. Fortunately, doing so for this problem is pretty simple: 90 minutes = 1.5 hours. Now you can plug the numbers into the distance formula, $d = rt$ (where d equals distance, r equals rate, and t equals time), using 1.5 for t:

$$d = 70(1.5) = 105 \text{ miles}$$

16. **D. 7.3 pounds**

    To find the average, add up all the weights and then divide by 5.

    $$\frac{8.1+7.2+6.5+4.4+10.3}{5}=\frac{36.5}{5}$$

    You can use long division to find the answer.

    $$
    \begin{array}{r}
    7.3 \\
    5\,\overline{)\,36.5} \\
    -35 \\
    \hline
    15 \\
    -15 \\
    \hline
    0
    \end{array}
    $$

    The average weight is 7.3 pounds.

17. **A. –20° Fahrenheit**

    When the temperature drops, it means you are subtracting. So you want to subtract 8° Fahrenheit from –12° Fahrenheit. If you find subtracting negatives a little confusing, think of it this way: Subtracting 8 from the point labeled –12 means moving 8 units below –12. So $-12 - 8 = -20$.

18. **C. $33\frac{3}{5}$ grams**

    Here, you need to multiply $1\frac{1}{5}$ by 28. But first, you want to write $1\frac{1}{5}$ as an improper fraction: $1\frac{1}{5}=\frac{5\times1+1}{5}=\frac{6}{5}$. Now you can multiply to get the answer:

    $$\frac{6}{5}\times28=\frac{6}{5}\times\frac{28}{1}=\frac{168}{5}=33\frac{3}{5}\text{ grams}$$

19. **B. 42 in**

    Solve the inequality by isolating x:

    $$
    \begin{aligned}
    2x-84&>0 \\
    2x&>84 \\
    x&>42
    \end{aligned}
    $$

    If a person's height x must be greater than 42, a person with a height of 42 inches can't ride the roller coaster.

    Make sure you read the questions carefully because the folks who write ASVAB questions construct them so you can get hung up on the details. For some questions, you might go back and read the question one more time after you work out the math to make sure you know what answer is expected.

20. **B. 36 ft**

    This problem uses two formulas. First, use the area formula, $A = lw$, to find the length l of the flatbed. Substitute known values into the formula and solve for l:

    $$
    \begin{aligned}
    A&=lw \\
    72&=l(6) \\
    \frac{72}{6}&=l \\
    12&=l
    \end{aligned}
    $$

Now substitute $w = 6$ and $l = 12$ into the perimeter formula, $P = 2l + 2w$:

$P = 2(12) + 2(6) = 24 + 12 = 36$ feet

21. C. $312.50

The formula to determine the area of a rectangle is $a = lw$. Substitute known values to find the area.

$a = 10 \times 25 = 250$ square ft.

Patrick charges $1.25 per square foot, so he'd require a total of $250(\$1.25) = \$312.50$ to paint the wall.

22. B. $64.00

The best way to solve this problem is to first find the amount of the discount: $0.2(80) = \$16$. Now you can subtract that amount from the original price to find the current cost: $\$80 - \$16 = \$64$.

23. D. 12

Let $x = $ Kiki's age. James is twice as old as Kiki, so his age is $2x$. Kiki's age in 5 years is $x + 5$, and James's age in 5 years is $2x + 5$. In 5 years, the sum of their ages is 28. Use these expressions to make an equation:

$$x + 5 + 2x + 5 = 28$$
$$3x + 10 = 28$$
$$3x = 18$$
$$x = 6$$

Because Kiki is 6 years old, James's age is $2(6) = 12$.

24. B. 20 yd

Let $x = $ the width of the playground. This means that the length is $x + 5$. The formula for the area of a rectangle is $a = lw$. Substitute all known values into the formula and simplify:

$$300 = x(x + 5)$$
$$300 = x^2 + 5x$$
$$0 = x^2 + 5x - 300$$

$x^2 + 5x - 300 = 0$ is a quadratic equation because it is in the form $ax^2 + bx + c = 0$. You can solve it by factoring. To factor $x^2 + 5x - 300$, you need to think of two numbers that multiply to be -300 and add to be 5. The only two numbers that fit this description are 20 and -15.

$$0 = x^2 + 5x - 300$$
$$0 = (x + 20)(x - 15)$$

Now set each factor equal to 0 and solve for x:

$$x + 20 = 0$$
$$x = -20$$
$$x - 15 = 0$$
$$x = 15$$

Because a distance can't be negative, the width is 15 yards. So the length is $15 + 5 = 20$ yards.

25. **C. 14**

First, find the number of blue cars in the lot. Because 30 percent of the cars in the lot are blue, the number of blue cars is equal to 0.3(140) = 42. Next, find the number of red cars in the lot. Because 20 percent of the cars in the lot are red, the number of red cars is 0.2(140) = 28. Now subtract the number of red cars from the number of blue cars: 42 – 28 = 14 more blue cars than red cars.

26. **A. 5° Fahrenheit**

First, divide –15 by 5. Remember that a negative number divided by a positive number is negative: $\frac{-15}{5} = -3$. Next, multiply the result by 9. Remember that a negative number times a positive number is negative: $-3(9) = -27$. For the final step, add 32 and –27. Remember that adding a negative is the same as subtracting a positive: $32 + (-27) = 32 - 27 = 5°F$.

27. **C. 6 packages of hot dogs, 8 packages of buns, and 3 packages of chips**

This problem involves finding the least common multiple, or LCM, of three numbers. To find the LCM, write out multiples of each number and find the first multiple that they all have in common:

Hot dogs: 8, 16, 24, 43, 40, 48

Buns: 6, 12, 18, 24, 30, 36, 42, 48

Chips: 16, 32, 48

The LCM of 8, 6, and 16 is 48, so you need 48 of each item. For each item, count how many multiples it took to get to 48:

Hot dogs: 8, 16, 24, 43, 40, 48 (6 packages)

Buns: 6, 12, 18, 24, 30, 36, 42, 48 (8 packages)

Chips: 16, 32, 48 (3 packages)

28. **B. 100 revolutions**

First, find the circumference of each wheel. The formula for the circumference of a circle is $C = \pi d$, so the circumference of a wheel is $C = 3.14(20) = 62.8$ inches. Every time a wheel makes a full revolution, the bicycle moves exactly 62.8 inches. Divide the total distance traveled by the circumference to find the total number of revolutions: $\frac{6,280}{62.8} = 100$. So each wheel made 100 full revolutions.

29. **D. $7**

Let x = the cost of a child's ticket. Alexa has sold a total of $10x$ dollars in children's tickets. An adult ticket costs 40 percent more, which is $0.4x$, so the cost of an adult ticket is $x + 0.4x = 1.4x$. So Alexa has sold $12(1.4x)$ dollars in adult tickets. Make an equation and solve for x:

$$10x + 12(1.4x) = 134$$
$$10x + 16.8x = 134$$
$$26.8x = 134$$
$$x = \frac{134}{26.8}$$
$$x = 5$$

Children's tickets sell for $5, so each adult ticket sells for 1.4(5) = $7.

30. **A. 10 quarters**

    Let q equal the number of quarters and d equal the number of dimes. The value of the quarters is $25q$, and value of the dimes is $10d$. Because you know there are 8 nickels, you know the value of the nickels is 5(8). The sum of the values of the quarters, dimes, and nickels is equal to 340. Write an equation:

    $$25q + 10d + 5(8) = 340$$

    Because there are twice as many quarters as there are dimes, you can substitute $q = 2d$ into the equation and solve for d:

    $$25\,(2d) + 10d + 5(8) = 340$$
    $$50d + 10d + 40 = 340$$
    $$60d + 40 = 340$$
    $$60d = 300$$
    $$d = 5$$

    There are 5 dimes, so there are 2(5) = 10 quarters.

Part 2: Word Knowledge

Scoring well on the Word Knowledge subtest is crucial to scoring high on the AFQT and getting into the military branch of your choice. If your score is weak in this area, spend time reviewing the material and improving your vocabulary (see Chapter 4).

Other great references that can help you improve your score in this area are *Vocabulary For Dummies,* by Laurie E. Rozakis, and *SAT Vocabulary For Dummies,* by Suzee Vlk (both published by Wiley). Plus, see Chapter 5 for more practice questions.

1. **D. lie**

    Perjury is a noun that means a lie told after taking an oath.

2. **B. vibrant**

    Used as an adjective, *dynamic* means full of energy and vigorous activity.

3. **B. maintain**

    Used as a verb, *abandon* means to cease or to leave behind.

4. **A. major**

    Momentous is an adjective that means extremely important or significant.

5. **C. critical**

    Vital is an adjective that describes something crucial or very important.

6. **B. hum**

    Used as a verb, *drone* means to make a low-pitched humming noise.

7. **D. restrain**

    Stifle is a verb that means to repress or prevent.

8. **B. charming**

   Quaint is an adjective that means having an old-fashioned or pleasant quality.

9. **C. pointless**

   Futile is an adjective that describes something useless or fruitless.

10. **B. nonsense**

    Drivel is a noun that means something foolish or without sense.

11. **A. label**

    Used as a noun, *stereotype* means an oversimplified categorization of a person or group.

12. **A. protect**

    Betray is a verb that means to harm or to be disloyal.

13. **A. stroll**

    Amble is a verb that means a leisurely walk for pleasure.

14. **C. gain**

    Garner is a verb that means to acquire or gather.

15. **D. dull**

    Monotonous is an adjective that means repetitive or dull.

16. **B. questionable**

    As used in this sentence, *dubious* is an adjective that describes something suspect or untrustworthy.

17. **C. isolate**

    Used as a verb, *quarantine* means to detain someone from the public or away from others.

18. **A. condemn**

    Endorse is a verb that means to give support to.

19. **C. reduce**

    Mitigate is a verb meaning to lessen or decrease.

20. **A. content**

    Complacent is an adjective that means unworried or self-satisfied.

21. **C. surrender**

    Dominate is a verb that means to take over or dictate.

22. **B. seize**

    Commandeer is a verb that means to take or confiscate something by force.

23. **D. justify**

    Vindicate is a verb that means to prove that something is correct or justified.

24. **C. devoted**

    Staunch is an adjective that means loyal or steadfast.

25. **B. commonplace**

    Colloquial is an adjective that describes something usual or informal.

26. **A. shrivel**

    Atrophy is a verb that means to waste away or deteriorate.

27. **D. rebel**

    Insurgent is a noun that represents somebody who rebels against authority.

28. **B. enlarge**

    Augment is a verb that means to add to something or to expand.

29. **B. variable**

    Intermittent is an adjective that means occurring at sporadic times.

30. **D. predicament**

    Quandary is a noun that represents a dilemma or difficult situation.

31. **C. unemotional**

    Stoic is an adjective that describes someone patient or impassive.

32. **B. dislike**

    Aversion is a noun that means a distaste for something.

33. **A. gaudy**

    Garish is an adjective that means overly ornate or bright.

34. **C. brave**

    Intrepid is an adjective that means courageous or fearless.

35. **D. yield**

    Vanquish is a verb that means to overcome or defeat.

Part 3: Paragraph Comprehension

Those ASVAB folks sure don't give you much time to read all those paragraphs, do they? But, with a little practice, anyone can improve his reading speed and comprehension skills. The material in Chapter 6 can be helpful in these endeavors. There are also more practice questions in Chapter 7.

1. **D. Fiddles and violins are the same instrument.**

    Both the opening and closing sentences in this paragraph state the main point. The different styles of music are secondary information.

2. **A. smoothly**

    Fluidly is an adjective that means gracefully or flowing.

3. **C. Acupuncture has become trendy in spa settings.**

   Although the passage doesn't directly define the term, the use of the term "popular" indicates that Choice (C) is the only choice that makes sense.

4. **C. hundreds of thousands**

   The passage says that the number of children with peanut allergies is in the "hundreds of thousands."

5. **B. It could reduce their anxiety about exposure.**

   The research mentioned in the passage indicates that reduced sensitivity is the possible outcome of the treatment. This reduced sensitivity helps decrease the risk of a negative reaction, which could relieve parents' concerns about a reaction from secondary sources of peanuts.

6. **C. because of urban sprawl**

   The last sentence in the passage specifically states that the main cause is urban sprawl, so you can quickly scan and find the answer if you don't remember it from reading.

7. **C. bizarre**

   Outlandish is an adjective that means peculiar or unusual.

8. **B. 15**

   The passage states that he played with the Yankees from 1923 to 1938. Simple subtraction finds you the correct answer.

9. **C. They learn to ski more easily.**

   The passage provides examples of why children learn to ski more quickly than adults do, but it makes no other judgments about their abilities.

10. **A. being less fearful**

    In the passage, many of the factors that make skiing more difficult for adults involve some kind of fear (fear of falling, fear of injury, fear of medical bills). None of the other answer choices fits the information in the passage.

11. **B. prime**

    Heyday is a noun that means at the height or top of a situation or timeline.

12. **C. nervous**

    The passage describes the fidgety behavior or last-minute preparation of the children as they wait in line. These are signs of nervousness.

13. **D. She achieved the highest score given in Olympic gymnastics.**

    The passage states that Comaneci was the first female gymnast to receive a perfect ten for her performance, which she did seven times at the Montreal games. Choice (D) provides this answer.

14. **A. 1989**

    You can find the answer to this question at the end of the passage, where it specifically states she "found her freedom in 1989 when she defected to the United States."

15. **A. lack of knowledge about prices**

    The passage states that more Americans would likely drive NGVs if they knew about the savings, so their lack of knowledge must be what's keeping them from getting on the NGV bandwagon.

Part 4: Mathematics Knowledge

Many people find the Mathematics Knowledge subtest to be more difficult than the Arithmetic Reasoning subtest, but doing well on this subtest is just as important. If you missed more than a few answers, or you ran out of time before you finished, you have a date with the books (Chapter 8 is a great place to start). Getting in touch with a math teacher at your high school or a local community college (or at least finding a good basic-algebra textbook) can help. You can also try out the following *For Dummies* books: *Algebra I For Dummies* and *Algebra II For Dummies*, both by Mary Jane Sterling; *Geometry For Dummies*, 2nd Edition, and *Calculus For Dummies*, both by Mark Ryan and *SAT II Math For Dummies*, by Scott Hatch (all published by Wiley). Chapter 9 also has some additional practice questions.

1. **B. 54**

   When a numerical expression just has addition and subtraction, you perform operations from left to right; in this problem, that means you subtract before adding. So $45 - 6 + 15 = 39 + 15 = 54$.

2. **A. 216**

   Write 30 percent as a decimal: 30 percent = 0.3. Multiply 0.3 by 720: $0.3(720) = 216$.

3. **D. characteristic**

   In a logarithm, the number to the left of the decimal (the whole number part) is called the *characteristic*. It shows the position of the decimal point in the associated number. (The numbers to the right of the decimal point are the *mantissa*, in case that question comes up on the actual test.)

4. **A. 2.6 percent**

   To turn a decimal into a percent, simply move the decimal point two places to the right (which is the same thing as multiplying by 100).

5. **C. 235,000**

   For the given number, 8 is in the ones place, 7 is in the tens place, 6 is in the hundreds place, and 4 is in the thousands place. You round 4 up to 5 because the digit one place to the right of it (6) is 5 or greater. So 234,678 rounds to 235,000.

6. **D. 2**

   The first digit after the decimal point is in the tenths place, and the second digit is in the hundredths place. So 2 is in the hundredths place.

7. **B. 24**

   4! means the factorial of 4. You find it by multiplying all the whole numbers from 1 to 4:

   $$4 \times 3 \times 2 \times 1 = 24$$

8. **A. −4**

   Evaluate means to substitute the given value of *m* into the expression and then simplify the result. Remember that a positive number divided by a negative number results in a negative number.

   $$\frac{28}{-7} = 28 \div (-7) = -4$$

9. **A. –38**

Isolate the variable, m, by adding 17 to each side of the equation.

$$-55 = m - 17$$
$$-55 + 17 = m$$
$$-38 = m$$

10. **C. 15 percent**

Subtract the original number from the new number to get the difference: $23 - 20 = 3$.

Then divide the difference (3) by the original number (20) to determine the percent increase: $3 \div 20 = 0.15 = 15$ percent.

11. **D. 4.36×10^{-6}**

A number written in scientific notation is a number between 1 and 10 multiplied by a power of 10. To make a number between 1 and 10, move the decimal point six places to the right to get 4.36. You find the power of 10 by taking the number of spaces you moved the decimal and determining whether it should be positive or negative based on which direction you moved it. Because you moved it to the right (that is, the given number is less than 1), the power of 10 must be negative: 10^{-6}.

12. **B. Point B**

First, notice that the x-coordinate is –3. This means that from the origin (0, 0), you move to the left three units. The y-coordinate is 2, so you then move up two units. That puts you at point B.

13. **C. $\frac{5}{6}$**

Write each mixed number as an improper fraction:

$$5\frac{1}{3} = \frac{3 \times 5 + 1}{3} = \frac{15 + 1}{3} = \frac{16}{3}$$
$$4\frac{1}{2} = \frac{2 \times 4 + 1}{2} = \frac{8 + 1}{2} = \frac{9}{2}$$

The common denominator is 6. Rewrite each fraction with the common denominator:

$$\frac{16}{3} - \frac{9}{2} = \frac{16 \cdot 2}{3 \cdot 2} - \frac{9 \cdot 3}{2 \cdot 3}$$
$$= \frac{32}{6} - \frac{27}{6}$$
$$= \frac{5}{6}$$

14. **D. $-21m$**

This is basically just three values being multiplied together: 7, –3, and m. However, because you don't know the value of m, you only need to multiply 7 and –3. Remember that a positive number times a negative number is a negative number:

$$7(-3m) = 7(-3)m = -21m$$

15. **A. 19**

In any triangle, any side length must be less than the sum of the other two side lengths. So that means y has to be less than $14 + 6 = 20$. All the answer choices are greater than 20 except 19.

16. **B. 18**

Use the order of operations, which says to simplify inside the parentheses first, compute all exponents next, multiply and divide from left to right after that, and then add and subtract from left to right:

$$10 + 2(5-3)^2 = 10 + 2(2)^2$$
$$= 10 + 2(4)$$
$$= 10 + 8$$
$$= 18$$

17. **C. 16**

Remember that dividing by a fraction is the same as multiplying by the reciprocal of the fraction. So dividing 12 by $\frac{3}{4}$ is the same as multiplying 12 by $\frac{4}{3}$.

$$12 \div \frac{3}{4} = 12 \times \frac{4}{3}$$
$$= \frac{12}{1} \times \frac{4}{3}$$
$$= \frac{48}{3}$$
$$= 16$$

18. **D. p^8**

A square root is a number that when multiplied by itself equals the number under the radical sign. When the base is the same, you add the exponents to multiply, so $p^4 \times p^4 = p^{4+4} = \sqrt{p^8}$.

19. **B. –22**

Let x = the number you want to find. Remembering that "12 less than the product" means to subtract 12 from the product, write an equation: $x = 4(-2.5) - 12$.

Now, solve the equation, following the order of operations by multiplying first and then subtracting:

$$x = 4(-2.5) - 12$$
$$x = -10 - 12$$
$$x = -22$$

20. **D. 30°, 60°, 90°**

Remember that for any triangle, the sum of the three angle measures is always 180°. You can make an equation by adding the three expressions shown in the diagram and setting the sum equal to 180°. Then, solve the equation.

$$x + 2x + 3x = 180$$
$$6x = 180$$
$$x = 30$$

So the measures of the angles are

$$x = 30°$$
$$(2x)° = (2 \cdot 30)° = 60°$$
$$(3x)° = (3 \cdot 30)° = 90°$$

21. **A. $9x^2 - 4x - y$**

For problems like this one, the first thing you want to do is remove the parentheses. Remember that when you have a subtraction sign to the left of a set of parentheses, you need to change the sign of all the terms inside the parentheses. Then combine like terms and simplify:

$$\left(3x^2 - 4x + y\right) - \left(2y - 6x^2\right) = 3x^2 - 4x + y - 2y + 6x^2$$
$$= 9x^2 - 4x - y$$

22. **B. 4×10^5**

First, write this problem as a fraction:

$$\frac{4.8 \times 10^{-4}}{1.2 \times 10^{-9}}$$

Now, separate that fraction into a product of two fractions:

$$\frac{4.8}{1.2} \times \frac{10^{-4}}{10^{-9}}$$

The first fraction simplifies to 4, because $4.8 \div 1.2 = 4$. Because the bases are the same in the second fraction, subtract the exponents:

$$\frac{4.8}{1.2} \times \frac{10^{-4}}{10^{-9}} = 4 \times 10^{-4-(-9)} = 4 \times 10^{-4+9} = 4 \times 10^5$$

23. **C. 4**

Simplify everything under the radical sign first, using the order of operations. For this problem, that means computing the exponent first, multiplying next, and then subtracting:

$$\sqrt{66 - 2 \cdot 5^2} = \sqrt{66 - 2 \cdot 25}$$
$$= \sqrt{66 - 50}$$
$$= \sqrt{16}$$

Then, find the square root of the result:

$$\sqrt{16} = 4.$$

24. **D. –22**

First, substitute the given values of x and y into the expression: $\frac{45}{-5} - \frac{39}{3}$. Then use the order of operations to simplify. Remember that you have to divide the fractions before you subtract. Also, remember that a positive number divided by a negative number produces a negative number:

$$\frac{45}{-5} - \frac{39}{3} = 45 \div (-5) - 39 \div 3$$
$$= -9 - 13$$
$$= -22$$

25. **C. $(9\pi + 6m\pi)$ cm^2**

A good strategy for this problem is to find the area of each circle and then subtract. Use formula for the area of a circle, $A = \pi r^2$.

Area of smaller circle:

$$A_1 = \pi \cdot m^2 = m^2\pi$$

Area of larger circle:

$$\begin{aligned} A_2 &= \pi(3+m)^2 \\ &= \pi\,(3+m)(3+m) \\ &= \pi\,(9+6m+m^2) \\ &= \pi \cdot 9 + \pi \cdot 6m + \pi \cdot m^2 \\ &= 9\pi + 6m\pi + m^2\pi \end{aligned}$$

Now subtract the area of the smaller circle from the area of the larger circle:

$$9\pi + 6m\pi + m^2\pi - m^2\pi = 9\pi + 6m\pi.$$

Answer Key

Part 1: Arithmetic Reasoning

1. B	7. A	13. C	19. B	25. C
2. C	8. D	14. C	20. B	26. A
3. A	9. C	15. D	21. C	27. C
4. C	10. A	16. D	22. B	28. B
5. B	11. B	17. A	23. D	29. D
6. C	12. A	18. C	24. B	30. A

Part 2: Word Knowledge

1. D	8. B	15. D	22. B	29. B
2. B	9. C	16. B	23. D	30. D
3. B	10. B	17. C	24. C	31. C
4. A	11. A	18. A	25. B	32. B
5. C	12. A	19. C	26. A	33. A
6. B	13. A	20. A	27. D	34. C
7. D	14. C	21. C	28. B	35. D

Part 3: Paragraph Comprehension

1. D	4. C	7. C	10. A	13. D
2. A	5. B	8. B	11. B	14. A
3. C	6. C	9. C	12. C	15. A

Part 4: Mathematics Knowledge

1. B	6. D	11. D	16. B	21. A
2. A	7. B	12. B	17. C	22. B
3. D	8. A	13. C	18. D	23. C
4. A	9. A	14. D	19. B	24. D
5. C	10. C	15. A	20. D	25. C

Chapter 18

Practice Exam 4

· ·

*W*hen you've taken all four practice AFQT exams in this book, you should be ready to tackle the actual Armed Services Vocational Aptitude Battery (ASVAB) and impress all those military recruiters when you ace the four subtests that make up the AFQT. If you still want some more practice after this exam, or you want to study for the other ASVAB sub-tests as well, might I humbly suggest *ASVAB For Dummies* (Wiley)?

The four sections that follow represent the four subtests of the ASVAB that make up your all-important AFQT score. This is the score that determines whether you're qualified to join the military branch of your choice (see Chapter 2). The four subtests are Arithmetic Reasoning, Word Knowledge, Paragraph Comprehension, and Mathematics Knowledge.

Use the answer key and explanations in Chapter 19 to score the following sections. *Remember:* On the actual ASVAB, harder questions are worth more points than easier questions when you determine your AFQT score.

Take the final practice exam a day or two before the ASVAB to make sure you're ready and to boost your confidence. If you don't score well, you may want to consider asking your recruiter to reschedule your ASVAB test for a later date to give you more time to study.

Ready to get started? Okay, hold your No. 2 pencil in the air. (Not really — your friends might start talking about you). Ready, set, go!

Answer Sheet for Practice Exam 4

Part 1: Arithmetic Reasoning

1. Ⓐ Ⓑ Ⓒ Ⓓ   8. Ⓐ Ⓑ Ⓒ Ⓓ   15. Ⓐ Ⓑ Ⓒ Ⓓ   22. Ⓐ Ⓑ Ⓒ Ⓓ   29. Ⓐ Ⓑ Ⓒ Ⓓ
2. Ⓐ Ⓑ Ⓒ Ⓓ   9. Ⓐ Ⓑ Ⓒ Ⓓ   16. Ⓐ Ⓑ Ⓒ Ⓓ   23. Ⓐ Ⓑ Ⓒ Ⓓ   30. Ⓐ Ⓑ Ⓒ Ⓓ
3. Ⓐ Ⓑ Ⓒ Ⓓ   10. Ⓐ Ⓑ Ⓒ Ⓓ   17. Ⓐ Ⓑ Ⓒ Ⓓ   24. Ⓐ Ⓑ Ⓒ Ⓓ
4. Ⓐ Ⓑ Ⓒ Ⓓ   11. Ⓐ Ⓑ Ⓒ Ⓓ   18. Ⓐ Ⓑ Ⓒ Ⓓ   25. Ⓐ Ⓑ Ⓒ Ⓓ
5. Ⓐ Ⓑ Ⓒ Ⓓ   12. Ⓐ Ⓑ Ⓒ Ⓓ   19. Ⓐ Ⓑ Ⓒ Ⓓ   26. Ⓐ Ⓑ Ⓒ Ⓓ
6. Ⓐ Ⓑ Ⓒ Ⓓ   13. Ⓐ Ⓑ Ⓒ Ⓓ   20. Ⓐ Ⓑ Ⓒ Ⓓ   27. Ⓐ Ⓑ Ⓒ Ⓓ
7. Ⓐ Ⓑ Ⓒ Ⓓ   14. Ⓐ Ⓑ Ⓒ Ⓓ   21. Ⓐ Ⓑ Ⓒ Ⓓ   28. Ⓐ Ⓑ Ⓒ Ⓓ

Part 2: Word Knowledge

1. Ⓐ Ⓑ Ⓒ Ⓓ   8. Ⓐ Ⓑ Ⓒ Ⓓ   15. Ⓐ Ⓑ Ⓒ Ⓓ   22. Ⓐ Ⓑ Ⓒ Ⓓ   29. Ⓐ Ⓑ Ⓒ Ⓓ
2. Ⓐ Ⓑ Ⓒ Ⓓ   9. Ⓐ Ⓑ Ⓒ Ⓓ   16. Ⓐ Ⓑ Ⓒ Ⓓ   23. Ⓐ Ⓑ Ⓒ Ⓓ   30. Ⓐ Ⓑ Ⓒ Ⓓ
3. Ⓐ Ⓑ Ⓒ Ⓓ   10. Ⓐ Ⓑ Ⓒ Ⓓ   17. Ⓐ Ⓑ Ⓒ Ⓓ   24. Ⓐ Ⓑ Ⓒ Ⓓ   31. Ⓐ Ⓑ Ⓒ Ⓓ
4. Ⓐ Ⓑ Ⓒ Ⓓ   11. Ⓐ Ⓑ Ⓒ Ⓓ   18. Ⓐ Ⓑ Ⓒ Ⓓ   25. Ⓐ Ⓑ Ⓒ Ⓓ   32. Ⓐ Ⓑ Ⓒ Ⓓ
5. Ⓐ Ⓑ Ⓒ Ⓓ   12. Ⓐ Ⓑ Ⓒ Ⓓ   19. Ⓐ Ⓑ Ⓒ Ⓓ   26. Ⓐ Ⓑ Ⓒ Ⓓ   33. Ⓐ Ⓑ Ⓒ Ⓓ
6. Ⓐ Ⓑ Ⓒ Ⓓ   13. Ⓐ Ⓑ Ⓒ Ⓓ   20. Ⓐ Ⓑ Ⓒ Ⓓ   27. Ⓐ Ⓑ Ⓒ Ⓓ   34. Ⓐ Ⓑ Ⓒ Ⓓ
7. Ⓐ Ⓑ Ⓒ Ⓓ   14. Ⓐ Ⓑ Ⓒ Ⓓ   21. Ⓐ Ⓑ Ⓒ Ⓓ   28. Ⓐ Ⓑ Ⓒ Ⓓ   35. Ⓐ Ⓑ Ⓒ Ⓓ

Part 3: Paragraph Comprehension

1. (A) (B) (C) (D)   8. (A) (B) (C) (D)   15. (A) (B) (C) (D)
2. (A) (B) (C) (D)   9. (A) (B) (C) (D)
3. (A) (B) (C) (D)   10. (A) (B) (C) (D)
4. (A) (B) (C) (D)   11. (A) (B) (C) (D)
5. (A) (B) (C) (D)   12. (A) (B) (C) (D)
6. (A) (B) (C) (D)   13. (A) (B) (C) (D)
7. (A) (B) (C) (D)   14. (A) (B) (C) (D)

Part 4: Mathematics Knowledge

1. (A) (B) (C) (D)   8. (A) (B) (C) (D)   15. (A) (B) (C) (D)   22. (A) (B) (C) (D)
2. (A) (B) (C) (D)   9. (A) (B) (C) (D)   16. (A) (B) (C) (D)   23. (A) (B) (C) (D)
3. (A) (B) (C) (D)   10. (A) (B) (C) (D)   17. (A) (B) (C) (D)   24. (A) (B) (C) (D)
4. (A) (B) (C) (D)   11. (A) (B) (C) (D)   18. (A) (B) (C) (D)   25. (A) (B) (C) (D)
5. (A) (B) (C) (D)   12. (A) (B) (C) (D)   19. (A) (B) (C) (D)
6. (A) (B) (C) (D)   13. (A) (B) (C) (D)   20. (A) (B) (C) (D)
7. (A) (B) (C) (D)   14. (A) (B) (C) (D)   21. (A) (B) (C) (D)

Part 1

Arithmetic Reasoning

Time: 36 minutes for 30 questions

Directions: Arithmetic Reasoning is the second subtest of the ASVAB. These questions are designed to test your ability to use mathematics to solve various problems that may be found in real life — in other words, math word problems.

Each question is followed by four possible answers. Decide which answer is correct, and then mark the corresponding space on your answer sheet. Use your scratch paper for any figuring you want to do. You may not use a calculator.

1. One pound is equal to 16 ounces. How many ounces are in 5 pounds?

 (A) 21 ounces

 (B) 3.2 ounces

 (C) 80 ounces

 (D) 64 ounces

2. Jason is reading a book that is 180 pages long. He is 40 percent of the way through the book. What page is he on?

 (A) page 40

 (B) page 72

 (C) page 45

 (D) page 76

3. If you toss two coins, what is the probability that both coins show tails?

 (A) 33 percent

 (B) 30 percent

 (C) 25 percent

 (D) 50 percent

4. In a triangle, one angle has a measure of 40°, and the other two angles have measures equal to each other. What is the measure of one of the two other angles?

 (A) 30°

 (B) 40°

 (C) 80°

 (D) 70°

5. Jake's truck gets 22 miles per gallon on the highway. How many miles on the highway can he travel on 4 gallons of gasoline?

 (A) 88 miles

 (B) 44 miles

 (C) 22 miles

 (D) 26 miles

6. Sergeant Williams cut a 24-foot rope into smaller ropes, each with a length of 4 feet. How many times did he cut the rope?

 (A) 4

 (B) 6

 (C) 3

 (D) 5

7. The refrigerator's temperature dropped from 32° Fahrenheit to 28° Fahrenheit. What is the percent decrease in temperature?

 (A) 15 percent

 (B) 4 percent

 (C) 25 percent

 (D) 12.5 percent

8. Carter has $6.70. Dirk has 4 times as much money as Carter. Harriet has half as much money as Dirk. How much money does Harriet have?

 (A) $26.80

 (B) $13.40

 (C) $5.35

 (D) $10.70

Go on to next page

9. The ages of a group of adults are 24, 26, 37, 23, and 40. What is the average age for this group?

   (A) 26

   (B) 32

   (C) 30

   (D) 28

10. A pitcher has 2.5 gallons of juice. Twenty-five people share all the juice equally. How much juice does each person get?

   (A) 0.1 gallon

   (B) 0.25 gallon

   (C) 0.01 gallon

   (D) 0.2 gallon

11. Timothy's age is one more than twice Sam's age. The sum of their ages is 31. What is Sam's age?

   (A) 21

   (B) 10

   (C) 11

   (D) 16

12. The value of a new car depreciates 10 percent each year after it was purchased. What is the car's value two years after it is purchased new, if the initial value is $14,000?

   (A) $11,340

   (B) $11,200

   (C) $11,034

   (D) $10,955

13. The formula $W = 0.5n + 47$ gives the percent of women (W) in a certain country who owned a laptop computer n years after the year 2000. In what year did 50 percent of women in this country own a laptop computer?

   (A) 2004

   (B) 2006

   (C) 2011

   (D) 2008

14. A rhombus has two interior angle measurements of 87° and 93°. Which of the following can be a measure of one of the remaining angles?

   (A) 6°

   (B) 90°

   (C) 93°

   (D) 180°

15. To make a certain type of juice, the ratio of water to juice concentrate is 8 to 1. How much concentrate should be added to 6 gallons of water?

   (A) $\frac{2}{3}$ gallon

   (B) 2 gallons

   (C) $1\frac{1}{3}$ gallons

   (D) $\frac{3}{4}$ gallon

16. Lillian invests $5,000 into a savings account. After one year, she earns $100 in interest. What is the annual interest rate for the account?

   (A) 0.2 percent

   (B) 0.5 percent

   (C) 2 percent

   (D) 5 percent

17. Membership in a club has doubled every 2 years. The club started in 2002 with 42 members. How many members were in the club in 2008?

   (A) 672

   (B) 1,344

   (C) 336

   (D) 168

18. The high temperature (H) was ten degrees less than twice the low temperature (L). Which equation shows this relationship?

   (A) $H = 2L - 10$

   (B) $H = 10 - 2L$

   (C) $2H = L - 10$

   (D) $2H + L = 10$

Go on to next page

19. What is the area of the triangle?

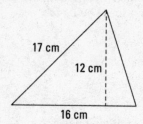

Illustration by Thomson Digital

(A) 136 cm²

(B) 96 cm²

(C) 102 cm²

(D) 45 cm²

20. The table shows how many men and women live in different regions of a town. How many more women live in the West region than men?

	East region	West region	South region
Men	320	110	421
Women	120	262	338

Illustration by Thomson Digital

(A) 110

(B) 372

(C) 262

(D) 152

21. Francis has two jobs. Last week, he earned $314 from both jobs, working 16 hours at the first job and 14 hours at the second job. He earns $10 an hour at his first job. What is his hourly rate at his second job?

(A) $12

(B) $11

(C) $9

(D) $8

22. A bag has 270 red, blue, and green marbles. The ratio of red to blue to green marbles is 1:3:5. How many blue marbles are in the bag?

(A) 30

(B) 90

(C) 150

(D) 50

23. A truck and a car leave from the same place at the same time. The truck takes a road that goes directly north, and the car takes a road that goes directly east. The truck travels at an average speed of 30 miles per hour, and the car travels at an average speed of 40 miles per hour. How far apart are the vehicles 2 hours after departure?

(A) 10 miles

(B) 1,000 miles

(C) 100 miles

(D) 70 miles

24. Evan is twice as old as Joe. In two years, the sum of their ages will be 85. How old is Evan now?

(A) 27

(B) 29

(C) 54

(D) 56

25. Gregory started the day with $45.10 in his wallet. The first thing he did was buy breakfast for himself, which cost $8.50 after tax. He left a 20 percent tip. How much did Gregory have left after he paid for breakfast?

(A) $10.20

(B) $34.80

(C) $34.90

(D) $36.60

26. Kendra's first three quiz scores were 7, 6, and 10. On the fourth quiz, she earned twice as much as she did on the fifth quiz. Her average score on the first five quizzes was 7. What was her score on the fourth quiz?

(A) 6.5

(B) 7.5

(C) 4

(D) 8

Go on to next page

27. The floor plan of a laboratory is shown. Its area is 126 square meters. What is the length of *x*?

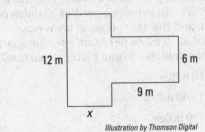

Illustration by Thomson Digital

(A) 6 m

(B) 4 m

(C) 5 m

(D) 10 m

28. The company truck weighs 3.5 tons when carrying forty 20-pound cylinder blocks. What is the weight of the truck when it isn't carrying a load?

(A) $3\frac{1}{5}$ tons

(B) $3\frac{7}{10}$ tons

(C) $3\frac{1}{10}$ tons

(D) 4 tons

29. Carla has $4 in quarters and dimes. She has 5 fewer quarters than dimes. How many quarters does she have?

(A) 8

(B) 10

(C) 15

(D) 20

30. A secret building has a front and a rear entrance. The front entrance requires a three-character code, where the first character must be an odd number but the next two characters can be any number 0 through 9. The rear entrance requires a two-character code, where the first character is a letter and the second character can be any number 0 through 9. How many possible entrance codes does the building have?

(A) 760

(B) 61

(C) 900

(D) 130,000

STOP DO NOT TURN THE PAGE UNTIL TOLD TO DO SO. DO NOT RETURN TO A PREVIOUS TEST.

Part 2

Word Knowledge

Time: 11 minutes for 35 questions

Directions: The Word Knowledge subtest is the third subtest of the ASVAB. The questions are designed to measure your vocabulary knowledge. You'll see three types of questions on this subtest. The first type simply asks you to choose a word or words that most nearly mean the same as the underlined word in the question. The second type includes an underlined word used in a sentence, and you are to choose the word or words that most nearly mean the same as the underlined word, as used in the context of the sentence. The third type of question asks you to choose the word that has the opposite or nearly opposite meaning as the underlined word. Each question is followed by four possible answers. Decide which answer is correct, and then mark the corresponding space on your answer sheet.

1. Condescend most nearly means:
   (A) share
   (B) conjoin
   (C) belittle
   (D) soften

2. He's a legend in the bluegrass community, with a career spanning 35 years.
   (A) star
   (B) fairytale
   (C) myth
   (D) antagonist

3. Lavish most nearly means:
   (A) soapy
   (B) thick
   (C) meek
   (D) extravagant

4. Retraction most nearly means:
   (A) withdrawal
   (B) application
   (C) memory
   (D) solitude

5. Decoy most nearly means:
   (A) message
   (B) trap
   (C) plan
   (D) scheme

6. Obsession most nearly means:
   (A) pastime
   (B) piece
   (C) fixation
   (D) apathy

7. Brawny most nearly means:
   (A) obese
   (B) scrawny
   (C) meager
   (D) hefty

8. The word most opposite in meaning to relocate is
   (A) rearrange
   (B) move
   (C) continue
   (D) remain

9. Lisa found washing dishes therapeutic because it allowed her to free her mind.
   (A) astounding
   (B) healing
   (C) obstructing
   (D) injurious

Go on to next page

10. Jason was <u>poised</u> to take over as captain this year.

    (A) perched

    (B) proper

    (C) ready

    (D) unqualified

11. The meaning of the poem was <u>obscure</u> and created a lot of debate.

    (A) clear

    (B) vague

    (C) obvious

    (D) pointed

12. Paolo wasn't ready to deal with the <u>ramifications</u> of his car accident.

    (A) consequences

    (B) prizes

    (C) presentations

    (D) rewards

13. The <u>eccentric</u> minister made the ceremony more enjoyable than your average church wedding.

    (A) foolish

    (B) conventional

    (C) peculiar

    (D) standard

14. The word most opposite in meaning to <u>meander</u> is

    (A) wander

    (B) hurry

    (C) dawdle

    (D) discourage

15. <u>Volatile</u> most nearly means:

    (A) speedy

    (B) steady

    (C) unlawful

    (D) unpredictable

16. The skaters had obviously done the work to <u>hone</u> their jumps since the last competition.

    (A) tarnish

    (B) maintain

    (C) polish

    (D) contain

17. Cary wanted to <u>broach</u> the topic, but Jeffrey wasn't paying attention.

    (A) mention

    (B) conclude

    (C) kill

    (D) belabor

18. The family was worried when the dog's behavior became <u>erratic</u>.

    (A) irrational

    (B) random

    (C) constant

    (D) even

19. <u>Obsolete</u> most nearly means:

    (A) absent

    (B) old

    (C) prominent

    (D) innovative

20. <u>Decorum</u> most nearly means:

    (A) design

    (B) festivities

    (C) servitude

    (D) respectability

21. My editing style tends to favor <u>brevity</u> over long-winded explanations.

    (A) rudeness

    (B) briefness

    (C) lengthy

    (D) continuous

22. The word most opposite in meaning to <u>mayhem</u> is

    (A) gathering

    (B) confusion

    (C) havoc

    (D) stability

23. <u>Hiatus</u> most nearly means:

    (A) gap

    (B) inequality

    (C) mismatch

    (D) shift

Go on to next page

24. <u>Cynical</u> most nearly means:
    (A) friendly
    (B) hopeful
    (C) pessimistic
    (D) depressed

25. <u>Riddled</u> most nearly means:
    (A) mysterious
    (B) inquisitive
    (C) full of
    (D) covered with

26. Sean was finally released after his <u>larceny</u> conviction four years ago.
    (A) gift
    (B) theft
    (C) help
    (D) skill

27. The word most opposite in meaning to <u>proposition</u> is
    (A) demand
    (B) suggestion
    (C) offer
    (D) plan

28. The movie gave a <u>poignant</u> portrayal of the fallen soldier.
    (A) lackluster
    (B) traumatic
    (C) moving
    (D) composed

29. I had to take a <u>respite</u> from work or I was never going to rest.
    (A) interval
    (B) start
    (C) end
    (D) continuation

30. The celebrity had to <u>debunk</u> the rumors of his death.
    (A) chide
    (B) shoot down
    (C) alarm
    (D) conceal

31. <u>Adamant</u> most nearly means:
    (A) erratic
    (B) flexible
    (C) fickle
    (D) resolute

32. The word most opposite in meaning to <u>malarkey</u> is
    (A) drivel
    (B) nonsense
    (C) justification
    (D) wisdom

33. The bobsledder won the bronze medal despite the <u>adversity</u> he had to overcome.
    (A) hardship
    (B) strength
    (C) death
    (D) fortune

34. The <u>defunct</u> band still sold records years after its split.
    (A) rising
    (B) extinct
    (C) promising
    (D) useless

35. <u>Origin</u> most nearly means:
    (A) section
    (B) closure
    (C) beginning
    (D) new

STOP DO NOT TURN THE PAGE UNTIL TOLD TO DO SO. DO NOT RETURN TO A PREVIOUS TEST.

Part 3
Paragraph Comprehension

Time: 13 minutes for 15 questions

Directions: Paragraph Comprehension is the fourth subtest on the ASVAB. The questions are designed to measure your ability to understand what you read. This section includes one or more paragraphs of reading material, followed by incomplete statements or questions. Read the paragraph and select the choice that best completes the statement or answers the question. Then mark the corresponding space on your answer sheet.

Questions 1, 2, and 3 refer to the following passage.

"November had come; the crops were in, and barn, buttery, and bin were overflowing with the harvest that rewarded the summer's hard work. The big kitchen was a jolly place just now, for in the great fireplace roared a cheerful fire; on the walls hung garlands of dried apples, onions, and corn; up aloft from the beams shone crook-necked squashes, juicy hams, and dried venison — for in those days deer still haunted the deep forests, and hunters flourished. Savory smells were in the air; on the crane hung steaming kettles, and down among the red embers copper saucepans simmered, all suggestive of some approaching feast."

–Louisa May Alcott

1. In this passage, <u>flourished</u> most nearly means

    (A) failed

    (B) prospered

    (C) congregated

    (D) killed

2. Where is the scene described in the passage taking place?

    (A) the kitchen

    (B) the forest

    (C) the barn

    (D) at a feast

3. What is happening in the passage?

    (A) The season is changing.

    (B) Hunters are looking for deer.

    (C) Farmers are harvesting their crops.

    (D) A feast is being prepared.

Question 4 refers to the following passage.

The topic of creating a high-speed rail system in the United States is the focus of the annual High-Speed Rail Summit in Washington, D.C. The purpose of this summit is to determine the most optimal and logical maneuvers that would allow a rail system to succeed on American soil. Critics have long contested the system as an expensive endeavor lacking the appropriate ridership numbers. Regardless, the summit participants will spend two full days hashing out the details to work toward a high-speed rail system in the future.

4. What is the main point of the passage?

    (A) to define what a high-speed rail system is

    (B) to explain why critics are against a high-speed rail system

    (C) to explain the purpose of the High-Speed Rail Summit

    (D) to suggest ways to improve ridership on a high-speed rail system

Go on to next page

Questions 5 and 6 refer to the following passage.

California is often the location for devastating natural events, such as earthquakes or droughts. However, the aftermath of those events can often be worse than the events themselves. For instance, the near-record drought in 2013 led to a wildfire season that began in May and continued until the end of the year. Fire season typically lasts from September to October, but in 2013, a fire in central California burned thousands of acres of land right before the Christmas holiday. Without rain, the number and severity of wildfires increased in 2013.

5. According to the passage, which of the following is a true statement?

   (A) California gets an average amount of rain.

   (B) Forest fires are rare.

   (C) Firefighters are often able to reduce the damage caused by forest fires.

   (D) The 2013 fire season was much longer than normal.

6. What caused the increase in forest fires in 2013?

   (A) careless campers

   (B) a lack of rain

   (C) lightning

   (D) heavily vegetated areas

Question 7 refers to the following passage.

Richard had never had rhythm and didn't enjoy dancing. He only went to the ballroom dance class to watch his wife perform. Then the instructor grabbed Richard's hands, pulling him onto the floor and showing him exactly what to do and how to do it. After that, Richard was dancing like a pro. He realized the secret to dancing wasn't rhythm; it was enjoying moving and being free.

7. According to this passage, Richard's lack of rhythm is

   (A) unimportant

   (B) his downfall

   (C) an embarrassment

   (D) hilarious

Question 8 refers to the following passage.

Making a good war movie is a tricky business. The subject matter is very dear to the hearts of many people, and accuracy is key. The combat scenes, soldiers, accommodations, and relationships among and throughout the different ranks must all be portrayed well to avoid negative backlash and ensure a profitable film.

8. According to the passage, which of the following is likely to make a war movie profitable?

   (A) length

   (B) emotional acting

   (C) historical accuracy

   (D) violence

Question 9 refers to the following passage.

Anyone can be a world-record holder if he or she has the wits and determination to do so. Guinness World Records has been making record holders out of ordinary citizens since 1955. All that's required is filling out an application stating which record you want to break or make and sending in the evidence of your achievement. If the judges approve of your evidence, you become a world-record holder, and the sky is now the limit.

9. According to the passage, what do you have to do to be recognized by Guinness World Records?

   (A) break a record in front of a Guinness judge

   (B) file an application and ask to be accepted

   (C) prove that you have broken a record

   (D) both Choice (B) and Choice (C)

Go on to next page

The fervor that each side brings to the Mac versus PC debate is so extreme that you'd think people had a personal stake in the matter. Despite the obvious popularity of Apple products, recent studies have shown that only a small fraction (about 15 percent) of the computers sold each year are Macs. Of course, there's only one Apple company and a multitude of PC manufacturers. Perhaps that's why many feel the Mac operating system is superior to Microsoft Windows. So how do you choose? Price and need are usually the best factors to consider. Why spend a lot of money if all you need is a word processor?

10. As used in this passage, the word <u>fervor</u> most nearly means

(A) passion

(B) illness

(C) cruelty

(D) refreshments

11. According to the passage, when choosing a new computer you should consider

(A) a brand's popularity and reliability

(B) price and need

(C) popularity and price

(D) none of the above

If you get a flat tire while driving, stay calm. As long as you have a spare that's full of air, you can fix the problem in no time. The most important thing is to pull off the road to a safe location away from passing cars and with the flat side away from the road, if possible. Use a tire iron to loosen the lug nuts before jacking the car up. Next, place the jack under the vehicle in the appropriate spot and crank it so the car is just a foot or two off the ground. Remove the lug nuts, replace the flat tire with the spare, and put the nuts back on. After you've released the car to the ground, tighten the lug nuts. If you try to tighten the nuts while the wheel is suspended, you won't have the proper resistance to get them as tight as you want. Now you're ready to drive off into the sunset.

12. The author is giving advice on

(A) jack safety

(B) proper lug nut resistance

(C) appropriate places to pull off the road

(D) changing a flat tire

The face of tennis was never the same after 14-year-old Venus Williams hit the scene in 1994. After she claimed the distinction of being the first African American woman to rank number one in the world, she and her sister Serena took over. Between the two of them, they dominated the Grand Slam circuit between 2000 and 2012, with 24 Grand Slam singles titles between them and doubles gold medals as a team in the 2000, 2008, and 2012 Summer Olympics. Their athleticism and aggressive playing style have been credited for changing the way women play tennis. They will forever be considered two of the greatest tennis players in history.

13. What year did the Williams sisters not win an Olympic gold medal?

(A) 2004

(B) 2000

(C) 2008

(D) 2012

14. How did the Williams sisters change the way women's tennis is played?

(A) by ranking number one

(B) with their uniforms

(C) by being sisters

(D) with their aggressive style

Go on to next page

Question 15 refers to the following passage.

The work of cobblers is very time consuming. They have to not only find the perfect materials but also size them perfectly, soften the leather for shaping, and attach the leather to the sole. Cobblers use more than 15 techniques when making shoes by hand. Most shoe shoppers have no idea how hard a cobbler's job is.

15. What is the main point of the passage?

(A) Cobblers use many techniques to make shoes.

(B) More people should become cobblers.

(C) Being a cobbler is hard work.

(D) Leather is the only material used to make shoes.

STOP DO NOT TURN THE PAGE UNTIL TOLD TO DO SO. DO NOT RETURN TO A PREVIOUS TEST.

Part 4

Mathematics Knowledge

Time: 24 minutes for 25 questions

Directions: Mathematics Knowledge is the fifth subtest on the ASVAB. The questions are designed to test your ability to solve general mathematical problems. Each question is followed by four possible answers. Decide which answer is correct, and then mark the corresponding space on your answer sheet. Use your scratch paper for any figuring you want to do. You may not use a calculator.

1. A circle has a diameter of 15 inches. What is its circumference?

   (A) 47.1 inches

   (B) 30 inches

   (C) 55.3 inches

   (D) 64.7 inches

2. $4x + 7xy + 6x =$

   (A) $17xy$

   (B) $10x + 7xy$

   (C) $17x + y$

   (D) $24x + 7xy$

3. Which is 8 inches less than 3 feet?

   (A) 28 in

   (B) 3.5 ft

   (C) 32 in

   (D) 2.8 ft

4. Which inequality represents all numbers m that are at least 14?

   (A) $m > 14$

   (B) $m < 14$

   (C) $m \geq 14$

   (D) $m \leq 14$

5. An angle has a measure of 37°. What is the measure of its complementary angle?

   (A) 63°

   (B) 53°

   (C) 143°

   (D) 163°

6. Round 120,459 to the nearest hundred.

   (A) 120,400

   (B) 120,460

   (C) 120,000

   (D) 120,500

7. $\sqrt{16} + \sqrt{100} =$

   (A) $\sqrt{116}$

   (B) 14

   (C) $\sqrt{14}$

   (D) 58

8. What is the least common multiple (LCM) of 12 and 14?

   (A) 26

   (B) 168

   (C) 2

   (D) 84

9. $\left(\frac{2x}{4}\right)^3 =$

   (A) $\frac{3x^3}{4}$

   (B) $\frac{x^3}{2}$

   (C) $2x^3$

   (D) $\frac{x^3}{8}$

10. $\frac{1}{5} + \frac{2}{7} =$

   (A) $\frac{1}{4}$

   (B) $\frac{2}{35}$

   (C) $\frac{3}{35}$

   (D) $\frac{17}{35}$

Go on to next page

11. Solve the equation $\frac{x^2}{2} = 8$.

    (A) 4 only

    (B) 4 and –4

    (C) 32 only

    (D) 8 and –8

12. Fifteen is what percent of 75?

    (A) 20 percent

    (B) 15 percent

    (C) 25 percent

    (D) 5 percent

13. $4(x + 1) + x =$

    (A) $x + 4$

    (B) $5x + 4$

    (C) $5x + 1$

    (D) $6x$

14. Eighty-five percent of 320 is

    (A) 85

    (B) 262

    (C) 305

    (D) 272

15. Given that $6m = 7n$, what is the ratio of n to m?

    (A) $\frac{7}{6}$

    (B) $\frac{6}{7}$

    (C) $\frac{1}{42}$

    (D) $\frac{13}{1}$

16. Two angles of a triangle measure 40° and 100°. What kind of triangle is it?

    (A) isosceles

    (B) obtuse

    (C) equilateral

    (D) right

17. What is the length a in the right triangle?

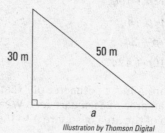

Illustration by Thomson Digital

    (A) 48.6 cm

    (B) 41.5 cm

    (C) 35 m

    (D) 40 m

18. Which fraction is the largest?

    (A) $\frac{1}{4}$

    (B) $\frac{7}{12}$

    (C) $\frac{2}{3}$

    (D) $\frac{5}{9}$

19. What is the product of $\sqrt{81}$ and $\sqrt{121}$?

    (A) 9,801

    (B) 40

    (C) 20

    (D) 99

20. What is the value of $(1 - x)^3$ if $4x - 1 = 19$?

    (A) 64

    (B) 125

    (C) –124

    (D) –64

21. The height of a right cylinder is $8x$, and the cylinder's radius is $\frac{x}{2}$. What is the volume of the cylinder?

    (A) $2\pi x^3$

    (B) $2\pi x^2$

    (C) $4\pi x^3$

    (D) $4\pi x$

Go on to next page

22. If $2p + \square + 5q = 14p + 15q$, then $\square = ?$

    (A) $12p + 10q$

    (B) $12p - 3q$

    (C) $7p + 3q$

    (D) $10p + 12q$

23. Square A has a perimeter of 8 feet. Square B has an area of 64 square feet. What is the ratio of the area of square A to the area of square B?

    (A) $\frac{1}{4}$

    (B) $\frac{1}{8}$

    (C) $\frac{1}{16}$

    (D) $\frac{3}{8}$

24. If $(x^9)(x^3) = x^{12}$, then $(x^{12}) \div (x^3) =$

    (A) x^4

    (B) x^{15}

    (C) x^9

    (D) x^6

25. What is the value of m?

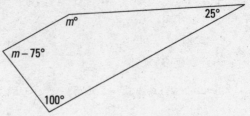

Illustration by Thomson Digital

    (A) $155°$

    (B) $125°$

    (C) $95°$

    (D) $80°$

STOP DO NOT TURN THE PAGE UNTIL TOLD TO DO SO. DO NOT RETURN TO A PREVIOUS TEST.

Chapter 19

Practice Exam 4: Answers and Explanations

. . . .

A re you ready to take the actual ASVAB yet and max out the AFQT score? I sure hope so. I hope you're feeling confident as well. If you still don't feel ready, you may want to look over the practice exams again, until you're comfortable with the types of questions that will be presented on the real test. You may also want to consider reading *ASVAB For Dummies* (Wiley) for another full-length AFQT practice exam, as well as three full-length ASVAB practice tests.

The answer keys in the following sections tell you how well you did on the final AFQT practice exam. ***Remember:*** Don't be too concerned about the percent right or wrong. On the actual test, harder questions are worth more points than easier questions when computing your AFQT score, so it's entirely possible to miss a few questions and still max out your AFQT score.

Part 1: Arithmetic Reasoning

How'd you do on this subtest? If you don't feel so good about the results, you may want to postpone taking the real ASVAB until you've gotten some more study time under your belt, and perhaps taken a math course or two at your neighborhood community college. You may also want to take another look at Chapters 8 and 10.

Other great resources to improve your math skills are *Math Word Problems For Dummies, Algebra I For Dummies,* and *Algebra II For Dummies,* all by Mary Jane Sterling; *Geometry For Dummies,* 2nd Edition, and *Calculus For Dummies,* both by Mark Ryan; and *SAT II Math For Dummies,* by Scott Hatch, JD, and Lisa Zimmer Hatch, MA — all published by Wiley.

1. **C. 80 ounces**

   Because 1 pound = 16 ounces, you can convert by multiplying 5 pounds by the conversion factor $\frac{16 \text{ ounces}}{1 \text{ pound}}$:

   $$5 \text{ pounds} \times \frac{16 \text{ ounces}}{1 \text{ pound}} = 5 \times 16 \text{ ounces}$$
   $$= 80 \text{ ounces}$$

2. **B. page 72**

   In order to find the page Jason is on, you need to find 40 percent of 180. Write 40 percent as a decimal and multiply by 180: 0.4(180) = 72. Jason is on page 72.

3. **C. 25 percent**

   There are four possible outcomes: two heads (HH), heads on the first coin/tails on the second (HT), tails on the first coin/heads on the second (TH), and two tails (TT). The desired outcome is TT. So the probability is 1/4 = 25 percent.

4. **D. 70°**

The sum of the angles of any triangle is 180°. You know one of the angles is 40°, so the sum of the remaining two angles is 140° (180° − 40° = 140°). Because the remaining two angles have equal measures, divide 140° by 2 to find the measure of one of the angles:

$$\frac{140°}{2} = 70°$$

5. **A. 88 miles**

If the truck gets 22 miles per gallon on the highway, that means it can go 22 miles on one gallon of gasoline. Multiply the mileage by 4 to find out how far Jake can travel using 4 gallons of gasoline: 4(22) = 88 miles.

6. **D. 5**

If you cut a 24-foot rope into 4-foot lengths, you will have six smaller ropes. To get these smaller ropes, Sergeant Williams would have to cut the rope five times. The following figure illustrates each of the cuts Sergeant Williams had to make at 4-foot increments. Sometimes drawing a picture can help you solve a problem.

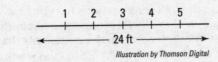

Illustration by Thomson Digital

7. **D. 12.5 percent**

To calculate percent decrease, divide the change in temperature (4° Fahrenheit) by the original temperature. Then convert the result to a percent:

$$\frac{4}{32} = \frac{1}{8} = 0.125 = 12.5\%$$

8. **B. $13.40**

First, multiply 4 times $6.70 to find out how much money Dirk has: 4($6.70) = $26.80. Harriet has half this amount:

$$\frac{1}{2}(\$26.80) = \frac{\$26.80}{2} = \$13.40$$

9. **C. 30**

To find the average age, add up all the ages and then divide by the number of adults in the group.

$$\frac{24 + 26 + 37 + 23 + 40}{5} = \frac{150}{5} = 30$$

10. **A. 0.1 gallon**

The word *share* is a clue that this problem uses division, so you need to divide 2.5 by 25.

$$\frac{2.5}{25} = \frac{25}{250} = \frac{1}{10} = 0.1$$

11. **B. 10**

   If x is Sam's age, then Timothy's age is $2x + 1$. Use the fact that the sum of their ages is 31 to set up an equation and solve for x:

   $$x + 2x + 1 = 31$$
   $$3x + 1 = 31$$
   $$3x = 30$$
   $$x = 10$$

   Sam is 10 years old.

12. **A. $11,340**

   If the car depreciates 10 percent in a year, the car's value after one year is 90 percent of what it was a year earlier. Repeat this twice to find the value of the car after two years:

   After one year: 0.9($14,000) = $12,600

   After two years: 0.9($12,600) = $11,340

   The value of the car after two years is $11,340.

13. **B. 2006**

   Because you are given a formula, you can substitute the known values and solve for n:

   $$W = 0.5n + 47$$
   $$50 = 0.5n + 47$$
   $$3 = 0.5n$$
   $$6 = n$$

   The problem states that n represents the number of years after the year 2000, so 50 percent of the women owned a laptop in the year 2006.

14. **C. 93°**

   A rhombus is a quadrilateral, a geometric shape with four sides with interior angles totaling 360°. A rhombus has equal opposite angles, so two angles are 93°, and the other two are 87°, totaling 360°.

15. **D. $\frac{3}{4}$ gallon**

   Let $x =$ the amount of concentrate that should be added. Write an equation and then cross multiply to solve for x.

   $$\frac{8}{1} = \frac{6}{x}$$
   $$8x = 6(1)$$
   $$x = \frac{6}{8}$$
   $$x = \frac{3}{4}$$

16. **C. 2 percent**

Use the interest formula ($I = Prt$), where I is the interest, P is the principal, r is the interest rate (as a decimal), and t is the time in years. Substitute the known values into the formula and solve for r:

$$100 = 5,000\,(r)\,(1)$$
$$100 = 5,000r$$
$$\frac{100}{5,000} = r$$
$$\frac{1}{50} = r$$
$$0.02 = r$$

Write 0.02 as a percent by moving the decimal point two places to the right (which is the same as multiplying by 100): $0.02 = 2$ percent.

17. **C. 336**

To determine club membership over this six-year period, it's best to work in increments. In 2004, after the first two years, the club's membership of 42 had doubled to 84. In 2006, the previous number of members doubled: $2(84) = 168$. Finally, in 2008, membership doubled again: $2(168) = 336$.

The easiest way to solve this problem may be to organize your work in a table:

Year	Number of members
2002	42
2004	2(42) = 84
2006	2(84) = 168
2008	2(168) = 336

Illustration by Thomson Digital

The club had 336 members in 2008.

18. **A. $H = 2L - 10$**

First, write twice the low temperature as $2L$. You know that H is 10 less than this amount, or $2L - 10$, so now you have your equation: $H = 2L - 10$.

19. **B. 96 cm²**

The formula for the area of a triangle is $A = \frac{1}{2}bh$, where b is the base and h is the height. The height is drawn perpendicular to the bottom side of the triangle (with a measure of 16 cm), so use the bottom as the base. Substitute $b = 16$ and $h = 12$ into the formula to find the area:

$$A = \frac{1}{2}bh = \frac{1}{2}(16)(12) = 8(12) = 96$$

20. **D. 152**

Looking at the table, you see that 262 women and 110 men live in the West region. To find how many more women there are than men, you need to subtract: $262 - 110 = 152$.

21. **B. $11**

Use Francis's hourly rate and the number of hours worked to find how much he earned at his first job: $16(\$10) = \$160$. Subtract that amount from the total pay to find how much he earned at his second job last week: $\$314 - \$160 = \$154$. Finally, divide $154 by 14 to find the hourly pay at his second job: $\$154 \div 14 = \$11$.

22. **B. 90**

If the ratio of red to blue to green marbles is 1:3:5, then there are x red marbles, $3x$ blue marbles, and $5x$ green marbles (x is some common multiple). Write an equation and solve for x:

$$x + 3x + 5x = 270$$
$$9x = 270$$
$$x = 30$$

This solution tells you there are 30 red marbles, which means that there are $3x = 3(30) = 90$ blue marbles.

23. **C. 100 miles**

First, use the distance formula, $d = rt$ (where d is the distance traveled, r is the rate of speed, and t is the time elapsed), to find how far each vehicle traveled in 2 hours:

Truck: $d = 30(2) = 60$ miles

Car: $d = 40(2) = 80$ miles

Now draw a diagram showing the paths of the two vehicles.

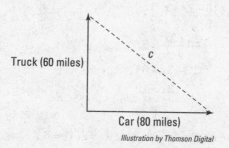

Truck (60 miles)

c

Car (80 miles)

Illustration by Thomson Digital

Looking at the diagram, you see a right triangle with the hypotenuse (c) missing, so it's Pythagorean theorem time.

$$c^2 = 60^2 + 80^2$$
$$c^2 = 3,600 + 6,400$$
$$c^2 = 10,000$$
$$c = \pm\sqrt{10,000} = \pm 100$$

Because distance is never negative, you use the positive answer. After 2 hours, the vehicles are 100 miles apart.

24. **C. 54**

Let Joe's age $= x$. Because Evan is twice as old as Joe, his age can be represented as $2x$. In two years, Joe's age will be $x + 2$, and Evan's age will be $2x + 2$. The sum of their ages together will equal 85.

Write your equation like this and solve for x:

$$(x + 2) + (2x + 2) = 85$$
$$3x + 4 = 85$$
$$3x + 4 - 4 = 85 - 4$$
$$3x = 81$$
$$\frac{3x}{3} = \frac{81}{3}$$
$$x = 27$$

Now that you know Joe's age, you can figure out Evan's:

$$27 \times 2 = 54$$

Check by plugging into the formula:

$$(27+2)+(2 \times 27+2)=85$$
$$29+56=85$$

25. **C. $34.90**

First, find out how much of a tip Gregory left by finding 20 percent of $8.50: $0.2(8.50) = 1.70$. So the total cost of breakfast after the tip was $8.50 + $1.70 = $10.20. Now, subtract the total amount paid from the amount in Gregory's wallet at the start of the day: $45.10 – $10.20 = $34.90 leftover after breakfast.

26. **D. 8**

Let x equal Kendra's score on the fifth quiz. Her score on the fourth quiz was twice that amount, so let $2x$ represent the fourth score. To find the average score, add up all the scores, and then divide by the number of quizzes taken.

$$\frac{7+6+10+2x+x}{5}=7$$
$$\frac{23+3x}{5}=7$$
$$23+3x=35$$
$$3x=12$$
$$x=4$$

Her score on the fourth quiz was $2(4) = 8$.

27. **A. 6 m**

For problems like this one, your best bet is to break the odd-shaped figure down into rectangles. You can break this figure into two rectangles and find their areas separately:

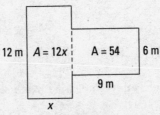

Illustration by Thomson Digital

Because the sum of the two areas is 126, you can write and solve an equation to find x:

$$12x+54=126$$
$$12x=72$$
$$x=6$$

28. **C. $3\frac{1}{10}$ tons**

First, find the weight of the truck in pounds because the weights of the cylinder blocks are in pounds. One ton is 2,000 pounds, so $3.5(2,000) = 7,000$ pounds. Now, each cylinder block weighs 20 pounds, so 40 cylinder blocks weigh $20(40) = 800$ pounds. So the total weight of the truck without the cylinder blocks is $7,000 – 800 = 6,200$ pounds. Divide the total weight by 2,000 to convert back to tons: $6,200 \div 2,000 = 3.1$ or $3\frac{1}{10}$.

29. **B. 10**

Let *d* equal the number of dimes Carla has; the number of quarters she has is *d* – 5. The values of the dimes and quarters are 10 cents and 25 cents, respectively, and the coins add up to $4 (or 400 cents). Write an equation and solve for *d*:

$$10d + 25(d-5) = 400$$
$$10d + 25d - 125 = 400$$
$$35d = 525$$
$$d = 15$$

Carla has 15 dimes, which means she has 15 – 5 = 10 quarters.

30. **A. 760**

The total number of codes includes all the codes for both the front and back entrances. To find the number of possible codes for each entrance, multiply the number of possibilities for each character of the code:

Front: 5 possible odd numbers × 10 possible numbers × 10 possible numbers = 500 possible combinations

Rear: 26 possible letters × 10 possible numbers = 260 possible combinations

So the total number of codes possible is 500 + 260 = 760.

Part 2: Word Knowledge

The Word Knowledge subtest, as with all the AFQT subtests, determines whether you qualify for enlistment. If you're not seeing the improvement in your scores that you need to see, work with a partner who can quiz you on vocabulary. Review your vocabulary words intensely, even several times a day, to ensure your success on this subtest. You may also want to reread the information in Chapter 4.

Also check out *Vocabulary For Dummies,* by Laurie E. Rozakis, and *SAT Vocabulary For Dummies,* by Suzee Vlk (both published by Wiley). Finally, see Chapter 5 for more practice questions.

1. **C. belittle**

   Condescend is a verb that means to talk down to someone.

2. **A. star**

   As used in this sentence, *legend* is a noun that refers to someone famous or popular in a certain field.

3. **D. extravagant**

   Lavish is an adjective that means in abundance.

4. **A. withdrawal**

   Retraction is a noun that means the taking back of a statement.

5. **B. trap**

   Decoy is a noun that means a distraction or trick.

6. **C. fixation**

   Obsession is a noun that means a preoccupation with something or someone.

7. **D. hefty**

   Brawny is an adjective that means muscular or appearing strong.

8. **D. remain**

   Relocate is a verb that means to change places.

9. **B. healing**

   Therapeutic is an adjective that describes something relating to good health or beneficial.

10. **C. ready**

    As used in this sentence, *poised* is an adjective that means to be in position or prepared.

11. **B. vague**

    As used in this sentence, *obscure* is an adjective that means unclear or ambiguous.

12. **A. consequences**

    Ramification is a noun that means a result or an outcome.

13. **C. peculiar**

    Eccentric is an adjective that describes something or someone unusual or odd.

14. **B. hurry**

    Meander is a verb that means to roam or stroll leisurely.

15. **D. unpredictable**

    Volatile is an adjective that means something unstable or explosive.

16. **C. polish**

    As used in this sentence, *hone* is a verb that means to improve or perfect something.

17. **A. mention**

    Broach is a verb that means to bring up or raise.

18. **B. random**

    Erratic is an adjective that describes something inconsistent or frequently changing.

19. **B. old**

    Obsolete is an adjective that means something outdated or no longer in use.

20. **D. respectability**

    Decorum is a noun that means appropriate behavior.

21. **B. briefness**

    Brevity is a noun that means something kept concise or short.

22. **D. stability**

    Mayhem is a noun that describes disruption or chaos.

23. **A. gap**

    Hiatus is a noun that means a break or pause in something continuous.

24. **C. pessimistic**

    Cynical is an adjective that means distrusting or having a negative outlook.

25. **C. full of**

    Riddled is an adjective that means containing a lot of something.

26. **B. theft**

    Larceny is a noun that describes the illegal removal of another's possessions.

27. **A. demand**

    Used as a noun, *proposition* means an idea or a proposal.

28. **C. moving**

    Poignant is an adjective that means something understanding and emotional.

29. **A. interval**

    Respite is a noun that means a brief break in something or a period of rest.

30. **B. shoot down**

    Debunk is a verb that means to expose false or exaggerated claims.

31. **D. resolute**

    Adamant is an adjective that means having an unyielding or unwavering opinion.

32. **D. wisdom**

    Malarkey is a noun that means rubbish or insincere talk.

33. **A. hardship**

    Adversity is a noun that represents a difficulty or misfortune.

34. **B. extinct**

    Defunct is an adjective that means no longer in existence.

35. **C. beginning**

    Origin is a noun that indicates where something started.

Part 3: Paragraph Comprehension

If you're struggling with this subtest, remember to take your time when you read the passages. And, after you read each question, you can quickly reread the passage just to make sure you're on the money. The information is in the paragraph; you just have to concentrate to pull it out. Turn to Chapter 6 if you still need additional help to pull off a good score on this subtest. You can also find more practice questions in Chapter 7.

1. **B. prospered**

    Flourished is a verb that means to thrive or do well.

2. **A. the kitchen**

    Although many things are being described in the passage, the scene remains the same: in the "big kitchen."

3. **D. A feast is being prepared.**

   Although Alcott is talking about the harvest and hunting, the only action taking place is the cooking of the feast, as stated in the last sentence: "all suggestive of some approaching feast." Sometimes reading through the answers and eliminating those that are obviously wrong is the best way to answer questions on the ASVAB.

4. **C. to explain the purpose of the High-Speed Rail Summit**

   Although the passage touches on many of the other answers, the focus remains on the summit.

5. **D. The 2013 fire season was much longer than normal.**

   The passage compares the typical fire season (September to October) to the 2013 fire season (May to December). None of the other choices is addressed.

6. **B. a lack of rain**

   The passage states that wildfire season started early due to a drought and later reinforces that the number of fires increased because of a lack of rain.

7. **A. unimportant**

   The last sentence states that the secret to dancing isn't rhythm, so the fact that Richard doesn't have any doesn't matter. The passage never says that Richard is embarrassed by his lack of rhythm or that it has harmed him in any way. Although watching Richard dance may be funny, the passage clearly says that the secret to dancing isn't rhythm; it's enjoying the movement and being free. That means Richard's lack of rhythm is unimportant.

8. **C. historical accuracy**

   The passage discusses the aspects that make a good and profitable war movie. It indicates that an accurate portrayal of war is important to "ensure a profitable film," so Choice (C) is the best answer.

9. **D. both Choice (B) and Choice (C)**

   The passage says aspiring record-holders have to do only two things: complete an application and submit evidence that they have broken the record. Breaking the record in front of a judge isn't required.

10. **A. passion**

    Even if you didn't know what *fervor* meant, the context in which the passage uses it can help you eliminate the incorrect choices. By reading the next part of the sentence, which says, "you'd think people had a personal stake in the matter," you can tell that people take it very seriously. That signifies that each side is very passionate about its beliefs.

11. **B. price and need**

    The passage poses the question, "So how do you choose?" and then answers it: "Price and need are usually the best factors to consider."

12. **D. changing a flat tire**

    This passage gives step-by-step instructions for changing a flat tire. Some of the other answer choices are mentioned, but they're part of the advice given about Choice (D).

13. **A. 2004**

    The Summer Olympics occur every four years. The passage lists every Summer Olympic year between 2000 and 2012 except for 2004. When the ASVAB asks you for specific dates, scan the paragraph for them rather than rereading the entire passage.

14. **D. with their aggressive style**

The end of the passage clearly tells you that the Williams sisters' "athleticism and aggressive playing style have been credited for changing the way women play tennis," which is exactly what the question asked.

15. **C. Being a cobbler is hard work.**

The first and last sentences both mention the laborious and difficult nature of shoemaking. Choice (A) is a fact mentioned in the passage, but it's in support of the idea that shoemaking is a tough job. On the ASVAB, many questions are easier than they look. By reading through your answer options, you can see that the passage doesn't say anything about the need for more people to take up cobbling (Choice (B)). You can also see that Choice (D) probably isn't correct because the passage doesn't say that leather is the only material used. Though Choice (A) may have tempted you, the passage as a whole is about how tough it is to be a cobbler, making Choice (C) the correct answer.

Part 4: Mathematics Knowledge

If you're missing too many math questions, you may need to take more drastic measures like enrolling in a basic algebra class at a local community college. If your scores are improving, keep hitting the books and testing yourself up until the day of the ASVAB. Chapter 8 will also be a good review.

If you want to increase your math skills, the following *For Dummies* books will help: *Algebra I For Dummies* and *Algebra II For Dummies,* by Mary Jane Sterling; *Geometry For Dummies,* 2nd Edition, and *Calculus For Dummies,* both by Mark Ryan; and *SAT II Math For Dummies,* by Scott Hatch (all published by Wiley). Chapter 9 also has some additional practice questions.

1. **A. 47.1 inches**

Using the circumference formula ($C = \pi d$), plug in the known values and solve:

$$C = \pi d$$
$$C = (3.14)(15)$$
$$C = 47.1$$

2. **B. $10x + 7xy$**

This expression has two like terms: $4x$ and $6x$. Combine them by adding their coefficients:

$$4x + 7xy + 6x = 4x + 6x + 7xy$$
$$= (4 + 6)x + 7xy$$
$$= 10x + 7xy$$

3. **A. 28 in**

Convert the 3 feet to inches by multiplying by 12: $3(12) = 36$ inches. Now, subtract 8 inches to get the answer: $36 - 8 = 28$.

4. **C. $m \geq 14$**

"All numbers that are at least 14" means all numbers greater than or equal to 14, which is represented by the symbol $\geq$. So the answer is $m \geq 14$.

5. **B. 53°**

Complementary angles have a sum of 90°. To find the measure of the complement of 37°, subtract from 90°: $90° - 37° = 53°$.

6. **D. 120,500**

Determine what your rounding digit is; you're rounding to the hundreds place, so you want the hundreds digit. Now look at the number immediately to the right of it. If that number is 4 or less, don't change the rounding digit. If the digit is 5 or more, the rounding digit rounds up by one number. Here, the number in the hundreds place is 4 and the number to the right is 5, so you round up.

7. **B. 14**

Here, you solve the square roots and then add. The square root of 16 is 4, and the square root of 100 is 10. So $\sqrt{16} + \sqrt{100} = 4 + 10 = 14$.

8. **D. 84**

One way to find the LCM of two numbers is to list all the multiples of each number and find the smallest number that is common to both:

12: 12, 24, 36, 48, 60, 72, 84

14: 14, 28, 42, 56, 70, 84

The LCM of 12 and 14 is 84.

9. **D. $\dfrac{x^3}{8}$**

First, reduce the fraction inside the parentheses:

$$\left(\frac{2x}{4}\right)^3 = \left(\frac{x}{2}\right)^3$$

Whenever you raise a fraction to a power, the exponent goes to the numerator and the denominator:

$$\left(\frac{x}{2}\right)^3 = \frac{x^3}{2^3} = \frac{x^3}{8}$$

10. **D. $\dfrac{17}{35}$**

You need to find the common denominator for these two fractions. The common denominator is the least common multiple of 5 and 7.

Multiples of 5: 5, 10, 15, 20, 25, 30, 35

Multiples of 7: 7, 14, 21, 28, 35

The common denominator for these two fractions is 35. Multiply the numerator and denominator of each fraction by the number that makes each denominator 35.

$$\frac{1}{5} + \frac{2}{7} = \frac{1 \cdot 7}{5 \cdot 7} + \frac{2 \cdot 5}{7 \cdot 5}$$
$$= \frac{7}{35} + \frac{10}{35}$$
$$= \frac{7+10}{35}$$
$$= \frac{17}{35}$$

11. **B. 4 and –4**

First, isolate the variable by multiplying both sides of the equation by 2:

$$2 \cdot \frac{x^2}{2} = 2 \cdot 8$$
$$x^2 = 16$$

Next, use the square root rule, which says if $x^2 = k$, then $x = \pm \sqrt{k}$:

$$x = \pm \sqrt{16}$$
$$x = \pm 4$$

12. **A. 20 percent**

    Begin by putting the problem into a fraction: $\frac{15}{75}$. Then divide the numerator by the denominator (you can simplify the fraction to $\frac{3}{15}$ first if that makes the division easier): $15 \div 75 = 0.2$. Finally, move the decimal point two spaces to the right, which is the same as multiplying by 100, to express the number as a percent: 20 percent.

13. **B. $5x + 4$**

    To simplify an expression like this one, first use the distributive property to remove the parentheses:

    $$4(x + 1) + x = 4x + 4 + x$$

    This expression has two like terms: $4x$ and x. Combine the like terms by adding their coefficients:

    $$4x + 4 + x = (4 + 1)x + 4$$
    $$= 5x + 4$$

14. **D. 272**

    First, write 85 percent as a decimal: $\frac{85}{100} = 0.85$. Next, multiply 0.85 by 320: $0.85(320) = 272$.

15. **B. $\frac{6}{7}$**

    The goal here is to use the given equation to find the ratio $\frac{n}{m}$. Start by dividing both sides of the equation by m: $6 = \frac{7n}{m}$. To get $\frac{n}{m}$ alone, get rid of the 7 by multiplying both sides by $\frac{1}{7}$:

    $$\frac{1}{7} \cdot \frac{6}{1} = \frac{1}{7} \cdot \frac{7n}{m}$$
    $$\frac{6}{7} = \frac{1}{7} \cdot \frac{7n}{m}$$
    $$\frac{6}{7} = \frac{n}{m}$$

16. **A. isosceles**

    The sum of the angles of a triangle is 180°. To find the measure of the third angle, subtract the known angles from 180°: $180° - 100° - 40° = 40°$. Because two of the angles of the triangle have the same measure, the sides opposite them are the same length. A triangle with two equal sides is an isosceles triangle.

17. **D. 40 m**

    Use the Pythagorean theorem ($a^2 + b^2 = c^2$) and the known values to find a:

    $$a^2 + 30^2 = 50^2$$
    $$a^2 + 900 = 2,500$$
    $$a^2 = 1,600$$
    $$a = \pm 40$$

Use the positive answer because a length is never negative.

18. **C.** $\frac{2}{3}$

    Comparing fractions is too difficult when all the denominators are different. Find the least common denominator by taking the least common multiple of all the denominators; in this case, that's 36. Rewrite the fractions with the common denominator, multiplying the numerators and denominators by the number that makes the denominator 36:

    $$\frac{1}{4} = \frac{1 \cdot 9}{4 \cdot 9} = \frac{9}{36}$$

    $$\frac{7}{12} = \frac{7 \cdot 3}{12 \cdot 3} = \frac{21}{36}$$

    $$\frac{2 \cdot 12}{3 \cdot 12} = \frac{24}{36}$$

    $$\frac{5}{9} = \frac{5 \cdot 4}{9 \cdot 4} = \frac{20}{36}$$

    The largest fraction is the one with the greatest numerator: $\frac{24}{36} = \frac{2}{3}$

19. **D. 99**

    The square root of 81 is 9, and the square root of 121 is 11, because $9 \times 9 = 81$ and $11 \times 11 = 121$. The product of those two numbers (9×11) is 99.

20. **D. –64**

    The first thing you need to do is find the value of x by solving the given equation:

    $$4x - 1 = 19$$
    $$4x = 20$$
    $$x = 5$$

    Now you can substitute 5 for x in the expression $(1 - x)^3$ and simplify to find the answer. Remember to simplify inside the parentheses before simplifying exponents.

    $$(1 - 5)^3 = (-4)^3$$
    $$= (-4)(-4)(-4)$$
    $$= -64$$

21. **A. $2\pi x^3$**

    This problem uses the formula for the volume of a right cylinder: $V = \pi r^2 h$. You're given the values of h and r in terms of x, so you can just substitute those values in place of r and h in the formula:

    $$V = \pi r^2 h$$
    $$= \pi \left(\frac{x}{2}\right)^2 (8x)$$
    $$= \pi \left(\frac{x^2}{4}\right) (8x)$$
    $$= \frac{\pi \cdot x^2 \cdot 8x}{4}$$
    $$= \frac{8\pi x^3}{4}$$
    $$= 2\pi x^3$$

22. **A. $12p + 10q$**

    The goal is to find what goes in place of $\square$ so the left side of the equation is equal to the right side of the equation. The p component of the answer has to equal $14p$ when added to $2p$; therefore, the p component has to be $12p$. The q component of the answer has to equal $15q$ when added to $5q$; that means the q component is $10q$. So $\square = 12p + 10q$.

23. **C. $\dfrac{1}{16}$**

    You already know the area of square B, so you need to find the area of square A. To do that, you need to find the side length of square A based on what you know about the square's perimeter. The formula for the perimeter of a square is $P = 4s$. Substitute the known values for square A and then solve for s:

    $$P = 4s$$
    $$8 = 4s$$
    $$2 = s$$

    Now you can use the area formula for a square, $a = s^2$:

    $$a = s^2$$
    $$a = (2)^2$$
    $$a = 4$$

    Finally, you can express the ratio of the area of square A to the area of square B with a fraction:

    $$\frac{\text{Area of square A}}{\text{Area of square B}} = \frac{4}{64} = \frac{1}{16}$$

24. **C. x^9**

    When multiplying exponents, you add. When dividing exponents, you subtract:

    $$\left(x^{12}\right) \div \left(x^3\right) = x^{12-3}$$
    $$= x^9$$

25. **A. $155°$**

    This figure is a quadrilateral, which means the sum of its angles is $360°$. Because m is equal to is $360°$ minus the other three angles, plug in the values and solve:

    $$m = 360 - 25 - 100 - (m - 75)$$
    $$m = 360 - 125 - m + 75$$
    $$m = 360 - 50 - m$$
    $$2m = 310$$
    $$\frac{2m}{2} = \frac{310}{2}$$
    $$m = 155$$

Answer Key

Part 1: Arithmetic Reasoning

1. C	7. D	13. B	19. B	25. C
2. B	8. B	14. C	20. D	26. D
3. C	9. C	15. D	21. B	27. A
4. D	10. A	16. C	22. B	28. C
5. A	11. B	17. C	23. C	29. B
6. D	12. A	18. A	24. C	30. A

Part 2: Word Knowledge

1. C	8. D	15. D	22. D	29. A
2. A	9. B	16. C	23. A	30. B
3. D	10. C	17. A	24. C	31. D
4. A	11. B	18. B	25. C	32. D
5. B	12. A	19. B	26. B	33. A
6. C	13. C	20. D	27. A	34. B
7. D	14. B	21. B	28. C	35. C

Part 3: Paragraph Comprehension

1. B	4. C	7. A	10. A	13. A
2. A	5. D	8. C	11. B	14. D
3. D	6. B	9. D	12. D	15. C

Part 4: Mathematics Knowledge

1. A	6. D	11. B	16. A	21. A
2. B	7. B	12. A	17. D	22. A
3. A	8. D	13. B	18. C	23. C
4. C	9. D	14. D	19. D	24. C
5. B	10. D	15. B	20. D	25. A

Part V
The Part of Tens

Visit www.dummies.com/extras/asvabafqt for a free article that suggests ways parents can help their children study for the AFQT.

In this part . . .

- Check out ten tips for getting a better score on the AFQT.

- Discover more than ten resources that will give you more information about the military and the ASVAB and help you get ready to take one of the most important exams of your life.

Chapter 20

Ten Tips for a Better AFQT Score

. . . .

In This Chapter

▶ Setting up a study plan

▶ Using the practice examinations

▶ Boosting your math and communicative scores

. . . .

The U.S. military enlists around 265,000 new troops each and every year, counting the active and reserve components. And all those men and women share one thing in common: They all earned a qualifying score on the AFQT. (See Chapter 2 for qualifying AFQT scores for each service.)

Many people score very high, which makes their families proud and their recruiters smile. It also opens up a new world of special enlistment programs and enlistment incentives that are available only to those who score well on the AFQT.

I'm sure you want to be counted among that group; otherwise, why would you be reading this book? If so, this chapter will be a big help. Here, I list ten surefire ways to maximize your AFQT score and get you on your way to a satisfying and successful military career.

Take Your Time

Don't cram. I don't care whether you call it a "power study," "mega-brain feeding," or "mugging"; study after study has shown that it doesn't work. For example, a 2007 study conducted by University of South Florida psychologist Doug Rohrer determined that last-minute studying reduces retention of material and may hinder the learning process. If you don't plan for adequate study time, your test scores will suffer the consequences.

 Rome wasn't built in a day, but it took only a few hours for the city to crash and burn. If you develop a solid study plan and stick with it for six to eight weeks, you'll score much higher on the AFQT than if you try to pack four subjects' worth of knowledge into your brain in one or two days. Plus, you won't walk into the testing center with your eyes red and your brain fried.

Make a Study Plan

You wouldn't expect the U.S. military to fight a war without a plan, would you? It would be disorganized chaos, and probably nothing would be achieved. The same is true when studying for the AFQT (or doing anything else, for that matter). If you try to study without a plan, you'll wind up wandering here and there, reading this and that, but you won't really accomplish anything. To lay out your plan, try making a timeline of how much time you have between now and the test. Make a schedule of days and opportunities during the week you can commit study time. The more time you can commit to, the better your AFQT score will be.

Start by studying the subjects you find the hardest, and spend extra time on those areas. You're only as strong as your weakest subject. When you focus on the areas where you need the most improvement, you increase your entire score. After you feel confident in your weakest areas, start perfecting and reviewing the areas you consider less problematic.

Use the Practice Exams to Your Advantage

If you bought this book expecting the practice exams to include the exact same questions you'll see on the ASVAB, I'm afraid I have bad news: You won't see the same questions on the ASVAB that I include in this book (or any other ASVAB/AFQT preparation guide). Giving you the actual questions and answers in advance would be cheating — and illegal. The military classifies ASVAB tests as "official use only." That means only those with an official "need to know" have access to the test questions and answers, and that certainly doesn't include authors of ASVAB AFQT prep books.

The best I can do is to provide you with practice questions that are very similar to the ones you'll see on the ASVAB. In short, don't waste your time trying to memorize the questions and answers on the practice exams.

Even so, the practice exams are a very valuable study tool. Not only do they give you an idea about the type of questions you'll see and the test format, but they're also useful in determining what AFQT subject areas you need to spend the most time on.

Here are my recommendations for taking the exams:

- **Practice Exam 1:** Take this test before you set up your study plan. You can use the results of Practice Exam 1 to determine which areas of the AFQT you need to spend the most time on.

- **Practice Exam 2:** Use this test as a progress check after a week or two of study. Adjust your study plan accordingly.

- **Practice Exam 3:** Take this practice exam about a week before you're scheduled to take the actual ASVAB. Use the results to determine which AFQT subjects need a little extra attention.

- **Practice Exam 4:** Take the final practice exam a day or two before the ASVAB to make sure you're ready and to boost your confidence.

If you've already taken some or all of the exams and you didn't follow this schedule, that's okay, too. The key is to take the exams and learn from them. You may even find repeating each test and comparing your scores helpful. It's a good way to show personal progress.

Memorize Basic Math Formulas

The Arithmetic Reasoning and Mathematics Knowledge subtests require you to know many standard mathematical formulas used in geometry and algebra. As a minimum, you should have the following committed to memory by the time you sit down to take the ASVAB:

- **Perimeter of a square:** $p = 4s$, where $s =$ one side of the square
- **Area of a square:** $a = s^2$

- ✔ **Diagonal of a square:** $d = s\sqrt{2}$
- ✔ **Perimeter of a rectangle:** $p = 2l + 2w$, where l = the length and w = the width of the rectangle
- ✔ **Area of a rectangle:** $a = lw$
- ✔ **Diagonal of a rectangle:** $d = \sqrt{l^2 + w^2}$
- ✔ **Perimeter of a triangle:** $p = s_1 + s_2 + s_3$, where s = the length of each side of the triangle
- ✔ **Area of a triangle:** $a = \frac{1}{2}bh$, where b = the length of the triangle's base (bottom) and h = the height of the triangle
- ✔ **Radius of a circle:** $r = \frac{1}{2}d$, where d = the diameter of the circle
- ✔ **Diameter of a circle:** $d = 2r$
- ✔ **Circumference of a circle:** $c = 2\pi r$
- ✔ **Area of a circle:** $a = \pi r^2$
- ✔ **Volume of a cube:** $v = s^3$, where s = the length of one side of the cube
- ✔ **Volume of a rectangular box:** $v = lwh$, where l = the length, w = the width, and h = the height of the box
- ✔ **Volume of a cylinder:** $v = \pi r^2 h$, where r = the radius of the cylinder and h = the height of the cylinder
- ✔ **Surface area of a cube:** $SA = 6s^2$
- ✔ **Surface area of a rectangular box:** $SA = 2lw + 2wh + 2lh$
- ✔ **Distance formula:** $d = rt$, where d = distance, r = rate, and t = time
- ✔ **Interest formula:** $I = Prt$, where I = interest, P = principal, r = rate, and t = time

Memorize the Math Order of Operations

When a math problem asks you to perform more than one operation, you need to perform the operations in the set-in-stone correct order:

1. **Start with calculations in brackets or parentheses.**

   Note: When you have *nested* parentheses or brackets — parentheses or brackets inside other parentheses or brackets — do the inner ones first and work your way out.

2. **Work on terms with exponents and roots.**

3. **Do all the multiplication and division, in order from left to right.**

4. **Finish up with addition and subtraction, also in order from left to right.**

A helpful memory device for the order of operations is "Please Excuse My Dear Aunt Sally" or the acronym PEMDAS. It stands for parentheses, exponents, multiplication/division, and addition/subtraction. Remembering one or both of these will ensure you follow the proper steps in the math problem.

Boost Your Vocabulary

The Word Knowledge subtest is nothing more than a vocabulary test. This subtest contains questions that usually ask you to find the word that is "closest in meaning" to a given word. You may also have to find the *antonym,* or opposite, of a given word. The more words you know, the better you'll do on this subtest. It's that simple. (For details on how to increase your vocabulary, check out Chapter 4.)

Comprehend What You Read

To do well on the Paragraph Comprehension subtest, you must be able to read a paragraph, understand the information, and then correctly answer questions about the material. Generally, paragraph comprehension questions fall into four categories: inferring the main point or idea, analyzing the data, finding specific information, and identifying vocabulary in context. Understanding how to pick apart this information from your reading material is vital to a successful AFQT score.

Sharpen your comprehension daily by reading a paragraph in a book, newspaper, or magazine and then asking a friend to question you about information included in that paragraph.

Arrive at the Test Site Refreshed and Prepared

Don't let the recruiter schedule you to take the ASVAB until you're sure you're ready. Recruiters sometimes have a habit of trying to get you tested as soon as possible so they can fill their recruiting goals. However, if you don't achieve a qualifying AFQT score, you waste your time, your recruiter's time, and the military's time. *Remember:* You may have to wait for up to six months for a retest. Make sure you're ready. (For more on retesting, turn to Chapter 2.)

The ASVAB test day can be drawn out and overwhelming, especially if nerves and stomach butterflies come out of nowhere or you struggle to use brainpower for an extended period of time. Give yourself a head start against the fatigue factor by arriving well rested and motivated. Get a good night's sleep on the night before the test. If you're traveling to the test site in a bus or car, try to get a quick catnap during the journey — as long as you're not the one doing the driving, of course!

Try to eat a light meal or snack just before the test, along with drinking enough water. You don't want to become dehydrated or have your grumbling stomach to distract you from solving a quadratic equation.

Watch the Clock

You only have a limited amount of time to complete each subtest, but don't worry about it. The more you panic, the more likely you are to make mistakes. Just work at a steady pace, and you'll do fine. Chapter 2 breaks down how much time you have for the number of questions on each subtest (for both the paper and computerized tests).

If you're taking the computerized version of the ASVAB (CAT-ASVAB), you'll see a counter on the screen, counting down the time remaining on the subtest. If you're taking the paper version of the ASVAB, a clock will be clearly visible on the wall, and the test proctor will post the start and stop time of the subtest where you can easily see them.

Don't spend too much time on one question. If you're drawing a blank, make a guess and move on. Keep in mind that if you're taking the CAT-ASVAB, you can't go back to change your answers or review any questions if you finish early, so make your guess a good one! (I explain how to do that in the next section.)

Guess Smart

Despite your extensive study, you may stumble on a question that has you stumped. Prepare for plan B by knowing how to use the process of elimination. If you're stuck on a question, try to eliminate any answers that you know to be wrong instead of making a wild guess. If you can eliminate even one wrong answer, you increase your chances of guessing the right answer from one in four to one in three. If you can eliminate two wrong answers, your chances increase to 50/50. (For more tips on intelligent guessing, see Chapter 3.)

Chapter 21

Ten Topics to Explore

I'll be the first to admit that *ASVAB AFQT For Dummies*, 2nd Edition, is a great book — quite possibly the greatest book ever published (my well-known modesty aside). However, I can't pack everything you need to know about math, vocabulary, reading, and joining the military into 336 pages. You may have to rely on some outside help.

If you need to brush up on some of your skills before taking the ASVAB and maxing out your AFQT score, reading the appropriate chapters in this book is a great place to start. But you may need or want more work in a particular subject area, or you may want to know more about the military or even the entire ASVAB. This chapter helps point you in the right direction. Here I list places you can get additional information.

For More about the ASVAB

This book is about boosting your Armed Forces Qualification Test (AFQT) score, but this score comprises only four of the nine ASVAB subtests. The AFQT score is important because it determines whether you're qualified to join the military (see Chapter 2), but the other ASVAB subtests determine which military jobs you qualify for.

If you want to brush up on all the ASVAB subtests, an excellent resource is my own *ASVAB For Dummies* (Wiley), if I do say so myself. You can pick up a copy at your favorite bookstore or at www.dummies.com.

For More about the Military

If you're thinking about joining the military, presumably you want to learn more about how the military operates. The following websites are great resources:

▶ **About.com:** Much as I'd like to, I don't spend all my time writing *For Dummies* books. I spend much of my time running a military information website. Here you can find a huge vault of invaluable information about military careers, including basic training insight, military job descriptions, promotion tips, assignments, and military pay and benefits. The site even has a discussion board where you can get your questions answered and talk with current military members and veterans from all the service branches. Point your browser to http://usmilitary.about.com.

▶ **Department of Defense:** To figure out what the military is up to, you can stop by the official website of the Department of Defense. The site is a treasure trove of articles and photos about the military. Go to www.defense.gov.

✔ **Army recruiting:** If you're thinking about joining the Army, the Army's recruiting website is an essential first stop. Here you can read about Army enlistment qualifications and Army careers, and even chat online with an Army recruiter. Visit www.goarmy.com.

✔ **Air Force recruiting:** If you want to soar with the eagles (F-15 Eagles, of course), you should check out the Air Force recruiting website at www.airforce.com.

✔ **Navy recruiting:** If you aren't the claustrophobic type and you're thinking of a career aboard a submarine (or maybe an aircraft carrier), head to the official Navy site at www.navy.com.

✔ **Marine Corps recruiting:** The Marines have a few good men (and women) standing by at the Marine Corps recruiting website to help you become one of the proud few. Check them out at www.marines.com.

✔ **Coast Guard recruiting:** The Coast Guard is a military service, but it doesn't belong to the Department of Defense. Instead, it's under the purview of the Department of Homeland Security. You can find out about joining the Coast Guard at www.gocoastguard.com.

For More about Math

The Mathematics Knowledge and Arithmetic Reasoning subtests on the ASVAB make up half of your AFQT score. If you want to do well on these tests but haven't used your math skills since you got that nifty calculator, check out the following resources:

✔ **A slew of *For Dummies* math books:** *Algebra I For Dummies* and *Algebra II For Dummies,* both by Mary Jane Sterling; *Geometry For Dummies,* 2nd Edition, and *Calculus For Dummies,* both by Mark Ryan; and *SAT II Math For Dummies,* by Scott Hatch, JD, and Lisa Zimmer Hatch, MA — all published by Wiley — are great places to start. Check your favorite bookstore or visit www.dummies.com.

✔ **AAA Math:** AAA Math can help you review math problems from kindergarten through eighth grade. The website features a comprehensive set of interactive arithmetic lessons, with unlimited free online practice. Visit www.aaamath.com.

For More about Math Word Problems

Solving math word problems requires a special set of skills. You have to know basic math, analyze the problem, determine how to set up an equation, and then solve it. *Algebra I For Dummies, Algebra II For Dummies,* and *Geometry For Dummies* (see the preceding section) can be a great help in understanding word problems, but you may want to start with *Math Word Problems For Dummies* by Mary Jane Sterling (Wiley). Also, check out Purplemath at www.purplemath.com/modules/index.htm.

For More about Vocabulary

You can't get a good score on the AFQT without doing well on the Word Knowledge subtest. These resources can help you boost your vocabulary knowledge:

✔ ***Vocabulary For Dummies* by Laurie E. Rozakis and *SAT Vocabulary For Dummies* by Suzee Vlk (both published by Wiley):** Head to your favorite bookstore or www.dummies.com.

- ✔ **FreeVocabulary.com:** This site (`http://freevocabulary.com/`) has more than 5,000 vocabulary words and their definitions — a great resource if you're looking to improve your vocabulary.

- ✔ **ImprovingVocabulary.org:** This site (`http://improvingvocabulary.org/`) offers free tips for improving your vocabulary. If you want, you can purchase its software program, which is designed to make you a word wizard in no time.

For More about Reading Comprehension

If you need to brush up on your reading skills for the Paragraph Comprehension subtest or you just want to speed-read your way through *War and Peace,* try these sites:

- ✔ **MrNussbaum.com:** This site has dozens of reading comprehension exercises at your fingertips. Take a look at `http://mrnussbaum.com/readingpassageindex/`.

- ✔ **Resource Room:** This site offers tips, techniques, and exercises to help improve your reading comprehension skills. Go to `www.resourceroom.net/comprehension`.

For More about Test Taking

The best way to prepare for the AFQT is to develop a sound study plan. However, even with the best preparation, a question or two may trip you up. Chapter 2 has some great tips to help you take the test. Here are some other resources:

- ✔ **TestTakingTips.com:** This site (`http://testtakingtips.com/`) offers tips and techniques for studying, note taking, reducing test anxiety, and taking tests.

- ✔ **Study Guides and Strategies:** This site gives ten great tips for terrific test taking. Check it out at `www.studygs.net/tsttak1.htm`.

Playing at Public Libraries

Remember when you learned math and English in high school? You were taught from standard textbooks. Those same textbooks are a great resource to help you review, but have you ever priced a standard textbook in a bookstore? Holy cow! No wonder the American education system always seems to be out of money.

If only you knew a place where you could borrow math and English high-school and college textbooks for free. Wait a minute — you do! It's the public library, and most towns and cities have one. Not only can you borrow standard textbooks, but libraries also offer you a calm and quiet place to study, away from the hustle and bustle and demands of daily life.

Consorting with Colleges

Some people just aren't good at studying on their own. They prefer organized classrooms, specific assignments, and teachers to explain things. If you're one of these people, you may want to consider enrolling in a math, vocabulary, or reading course at your local community college. Who knows? You may even qualify for state or federal student aid and be able to take college courses for free!

Supplementing your AFQT knowledge through college courses offers a couple of big advantages:

✔ If you have a GED and get at least 15 college credits, you boost your chances of being accepted for enlistment by a factor of at least 10.

✔ If you get more than 30 college credits, you may qualify for advanced enlistment rank.

Trying Out a Tutor

Colleges and universities usually have a group of highly intelligent students who are eager to supplement their incomes by tutoring other students in a variety of subjects. Even if you decide not to enroll in college courses, having the extra company may be helpful. Studying in groups has been proven to help with memory retention.

To find a tutor in your area, visit the administration office of your local college or university. Or just walk around campus and look at the bulletin boards — students often advertise their tutoring services on fliers.

Appendix

Matching ASVAB Scores to Military Jobs

• •

*T*he military has hundreds of enlisted job opportunities, ranging from washing and sewing clothing items to translating foreign languages. Each of the military services has established its own individual *line score* requirements (a combination of various ASVAB subtest scores) for specific enlisted jobs. The tables in this appendix show the minimum line scores that the services have established for entry-level enlisted jobs.

Just because you achieve the minimum ASVAB line score for the job of your choice doesn't mean you'll absolutely get that job. Other factors are considered, including the current needs of the service, security clearance qualification, and medical exam results.

The charts in this appendix are as accurate as they can be at press time. However, military jobs and qualification standards are subject to change with little or no notice. For the most up-to-date information and for complete job descriptions and qualification factors, see your local military recruiter or visit the military enlisted-job pages on the About.com U.S. Military Information site (`usmilitary.about.com`).

Army Enlisted Jobs

The Army calls its enlisted jobs *Military Occupational Specialties* (MOSs), and more than 150 such specialties exist for entry-level recruits. Table A-1 shows entry-level Army MOSs and the ASVAB line scores required to qualify for the jobs. Scan the table and see whether you find a job that interests you.

Line scores are abbreviated as follows: Clerical (CL), Combat (CO), Electronics (EL), Field Artillery (FA), General Maintenance (GM), General Technical (GT), Mechanical Maintenance (MM), Operators and Food (OF), Surveillance and Communications (SC), and Skilled Technical (ST). See Chapter 2 for an explanation of which ASVAB subtest scores are used to calculate each of the line scores.

Table A-1		Army Enlisted Jobs and Required ASVAB Scores				
MOS	**Title**	**Score**	**MOS**	**Title**	**Score**	**MOS**	**Title**	**Score**
09L	Interpreter/ Translator	N/A	11B	Infantryman	CO-90	11C	Indirect Fire Infantryman	CO-90
12B	Combat Engineer	CO-98	12C	Bridge Crewmember	CO-87	12D	Diver	ST-106 or GM-98 and GT-107

(continued)

Table A-1 *(continued)*

MOS	Title	Score	MOS	Title	Score	MOS	Title	Score
12G	Quarrying Specialist	GM-93	12K	Plumber	GM-88	12M	Firefighter	GM-88
12N	Horizontal Construction Engineer	GM-90	12Q	Power Distribution Specialist	EL-93	12R	Interior Electrician	EL-93
12T	Technical Engineer	ST-101	12V	Concrete and Asphalt Equipment Operator	GM-88	12W	Carpentry and Masonry Specialist	GM-88
12Y	Geospatial Engineer	ST-95	13B	Cannon Crewmember	FA-95	13C	Tactical Automated Fire Control Systems Specialist	FA-95
13D	Field Artillery Automated Tactical Data Systems Specialist	FA-100	13E	Cannon Fire Direction Specialist	FA-95	13F	Fire Support Specialist	FA-100
13M	Multiple Launch Rocket System Crewmember	OF-105	13P	Multiple Launch Rocket System Operations/ Fire Direction Specialist	FA-100	13R	Field Artillery Firefinder Radar Operator	SC-98
13T	Field Artillery Surveyor/ Meteorological Crewmember	EL-95	14E	Patriot Fire Control Enhanced Operator/ Maintainer	MM-104	14G	Air Defense Battle Management System Operator	GT-98 and MM-99
14H	Air Defense Early Warning System Operator	GT-98 and MM-99	14J	Air Defense C41 Tactical Operations Center Enhanced Operator Maintainer	GT-98 and MM-99	14S	Air and Missile Defense (AMD) Crewmember	OF-85
14T	PATRIOT Launching Station Enhanced Operator/ Maintainer	OF-92	15B	Aircraft Power Plant Repairer	MM-104	15D	Aircraft Powertrain Repairer	MM-104
15E	Unmanned Aircraft Systems Repairer	EL-93 and MM-104	15F	Aircraft Electrician	MM-104	15G	Aircraft Structural Repairer	MM-104
15H	Aircraft Pneudraulics Repairer	MM-104	15J	OH-58D/ARH Armament/ Electrical/ Avionics Systems Repairer	EL-93 and MM-104	15M	Utility Helicopter Repairer (Reserves Only)	MM-104

MOS	Title	Score	MOS	Title	Score	MOS	Title	Score
15N	Avionic Mechanic	EL-93	15P	Aviation Operations Specialist	ST-91	15Q	Air Traffic Control Operator	ST-101
15R	AH-64 Attack Helicopter Repairer	MM-99	15S	OH-58D Helicopter Repairer	MM-100	15T	UH-60 Helicopter Repairer	MM-105
15U	CH-47 Helicopter Repairer	MM-104	15V	Observation/ Scout Helicopter Repairer	MM-102	15W	Unmanned Aerial Vehicle Operator	SC-102
15X	AH-64A Armament/ Electrical/ Avionic Systems Repairer	MM-102 and EL 98	15Y	AH-64D Armament/ Electrical/ Avionics Systems Repairer	EL-98 and MM-102	18B	Special Forces (Weapons)	GT-110 and CO-100
18C	Special Forces (Engineer)	GT-110 and CO-100	18D	Special Forces (Medical)	GT-100 and CO-87	18E	Special Forces (Communications)	GT-110 and SC-100
19D	Cavalry Scout	CO-90	19K	M1 Armor Crewman	CO-87	25B	Information Technology Specialist	ST-95
25C	Radio Operator/ Maintainer	SC-98 and EL-98	25F	Network Switching Systems Operator/ Maintainer	SC-105 and EL-102	25L	Cable Systems Installer/ Maintainer	SC-89 and EL-89
25M	Multimedia Illustrator	EL-93 and ST-91	25P	Microwave Systems Operator/ Maintainer	EL-107	25Q	Multichannel Transmission Systems Operator/ Maintainer	EL-98 and SC-98
25R	Visual Information Equipment Operator/ Maintainer	EL-107	25S	Satellite Communication Systems Operator/ Maintainer	EL-117	25U	Signal Support Systems Specialist	SC-92 and EL-93
25V	Combat Documentation/ Production Specialist	EL-93 and ST-91	35F	Intelligence Analyst	ST-101	35G	Geospatial Intelligence Imagery Analyst	ST-101
35M	Human Intelligence Collector	ST-101	35N	Signals Intelligence Analyst	ST-101	35P	Cryptologic Linguist	ST-91
35Q	Cryptologic Network Warfare Specialist	ST-105	35S	Signals Collector/ Analyst	ST-101	35T	Military Intelligence Systems Maintainer/ Integrator	ST-112
36B	Financial Management Technician	CL-101	37F	Psychological Operations Specialist	ST-101	38A	Civil Affairs Specialist	ST-100

(continued)

Table A-1 (continued)

MOS	Title	Score	MOS	Title	Score	MOS	Title	Score
38B	Intelligence and Combat Support	ST-96	42A	Human Resources Specialist	CL-90	42F	Information Systems Technician	CL-101
42L	Administrative Specialist	CL-95	42R	Band Member	N/A	46Q	Public Affairs Specialist	GT-107
46R	Public Affairs Broadcast Specialist Journalist	GT-107	56M	Chaplain Assistant	CL-90	68B	Orthopedic Specialist	ST-101 and GT-107
68C	Practical Nursing Specialist	ST-101 and GT-107	68D	Operating Room Specialist	ST-91	68E	Dental Specialist	ST-91
68F	Physical Therapy Specialist	ST-101 and GT-107	68G	Patient Administration Specialist	CL-90	68H	Optical Laboratory Specialist	GM-98
68J	Medical Logistics Specialist	CL-90	68K	Medical Laboratory Specialist	ST-106	68L	Occupational Therapy Specialist	ST-101 and GT-107
68M	Nutrition Care Specialist	OF-95	68N	Cardiovascular Specialist	ST-101 and GT-107	68P	Radiology Specialist	ST-106
68Q	Pharmacy Specialist	ST-95	68R	Veterinary Food Inspection Specialist	ST-95	68S	Preventive Medicine Specialist	ST-101
68T	Animal Care Specialist	ST-91	68U	Ear, Nose, and Throat & Hearing Readiness Specialist	ST-101 and GT-107	68V	Respiratory Specialist	ST-102
68W	Healthcare Specialist	ST-101 and GT-107	68X	Mental Health Specialist	ST-101	68Y	Eye Specialist	ST-101 and GT-107
69A	Biomedical Equipment Specialist	EL-107	74D	Chemical Operations Specialist	ST-91	88H	Cargo Specialist	GM-88
88K	Watercraft Operator	MM-99	88L	Watercraft Engineer	MM-99	88M	Motor Transport Operator	OF-85
88N	Transportation Management Coordinator	CL-95	88P	Railway Equipment Repairer	MM-97	88T	Railway Section Repairer	MM-87
88U	Railway Operations Crewmember	MM-92	89A	Ammunition Stock Control and Accounting Specialist	ST-91	89B	Ammunition Specialist	ST-91
89D	Explosive Ordnance Disposal (EOD) Specialist	ST-110	91A	M1 Abrams Tank System Maintainer	MM-99 or MM-88 and GT-92	91B	Wheeled Vehicle Mechanic	MM-92 or MM-87 and GT-85

MOS	Title	Score	MOS	Title	Score	MOS	Title	Score
91C	Utilities Equipment Repairer	GM-98 or GM-88 and GT-83	91D	Power Generation Equipment	GM-98 or GM-88 and GT-88	91E	Allied Trade Specialist	GM-98 or GM-88 and GT-92
91F	Small Arms/ Artillery Repairer	GM-93 or GM-88 and GT-85	91G	Fire Control Repairer	EL-98 or EL-93 and GT-88	91H	Track Vehicle Repairer	MM-92 or MM-87 and GT-85
91J	Quartermaster and Chemical Equipment Repairer	MM-92 or MM-87 and GT-85	91L	Construction Equipment Repairer	MM-92 or MM-87 and GT-85	91M	Bradley Fighting Vehicle System Maintainer	MM-99 or MM-88 and GT-92
91P	Artillery Mechanic	MM-99 or MM-88 and GT-88	91S	Stryker Systems Maintainer	MM-92 or MM-87 and GT-85	92A	Automated Logistical Specialist	CL-90
92F	Petroleum Supply Specialist	CL-86 and OF-85	92G	Food Service Specialist	OF-85	92L	Petroleum Laboratory Specialist	ST-91
92M	Mortuary Affairs Specialist	GM-88	92R	Parachute Rigger	GM 88 and CO 87	92S	Shower/Laundry and Clothing Repair Specialist	GM-84
92W	Water Treatment Specialist	GM-88	92Y	Unit Supply Specialist	CL-90	94A	Land Combat Electronic Missile System Repairer	EL-102
94D	Air Traffic Control Equipment Repairer	EL-102	94E	Radio and Communications Security Repairer	EL-102	94F	Computer/ Detection Systems Repairer	EL-102
94H	Test Measurement and Diagnostic Equipment Support Specialist	EL-107	94L	Avionic Communications Equipment Repairer	EL-98	94M	Radar Repairer	EL-107
94P	Multiple Launch Rocket System Repairer	EL-93	94R	Avionic and Survivability Equipment Repairer	EL-98	94S	Patriot System Repairer	EL-107
94T	Avenger System Repairer	EL-98	94Y	Integrated Family of Test Equipment Operator and Maintainer	N/A			

Air Force Enlisted Jobs

The United States Air Force has about 120 entry-level enlisted jobs for new recruits. The Air Force refers to enlisted jobs as *Air Force Specialty Codes* (AFSCs). Table A-2 shows the Air Force entry-level AFSCs and the line scores required to qualify for each job. The table is organized by AFSC number, so browse the table and see which AFSCs pique your interest.

Line scores are abbreviated as follows: General (G), Electronic (E), Mechanical (M), and Administrative (A). See Chapter 2 for information on which ASVAB subtest scores are used by the Air Force to calculate the various line scores.

Table A-2		Air Force Enlisted Jobs and Required ASVAB Scores				
AFSC	**Title**	**Score**	**AFSC**	**Title**	**Score**	**AFSC**	**Title**	**Score**
1A0X1	In-Flight Refueling	G-55	1A1X1	Flight Engineer	M-47 or E-38	1A2X1	Aircraft Loadmaster	G-57
1A3X1	Airborne Communications and Electronic Systems	E-70	1A4X1	Airborne Battle Management Systems	G-55	1A5X1	Airborne Missions Systems	E-70
1A7X1	Aerial Gunner	M-60 or E-45	1A8X1	Airborne Cryptologic Linguist	G-72	1C0X1	Airfield Management	A-41
1C1X1	Air Traffic Control	G-55 and M-55	1C2X1	Combat Control	G-44	1C3X1	Command Post	G-49
1C4X1	Tactical Air Command and Control	G-49	1C5X1	Aerospace Control and Warning Systems	G-55	1C6X1	Space Systems Operations	E-60
1C7X1	Airfield Management	G-50 and M-40	1N0X1	Operations Intelligence	G-57	1N1X1	Imagery Analysis	G-66
1N2X1	Communications Signals Intelligence Production	G-53	1N3XX	Cryptologic Linguist	G-72	1N4X1	Network Intelligence Analysis	G-62
1N5X1	Electronic Signal Intelligence Exploitation	G-72	1N6X1	Electronic Systems Security Assessment	G-62	1T0X1	Survival, Evasion, Resistance, and Escape Operations	G-55
1T1X1	Aircrew Life Support	G-34	1T2X1	Pararescue	G-44	1U0X1	Unmanned Aerospace Systems Sensor Operator	G-64 or E-54
1W0X1	Weather	G-66 and E-50	2A0X1	Avionics Test Stations and Components	E-70	2A3X1	A-10, F-15, and U-2 Avionics Systems	E-70
2A3X2	F-16, F-117, RQ-1, and CV-22 Avionics Systems	E-70	2A3X1	Tactical Aircraft Maintenance	M-47	2A5X1	Aerospace Maintenance	M-47

AFSC	Title	Score	AFSC	Title	Score	AFSC	Title	Score
2A5X2	Helicopter Maintenance	M-56	2A5X3	Integrated Avionics Systems	E-70	2A6X1	Aerospace Propulsion	M-56
2A6X2	Aerospace Ground Equipment	M-47 and E-28	2A6X3	Aircrew Egress Systems	M-56	2A6X4	Aircraft Fuel Systems	M-47
2A6X5	Aircraft Hydraulic Systems	M-56	2A7X1	Aircraft Metals Technology	M-47	2A7X2	Nondestructive Inspection	M-42
2A7X3	Aircraft Structural Maintenance	M-47	2A7X4	Survival Equipment	M-40	2E0X1	Ground Radar Systems	E-70
2E1X1	Satellite, Wideband, and Telemetry Systems	E-70	2E1X2	Meteorological and Navigations Systems	E-70	2E1X3	Ground Radio Communications	E-70
2E1X4	Visual Imagery and Intrusion Detection Systems	E-70	2E2X1	Computer, Network, Switching, and Cryptographic Systems	E-70	2E6X2	Communications Cable and Antenna Systems	M-47
2E6X3	Telephone Systems	E-45	2F0X1	Fuels	M-47 and G-38	2G0X1	Logistics Plans	A-56
2M0X1	Missile and Space Systems Electrical Maintenance	E-70	2M0X2	Missile and Space Systems Maintenance	M-47	2M0X3	Missile and Space Facilities	E-50
2P0X1	Precision Measurement Equipment Laboratory	E-70	2R0X1	Maintenance Data Systems Analysis	G-55	2R1X1	Maintenance Scheduling	G-44
2S0X1	Material Management	A-41 or G-44	2S0X2	Supply Systems Analysis	A-47	2T0X1	Traffic Management	A-35
2T1X1	Vehicle Operations	M-40	2T2X1	Air Transportation	M-47 and A-28	2T3X1	Special Purpose Vehicle and Equipment Maintenance	M-47
2T3X2	Special Vehicle Maintenance	M-40	2T3X5	Vehicle Body Maintenance	M-56	2T3X7	Vehicle Management and Analysis	A-41
2W0X1	Munitions Systems	M-55 or G-55	2W1X1	Aircraft Armament Systems	M-60 or E-45	2W2X1	Nuclear Weapons	M-60
3A0X1	Information Management	A-28	3C0X1	Computer Systems Operations	G-64	3C0X2	Computer Systems Programming	G-64

(continued)

Table A-2 *(continued)*

AFSC	Title	Score	AFSC	Title	Score	AFSC	Title	Score
3C1X1	Radio Communication Systems	A-41	3C1X2	Electromagnetic Spectrum Management	G-44	3C2X1	Computer Systems Control	E-70
3C3X1	Computer Systems Planning and Implementation	G-62	3M0X1	Services	G-24	3N0X1	Public Affairs	G-72
3N0X2	Radio and TV Broadcasting	G-72	3N1X1	Regional Band	A-21 or G-24	3P0X1	Security Forces	G-33
3E0X1	Electrical Systems	E-28	3E0X2	Electric Power Production	M-56 and E-40	3E1X1	Heating, Ventilation, Air Conditioning, and Refrigeration	M-47 or E-28
3E2X1	Pavement and Construction Equipment	M-40	3E3X1	Structural	M-47	3E4X1	Utilities Systems	M-47
3E4X2	Liquid Fuel Systems Maintenance	M-47	3E4X3	Pest Management	G-38	3E5X1	Engineering	G-49
3E6X1	Operations Management	G-44	3E7X1	Fire Protection	G-38	3E8X1	Explosive Ordnance Disposal	G-64 and M-60
3E9X1	Readiness	G-62	3S0X1	Personnel	A-41	3V0X1	Visual Information	G-44
3V0X2	Still Photograph	G-44	3V0X2	Visual Information Production-Documentation	G-62	4A0X1	Health Services Management	G-44
4A1X1	Medical Materiel	G-44	4A2X1	Biomedical Equipment	E-70 and M-60	4B0X1	Bioenvironmental Engineering	G-49
4C0X1	Mental Health Services	G-55	4D0X1	Diet Therapy	G-44	4E0X1	Public Health	G-44
4H0X1	Cardiopulmonary Lab	G-44	4J0X2	Physical Medicine	G-49	4M0X1	Aerospace Physiology	G-44
4N0X1	Aerospace Medical Service	G-44	4N1X1	Surgical Services	G-44	4P0X1	Pharmacy	G-44
4R0X1	Diagnostic Imaging	G-44	4T0X1	Medical Laboratory	G-62	4T0X2	Histopathology	G-44
4T0X3	Cytotechnology	G-44	4V0X1	Optometry	G-55	4Y0X1	Dental Assistant	G-44
4Y0X2	Dental Lab	G-66	5R0X1	Chaplain Assistant	G-44 or A-35	6C0X1	Contracting	G-72
6F0X1	Financial Management and Comptroller	G-57	9S100	Technical Applications Specialist	M-88 and E-85			

Navy Enlisted Jobs

The Navy calls its enlisted jobs *ratings* and has about 75 types of jobs available for entry-level recruits. This branch doesn't use line scores for job-qualification purposes. Instead, the Navy combines scores from the various ASVAB subtests for each of its enlisted ratings.

Table A-3 (in ratings order) shows combinations of ASVAB subtest scores that are required to qualify for Navy enlisted jobs. Peruse the list and see which jobs may best suit you. The ASVAB subtests are abbreviated as follows: General Science (GS), Arithmetic Reasoning (AR), Word Knowledge (WK), Paragraph Comprehension (PC), Auto & Shop Information (AS), Mathematics Knowledge (MK), Mechanical Comprehension (MC), Electronics Information (EI), Assembling Objects (AO), and Verbal Expression (VE).

Table A-3			Navy Enlisted Jobs and Required ASVAB Scores					
Rating	**Title**	**Score**	**Rating**	**Title**	**Score**	**Rating**	**Title**	**Score**
ABE	Aviation Boatswain's Mate — Equipment	VE + MR + MK + AS = 184	ABF	Aviation Boatswain's Mate — Fuels	VE + AR + MK + AS = 184	ABH	Aviation Boatswain's Mate — Handling	VE + AR + MK + AS = 184
AC	Air Traffic Controller	VE + AR + MK + MC = 220 or VE + MK + MC + CS = 220	AD	Aviation Machinist's Mate	VE + AR + MK + AS = 210 or VE + AR + MK + MC = 210	AE	Aviation Electrician's Mate	AR + MK + EI + GS = 222 or VE + AR + MK + MC = 222
AECF	Advanced Electronics Computer Field	AR + MK + EI + GS = 222	AG	(Aviation) Aerographer's Mate	VE + MK + GS = 162	AIR-CREW	Aircrew Program	VE + AR + MK + MC = 210 or VE + AR + MK + AS = 210
AM	Aviation Structural Mechanic	VE + AR + MK + AS = 210 or VE + AR + MK + MC = 210	AME	Aviation Structural Mechanic — Equipment	VE + AR + MK + AS = 210 or VE + AR + MK + MC = 210	AO	Aviation Ordnanceman	VE + AR + MK + AS = 185 or MK + AS + AO = 140

(continued)

Table A-3 *(continued)*

Rating	Title	Score	Rating	Title	Score	Rating	Title	Score
AS	Aviation Support Equipment Technician	VE + AR + MK + AS = 210 or VE + AR + MK + MC = 210	AT	Aviation Electronics Technician	AR + MK + EI + GS = 222 or VE + AR + MK + MC = 222	AW	Aviation Warfare Systems Operator	VE + AR + MK + MC = 210
AWF	Aircrewman Mechanical	VE + AR + MK + MC = 210	AWO	Aircrewman Operator	VE + AR + MK + MC = 210	AWR	Aircrewman Tactical Helicopter	VE + AR + MK + MC = 210
AWS	Aircrewman Helicopter	VE + AR + MK + MC = 210	AWV	Aircrewman Avionics	VE + AR + MK + MC = 210	AZ	Aviation Maintenance Administra-tionman	VE + AR = 102
BM	Boatswain's Mate	VE + AR + MK + AS = 175	BU	Builder	AR + MC + AS = 140	CE	Construction Electrician	AR + MK + EI + GS = 200
CM	Construction Mechanic	AR + MC + AS = 158	CS	Culinary Specialist	VE + AR = 89	CS(SS)	Culinary Specialist (Submarine)	AR + MK + EI + GS = 200 or VE + AR + MK + MC = 200
CTA	Cryptologic Technician — Administration	VE + MK = 105	CTI	Cryptologic Technician — Interpretive	VE + MK + GS = 165	CTM	Cryptologic Technician — Maintenance	MK + EI + GS + AR = 223
CTN	Cryptologic Technician — Networks	AR + 2MK + GS = 235 or VE + AR + MK + MC = 235	CTR	Cryptologic Technician — Collection	VE + AR = 110	CTT	Cryptologic Technician — Technical	VE + MK + GS = 162 or AR + MK + EI + GS = 223

Rating	Title	Score	Rating	Title	Score	Rating	Title	Score
DC	Damage Controlman	VE + MK + GS = 162 or AR + MK + EI + GS = 223	EA	Engineering Aide	AR + 2MK + GS = 210	EM	Electrician's Mate	VE + AR + MK + MC = 210
EN	Engineman	VE + AR + MK + AS = 195 or VE + AR + MK + AO = 200	EO	Equipment Operator	AR + MC + EI + GS = 204	EOD	Explosive Ordnance Disposal	AR + VE = 109 and MC = 51
ET	Electronics Technician	MK + EI + GS = 156 + AR = 223	ET(SS)	Electronics Technician (Submarine)	AR + MK + EI + GS = 222	FC	Fire Controlman	AR + MK + EI + GS = 218 and MK + EI + GS and MK = 57 and AR = 57
FT(SS)	Fire Control Technician (Submarine)	AR + MK + EI + GS = 222 or VE + AR + MK + MV = 222	GM	Gunner's Mate	AR + MK + EI + GS = 204	GSE	Gas Turbine Systems Technician — Electrical	VE + AR + MK + MC = 210

(continued)

Table A-3 *(continued)*

Rating	Title	Score	Rating	Title	Score	Rating	Title	Score
GSM	Gas Turbine Systems Technician — Mechanical	VE + AR + MK + AS = 195 or VE + AR + MK + AO = 200	HM	Hospital Corpsman	VE + MK + GS = 149	HT	Hull Technician	VE + MC + AS = 158
IC	Interior Communications Electrician	VE + AR + MK + MC = 210	IS	Intelligence Specialist	VE + AR = 108	IT	Information System Technician	AR + 2MK + GS = 222 or AR + MK + EI + GS = 222
LS	Logistics Specialist	VE + AR = 102	MA	Master at Arms	AR + WK = 95 and WK > 43	MC	Mass Communications Specialist	VE + AR = 115
MM	Machinist's Mate	VE + AR + MK + AS = 195 or VE + AR + MK + AO = 200	MM(SS)	Machinist's Mate (Submarine)	VE + AR + MK + MC = 210 or VE + AR + MK + AS = 210	MN	Mineman	VE + MC + AS = 158
MR	Machinery Repairman	VE + AR + MK + AS = 200 or MK + AS + AO = 150	MT	Missile Technician	AR + MK + EI + GS = 222 or VE + AR + MK + MC = 222	ND	Navy Diver	AR + VE = 103 and MC = 51
NUC	Nuclear Program	AR + MK + EI + GS = 252 or VE + AR + MK + MC = 252	OS	Operations Specialist	VE + MK + CS = 157 or AR + 2MK + GS = 210	PC	Postal Clerk	VE + AR = 108

Rating	Title	Score	Rating	Title	Score	Rating	Title	Score
PR	Aircrew Survival Equipmentman	VE + AR + MK + AS = 185 or MK + AS + AO = 140	**PS**	Personnel Specialist	VE + MK = 105	**QM**	Quartermaster	VE + AR = 96
RP	Religious Program Specialist	VE + MK = 105	**SH**	Ship Serviceman	VE + AR = 95	**SK**	Storekeeper	VE + AR = 103
SK(SS)	Storekeeper (Submarines)	AR + MK + EI + GS = 200 or VE + AR + MK + MC = 200	**SN(SS)**	Seaman (Submarine)	AR + MK + EI + GS = 200 or VE + AR + MK + MC = 200	**STG**	Sonar Technician (Surface)	AR + MK + EI + GS = 222
ST(SS)	Sonar Technician (Submarine)	AR + MK + EI + GS = 222 or VE + AR + MK + MC = 200	**SO**	Special Warfare Operator (SEAL)	GS + MC + EI = 165 or VE + MK + MC + CS = 220	**SW**	Steelworker	VE + MC + AS = 140
TM	Torpedoman's Mate	AR + 2MK + GS = 194	**UT**	Utilitiesman	AR + MK + EI + GS = 200	**YN**	Yeoman	VE + MK = 105
YN(SS)	Yeoman (Submarine)	AR + MK + EI + GS = 200 or VE + AR + MK + MC = 200						

Marine Corps Enlisted Jobs

The United States Marine Corps needs a few good men (and women) to fill about 120 enlisted entry-level job specialties. Like the Army, the Marine Corps calls its enlisted jobs *Military Occupational Specialties* (MOSs). The Marine Corps has only three line scores, and they're abbreviated in Table A-4 as follows: Mechanical Maintenance (MM), Electronics (EL), and General Technical (GT).

Table A-4			Marine Corps Enlisted Jobs and Required ASVAB Scores					
MOS	**Title**	**Score**	**MOS**	**Title**	**Score**	**MOS**	**Title**	**Score**
0121	Personnel Clerk	CL-100	0151	Administrative Clerk	CL-100	0161	Postal Clerk	CL-90
0231	Intelligence Specialist	GT-100	0241	Imagery Analysis Specialist	GT-100	0251	Interrogator/ Debriefer	GT-100
0261	Geographic Intelligence Specialist	EL-100	0311	Rifleman	GT-80	0313	LAV Crewman	GT-90
0321	Reconnaissance Man	GT-105	0341	Mortarman	GT-80	0351	Assaultman	GT-80
0352	Antitank Assault Guided Missileman	GT-90	0411	Maintenance Management Specialist	GT-100	0431	Logistics/ Embarkation and Combat Service Support (CSS) Specialist	GT-100
0451	Air Delivery Specialist	GT-100	0481	Landing Support Specialist	GT-95 and MM-100	0511	MAGTF Planning Specialist	GT-110
0612	Field Wireman	EL-90	0613	Construction Wireman	EL-90	0614	Unit Level Circuit Switch (ULCS) Operator/ Maintainer	EL-100
0621	Field Radio Operator	EL-90	0622	Mobile Multichannel Equipment Operator	EL-100	0624	High Frequency Communication Central Operator	EL-100
0626	Fleet SATCOM Terminal Operator	EL-100	0627	Ground Mobile Forces SATCOM Operator	EL-100	0811	Field Artillery Cannoneer	GT-90
0842	Field Artillery Radar Operator	GT-105	0844	Field Artillery Fire Control Man	GT-105	0847	Artillery Meteorological Man	GT-105
1141	Electrician	EL-90	1142	Electrical Equipment Repair Specialist	EL-100	1161	Refrigeration Mechanic	MM-105

MOS	Title	Score	MOS	Title	Score	MOS	Title	Score
1171	Hygiene Equipment Operator	MM-85	1181	Fabric Repair Specialist	MM-85	1316	Metal Worker	MM-95
1341	Engineer Equipment Mechanic	MM-95	1345	Engineer Equipment Operator	MM-95	1361	Engineer Assistant	GT-100
1371	Combat Engineer	MM-105	1391	Bulk Fuel Specialist	MM-85	1812	M1A1 Tank Crewman	GT-90
1833	Assault Amphibious Vehicle (AAV) Crewman	GT-90	2111	Small Arms Repairer/ Technician	MM-95	2131	Towed Artillery Systems Technician	MM-95
2141	Assault Amphibious Vehicle (AAV) Repairer/ Technician	MM-105	2146	Main Battle Tank (MBT) Repairer/ Technician	MM-105	2147	Light Armored Vehicle (LAV) Repairer/ Technician	MM-105
2161	Machinist	MM-105	2171	Electro-Optical Ordnance Repairer	MM-105 and EL-105	2311	Ammunition Technician	GT-100
2336	Explosive Ordnance Disposal Technician	GT-110	2621	Communications Signal Collection/ Manual Morse Operator/ Analyst	GT-100	2631	Electronic Intelligence (ELINT) Intercept Operator/ Analyst	GT-100
2651	Special Intelligence System Administrator/ Communicator	GT-100	267X	Cryptologic Linguist	GT-105	2811	Telephone Technician	EL-115
2818	Personal Computer (PC)/Tactical Office Machine Repairer	EL-115	2821	Computer Technician	EL-115	2822	Electronic Switching Equipment Technician	EL-115
2831	Multichannel Equipment Repairer	EL-115	2832	Multichannel Equipment Technician	EL-115	2834	Satellite Communications (SATCOM) Technician	EL-115
2841	Ground Radio Repairer	EL-115	2844	Ground Communications Organizational Repairer	EL-115	2846	Ground Radio Intermediate Repairer	EL-115

(continued)

Table A-4 *(continued)*

MOS	Title	Score	MOS	Title	Score	MOS	Title	Score
2871	Test Measurement and Diagnostic Equipment Technician	EL-115	2881	Communication Security Equipment Technician	EL-115	2886	Artillery Electronic System Repairer	EL-115
2887	Counter Mortar Radar Repairer	EL-115	3043	Supply Administration and Operations Clerk	GT-110	3051	Warehouse Clerk	GT-90
3052	Packaging Specialist	GT-80	3112	Traffic Management Specialist	GT-90	3361	Subsistence Supply Clerk	GT-90
3381	Food Service Specialist	GT-90	3432	Finance Technician	GT-110	3441	NAF Audit Technician	GT-110
3451	Fiscal/Budget Technician	GT-110	3521	Organizational Automotive Mechanic	MM-95	3531	Motor Vehicle Operator	MM-85
4066	Small Computer Systems Specialist	GT-110	4067	Programmer	GT-110	4113	Morale, Welfare, Recreation (MWR) Specialist	GT-110
4341	Combat Correspondent	GT-105 and VE-40	4421	Legal Services Specialist	GT-100	46XX	Visual Information	GT-100
55XX	Band	GT-50	5711	Nuclear Biological and Chemical (NBC) Defense Specialist	GT-110	5811	Military Police	GT-100
5821	Criminal Investigator	GT-110	5831	Correctional Specialist	GT-100	5937	Aviation Radio Repairer	EL-105
5942	Aviation Radar Technician	EL-105	5952	Air Traffic Control Navigational Aids Technician	EL-105	5953	Air Traffic Control Radar Technician	EL-105
5954	Air Traffic Control Communications Technician	EL-105	5962	Tactical Data Systems Equipment (TDSE) Repairer	EL-105	5963	Tactical Air Operations Module Repairer	EL-105
6042	Individual Material Readiness List (IMRL) Asset Manager	GT-100	6046	Aircraft Maintenance Administration Specialist	GT-100	6048	Flight Equipment Technician	MM-105

MOS	Title	Score	MOS	Title	Score	MOS	Title	Score
6061	Aircraft Intermediate Level Hydraulic/ Pneumatic Mechanic	MM-105	6071	Aircraft Maintenance Support Equipment (SE) Mechanic	MM-105	6091	Aircraft Intermediate Level Structures Mechanic	MM-105
611X	Helicopter Mechanic	MM-105	612X	Helicopter Power Plants Mechanic	MM-105	615X	Helicopter/ Tiltrotor Airframe Mechanic	MM-105
617X	Helicopter Crew Chief	MM-105	621X	Fixed-Wing Aircraft Mechanic	MM-105	622X	Fixed-Wing Aircraft Power Plants Mechanic	MM-105
6232	Fixed-Wing Aircraft Flight Mechanic	MM-105	625X	Fixed-Wing Aircraft Airframe Mechanic	MM-105	628X	Fixed-Wing Aircraft Safety Equipment Mechanic	MM-105
63XX	Aircraft Com- munications/ Navigation/ Electrical/ Weapon Systems Technician	EL-105	64XX	Aircraft Com- munications/ Navigation Systems Technician	EL-105	6511	Aircraft Ordnance Technician	GT-105
6672	Aviation Supply Clerk	GT-100	6673	Automated Information Systems (AIS) Computer Operator	GT-100	6821	Weather Observer	GT-105
7011	Expeditionary Airfield Systems Technician	MM-105	7041	Aviation Operations Specialist	GT-100	7051	Aircraft Firefighting and Rescue Specialist	MM-95
7212	Low Altitude Air Defense (LAAD) Gunner	GT-90	7234	Air Control Electronics Operator	GT-105	7242	Air Support Operations Operator	GT-100
7251	Air Traffic Controller	GT-105	7314	Unmanned Aerial Vehicle (UAV) Air Vehicle Operator	GT-105	7371	Aerial Navigator	GT-110
7381	Airborne Radio Operator/ Inflight Refueling Observer/ Loadmaster	GT-110						

Coast Guard Enlisted Jobs

The smallest U.S. Military service, the Coast Guard, has only 19 types of entry-level jobs for enlisted members. Like the Navy, the Coast Guard calls its enlisted jobs *ratings*. Also like the Navy, the Coast Guard doesn't use line scores for job qualification purposes. Instead, it uses the sums of various ASVAB subtest scores.

Table A-5 shows combinations of ASVAB subtest scores that are required to qualify for Coast Guard enlisted jobs. The ASVAB subtests are abbreviated as follows: General Science (GS), Arithmetic Reasoning (AR), Word Knowledge (WK), Paragraph Comprehension (PC), Auto & Shop Information (AS), Mathematics Knowledge (MK), Mechanical Comprehension (MC), Electronics Information (EI), Assembling Objects (AO), and Verbal Expression (VE).

Table A-5			**Coast Guard Enlisted Jobs and Required ASVAB Scores**					
Rating	*Title*	*Score*	*Rating*	*Title*	*Score*	*Rating*	*Title*	*Score*
AMT	Aviation Maintenance Technician	AR + MC + AS + EI = 213 (minimum AR = 52)	**AST**	Aviation Survival Technician	VE + MC + AS = 159 (minimum AR = 52)	**AV**	Avionics Technician	MK + EI + GS = 171 (minimum AR = 52)
BM	Boatswain's Mate	VE + AR = 101	**DC**	Damage Controlman	VE + MC + AS = 152	**EM**	Electrician's Mate	MK + EI + GS = 152 (minimum AR = 52)
ET	Electronics Technician	MK + EI + GS = 171 (minimum AR = 52) or AFQT = 66	**FS**	Food Service Specialist	VE + AR = 106	**GM**	Gunner's Mate	AR + MK + EI + GS = 208
HS	Health Services Technician	VE + MK + GS = 154	**IT**	Information Systems Technician	MK + EI + GS = 171 (minimum AR = 52)	**MK**	Machinery Technician	AR + MC + AS = 150 or VE + AR = 106

Rating	Title	Score	Rating	Title	Score	Rating	Title	Score
MST	Marine Science Technician	VE + AR = 115 (minimum MK = 58)	MU	Musician	N/A	OS	Operations Specialist	VE + AR = 106
PA	Public Affairs Specialist	VE + AR = 110 (minimum VE = 60)	PS	Port Security Specialist (CG Reserves Only)	VE + AR = 101	SK	Storekeeper	VE + AR = 106 (minimum VE = 52)
YN	Yeoman	VE + AR 106						

Index

• N •

• Y •

• Z •

About the Author

Rod Powers joined the Air Force in 1975, fully intending to become a spy. He was devastated to learn that he should've joined the CIA instead, because the military services don't have that particular enlisted job. Regardless, he fell in love with the military and made it both a passion and a career, retiring with 23 years of service. Rod spent 11 of those years as an Air Force first sergeant, helping to solve the problems of the enlisted corps.

Since his retirement from the military in 1998, Rod has become a world-renowned military careers expert. Through his highly popular U.S. Military Information website on About.com (http://usmilitary.about.com), Rod has advised thousands of troops about all aspects of U.S. armed forces career information. Rod has written several military books including *1,001 ASVAB Practice Questions For Dummies, ASVAB For Dummies, Veterans Benefits For Dummies,* and *Basic Training For Dummies,* all published by Wiley.

Rod is the proud father of twin girls, both of whom are enjoying successful careers in the Air Force while also being amazing wives and mothers. Rod is enjoying his role of grandpa to two new grandsons and one beautiful granddaughter. He currently resides in Daytona Beach, Florida, where he is attempting to prove that there's no such thing as too much sunshine.

Even today, Rod tries to run his life according to long-lived military ideals and standards, but he gets a bit confused as to why nobody will obey his orders anymore.

Dedication

To Connor, Marco, and Milani, my sweet grandchildren! Grandpa loves you and can't wait to buy you ice cream! To Charisa Raine, a little girl living with Angelman Syndrome. I know we will hear you speak one day. To my daughters, Jeanie and Chrissy. I love you, and I am very proud of you. To Bob Doyen, rest in peace.

Author's Acknowledgments

I would like to thank and acknowledge the men and women of our armed services.

Thank you, Vicki Adang, a superior editor, second to none, and her crew: Megan Knoll, Erin Calligan Mooney, Angie Papple Johnston, and Suzanne Langebartels. As always, a special thank you to my amazing agent, Barb Doyen. I am blessed to have you.

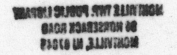

Publisher's Acknowledgments

Acquisitions Editor: Erin Calligan Mooney

Senior Project Editor: Victoria M. Adang

Copy Editors: Megan Knoll; Danielle Voirol

Contributor: LearningMate Solutions

Technical Editors: Angie Papple Johnston, Suzanne Langebartels

Project Coordinator: Patrick Redmond

Cover Image: Eagle with flag ©iStockphoto.com/ Michael Madsen; Monitor ©iStockphoto.com/ turbopixel

Apple & Mac

iPad For Dummies, 6th Edition
978-1-118-72306-7

iPhone For Dummies, 7th Edition
978-1-118-69083-3

Macs All-in-One For Dummies,
4th Edition
978-1-118-82210-4

OS X Mavericks For Dummies
978-1-118-69188-5

Blogging & Social Media

Facebook For Dummies, 5th Edition
978-1-118-63312-0

Social Media Engagement For Dummies
978-1-118-53019-1

WordPress For Dummies, 6th Edition
978-1-118-79161-5

Business

Stock Investing For Dummies,
4th Edition
978-1-118-37678-2

Investing For Dummies, 6th Edition
978-0-470-90545-6

Personal Finance For Dummies,
7th Edition
978-1-118-11785-9

QuickBooks 2014 For Dummies
978-1-118-72005-9

Small Business Marketing Kit
For Dummies, 3rd Edition
978-1-118-31183-7

Careers

Job Interviews For Dummies, 4th Edition
978-1-118-11290-8

Job Searching with Social Media
For Dummies, 2nd Edition
978-1-118-67856-5

Personal Branding For Dummies
978-1-118-11792-7

Resumes For Dummies, 6th Edition
978-0-470-87361-8

Starting an Etsy Business For Dummies,
2nd Edition
978-1-118-59024-9

Diet & Nutrition

Belly Fat Diet For Dummies
978-1-118-34585-6

Mediterranean Diet For Dummies
978-1-118-71525-3

Nutrition For Dummies, 5th Edition
978-0-470-93231-5

Digital Photography

Digital SLR Photography All-in-One
For Dummies, 2nd Edition
978-1-118-59082-9

Digital SLR Video & Filmmaking
For Dummies
978-1-118-36598-4

Photoshop Elements 12 For Dummies
978-1-118-72714-0

Gardening

Herb Gardening For Dummies,
2nd Edition
978-0-470-61778-6

Gardening with Free-Range Chickens
For Dummies
978-1-118-54754-0

Health

Boosting Your Immunity For Dummies
978-1-118-40200-9

Diabetes For Dummies, 4th Edition
978-1-118-29447-5

Living Paleo For Dummies
978-1-118-29405-5

Big Data

Big Data For Dummies
978-1-118-50422-2

Data Visualization For Dummies
978-1-118-50289-1

Hadoop For Dummies
978-1-118-60755-8

Language & Foreign Language

500 Spanish Verbs For Dummies
978-1-118-02382-2

English Grammar For Dummies,
2nd Edition
978-0-470-54664-2

French All-in-One For Dummies
978-1-118-22815-9

German Essentials For Dummies
978-1-118-18422-6

Italian For Dummies, 2nd Edition
978-1-118-00465-4

Math & Science

Algebra I For Dummies, 2nd Edition
978-0-470-55964-2

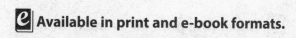 **Available in print and e-book formats.**

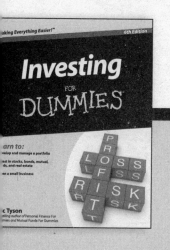
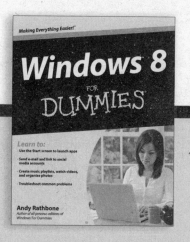

Available wherever books are sold. **For more information or to order direct visit www.dummies.com**

Anatomy and Physiology For Dummies, 2nd Edition
978-0-470-92326-9

Astronomy For Dummies, 3rd Edition
978-1-118-37697-3

Biology For Dummies, 2nd Edition
978-0-470-59875-7

Chemistry For Dummies, 2nd Edition
978-1-118-00730-3

1001 Algebra II Practice Problems For Dummies
978-1-118-44662-1

Microsoft Office

Excel 2013 For Dummies
978-1-118-51012-4

Office 2013 All-in-One For Dummies
978-1-118-51636-2

PowerPoint 2013 For Dummies
978-1-118-50253-2

Word 2013 For Dummies
978-1-118-49123-2

Music

Blues Harmonica For Dummies
978-1-118-25269-7

Guitar For Dummies, 3rd Edition
978-1-118-11554-1

iPod & iTunes For Dummies, 10th Edition
978-1-118-50864-0

Programming

Beginning Programming with C For Dummies
978-1-118-73763-7

Excel VBA Programming For Dummies, 3rd Edition
978-1-118-49037-2

Java For Dummies, 6th Edition
978-1-118-40780-6

Religion & Inspiration

The Bible For Dummies
978-0-7645-5296-0

Buddhism For Dummies, 2nd Edition
978-1-118-02379-2

Catholicism For Dummies, 2nd Edition
978-1-118-07778-8

Self-Help & Relationships

Beating Sugar Addiction For Dummies
978-1-118-54645-1

Meditation For Dummies, 3rd Edition
978-1-118-29144-3

Seniors

Laptops For Seniors For Dummies, 3rd Edition
978-1-118-71105-7

Computers For Seniors For Dummies, 3rd Edition
978-1-118-11553-4

iPad For Seniors For Dummies, 6th Edition
978-1-118-72826-0

Social Security For Dummies
978-1-118-20573-0

Smartphones & Tablets

Android Phones For Dummies, 2nd Edition
978-1-118-72030-1

Nexus Tablets For Dummies
978-1-118-77243-0

Samsung Galaxy S 4 For Dummies
978-1-118-64222-1

Samsung Galaxy Tabs For Dummies
978-1-118-77294-2

Test Prep

ACT For Dummies, 5th Edition
978-1-118-01259-8

ASVAB For Dummies, 3rd Edition
978-0-470-63760-9

GRE For Dummies, 7th Edition
978-0-470-88921-3

Officer Candidate Tests For Dummies
978-0-470-59876-4

Physician's Assistant Exam For Dummie
978-1-118-11556-5

Series 7 Exam For Dummies
978-0-470-09932-2

Windows 8

Windows 8.1 All-in-One For Dummies
978-1-118-82087-2

Windows 8.1 For Dummies
978-1-118-82121-3

Windows 8.1 For Dummies, Book + DVD Bundle
978-1-118-82107-7

Available in print and e-book formats.

Available wherever books are sold. **For more information or to order direct visit www.dummies.com**

Take Dummies with you everywhere you go!

Whether you are excited about e-books, want more from the web, must have your mobile apps, or are swept up in social media, Dummies makes everything easier.

  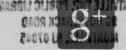

Leverage the Power

For Dummies is the global leader in the reference category and one of the most trusted and highly regarded brands in the world. No longer just focused on books, customers now have access to the For Dummies content they need in the format they want. Let us help you develop a solution that will fit your brand and help you connect with your customers.

Advertising & Sponsorships

Connect with an engaged audience on a powerful multimedia site, and position your message alongside expert how-to content.

Targeted ads • Video • Email marketing • Microsites • Sweepstakes sponsorship

For Dummies is a registered trademark of John Wiley & Sons, Inc.